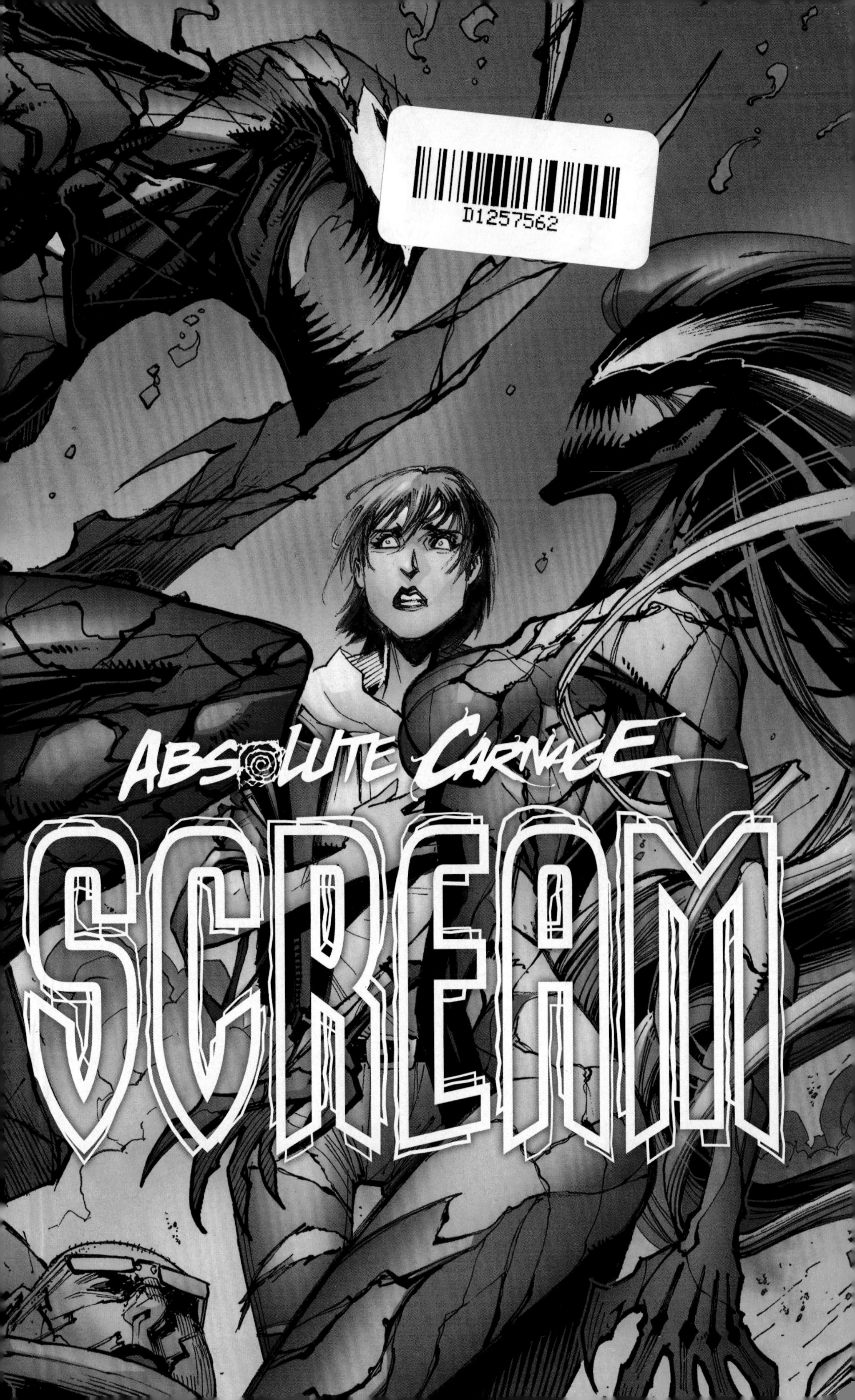
ABSOLUTE CARNAGE
SCREAM

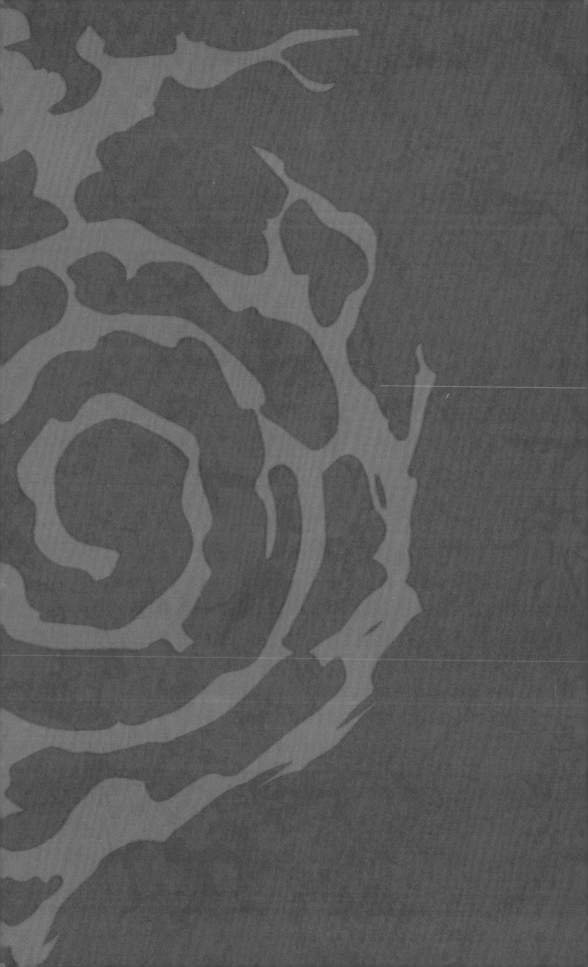

Years ago, the Life Foundation — a dangerous conglomerate that, for a time, focused its efforts on destroying Spider-Man — captured the Venom symbiote and forced it to spawn five offspring: **Scream, Lasher, Riot, Agony and Phage.**

Donna Diego was the original host to the Scream symbiote before her **murder at the hands of Eddie Brock.** Since her death, the whereabouts of the Scream symbiote have remained unknown…

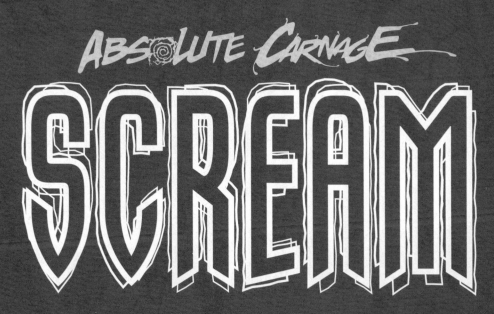

ABSOLUTE CARNAGE
SCREAM

Cullen Bunn
WRITER

Gerardo Sandoval with **Alex Arizmendi** (#2)
PENCILERS

Victor Nava (#1-2), **Gerardo Sandoval** (#2-3) & **Alex Arizmendi** (#2)
INKERS

Erick Arciniega
COLOR ARTIST

VC's Cory Petit
LETTERER

Gerardo Sandoval & **Jason Keith**
COVER ART

Separation Anxiety

Clay McLeod Chapman
WRITER

Brian Level
ARTIST

Jordan Boyd
COLOR ARTIST

VC's Travis Lanham
LETTERER

Philip Tan, Marc Deering & **John Rauch**
COVER ART

Danny Khazem
ASSISTANT EDITOR

Devin Lewis
EDITOR

Nick Lowe
EXECUTIVE EDITOR

Collection Editor **Jennifer Grünwald**
Assistant Editor **Caitlin O'Connell**
Associate Managing Editor **Kateri Woody**
Editor, Special Projects **Mark D. Beazley**

VP Production & Special Projects **Jeff Youngquist**
Book Designer **Adam Del Re**
SVP Print, Sales & Marketing **David Gabriel**
Director, Licensed Publishing **Sven Larsen**

Editor in Chief **C.B. Cebulski**
Chief Creative Officer **Joe Quesada**
President **Dan Buckley**
Executive Producer **Alan Fine**

ABSOLUTE CARNAGE: SCREAM. Contains material originally published in magazine form as ABSOLUTE CARNAGE: SCREAM (2019) #1-3 and ABSOLUTE CARNAGE: SEPARATION ANXIETY (2019) #1. First printing 2019. ISBN 978-1-302-92015-9. Published by MARVEL WORLDWIDE, INC., a subsidiary of MARVEL ENTERTAINMENT, LLC. OFFICE OF PUBLICATION: 135 West 50th Street, New York, NY 10020. © 2019 MARVEL No similarity between any of the names, characters, persons, and/or institutions in this magazine with those of any living or dead person or institution is intended, and any such similarity which may exist is purely coincidental. **Printed in Canada.** DAN BUCKLEY, President, Marvel Entertainment; JOHN NEE, Publisher; JOE QUESADA, Chief Creative Officer; TOM BREVOORT, SVP of Publishing; DAVID BOGART, Associate Publisher & SVP of Talent Affairs; DAVID GABRIEL, VP of Print & Digital Publishing; JEFF YOUNGQUIST, VP of Production & Special Projects; DAN CARR, Executive Director of Publishing Technology; ALEX MORALES, Director of Publishing Operations; DAN EDINGTON, Managing Editor; SUSAN CRESPI, Production Manager; STAN LEE, Chairman Emeritus. For information regarding advertising in Marvel Comics or on Marvel.com, please contact Vit DeBellis, Custom Solutions & Integrated Advertising Manager, at vdebellis@marvel.com. For Marvel subscription inquiries, please call 888-511-5480. **Manufactured between 11/22/2019 and 12/24/2019 by SOLISCO PRINTERS, SCOTT, QC, CANADA.**

10 9 8 7 6 5 4 3 2 1

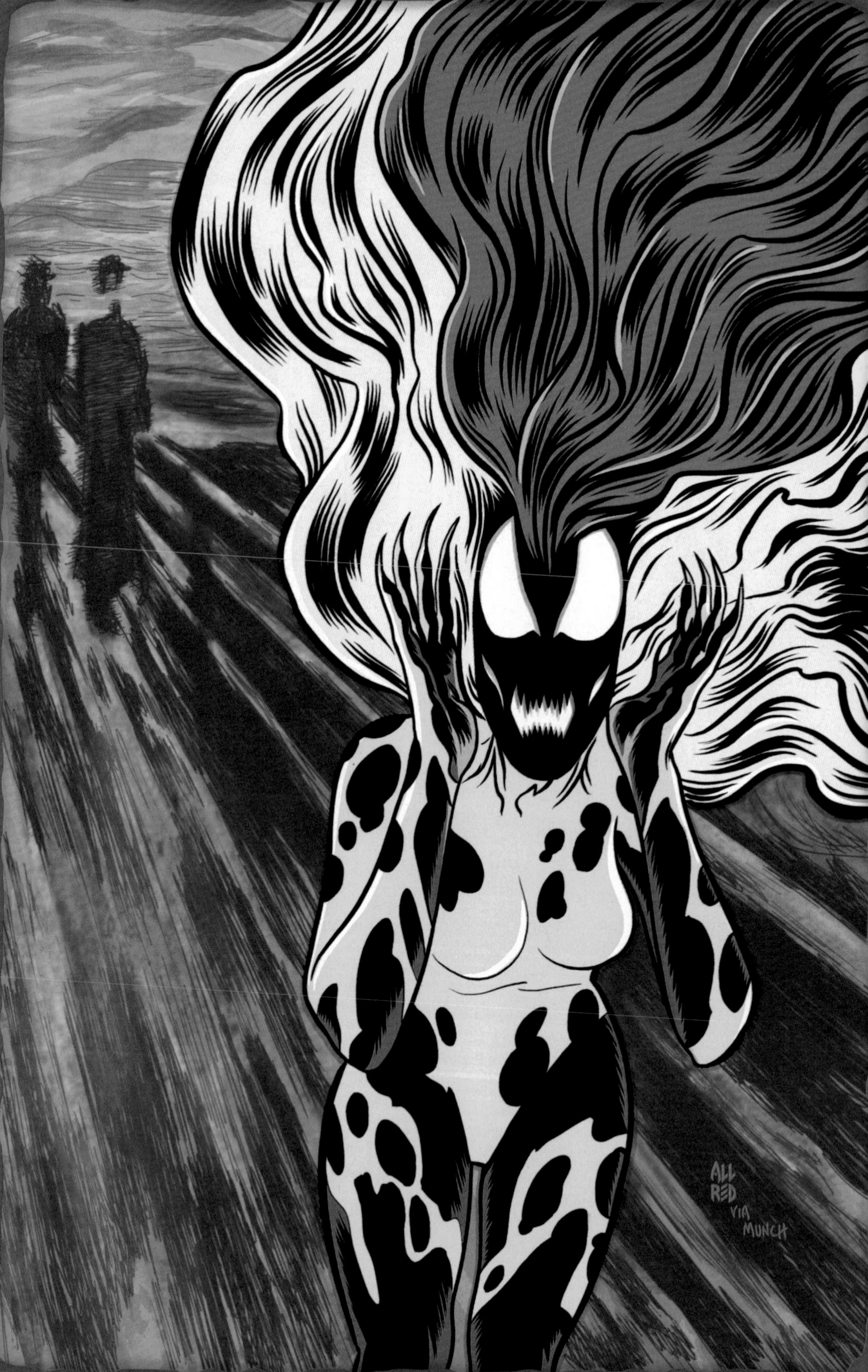
ALLRED
VIA
MUNCH

MICHAEL ALLRED & LAURA ALLRED

SCREAM #1 Codex Variant

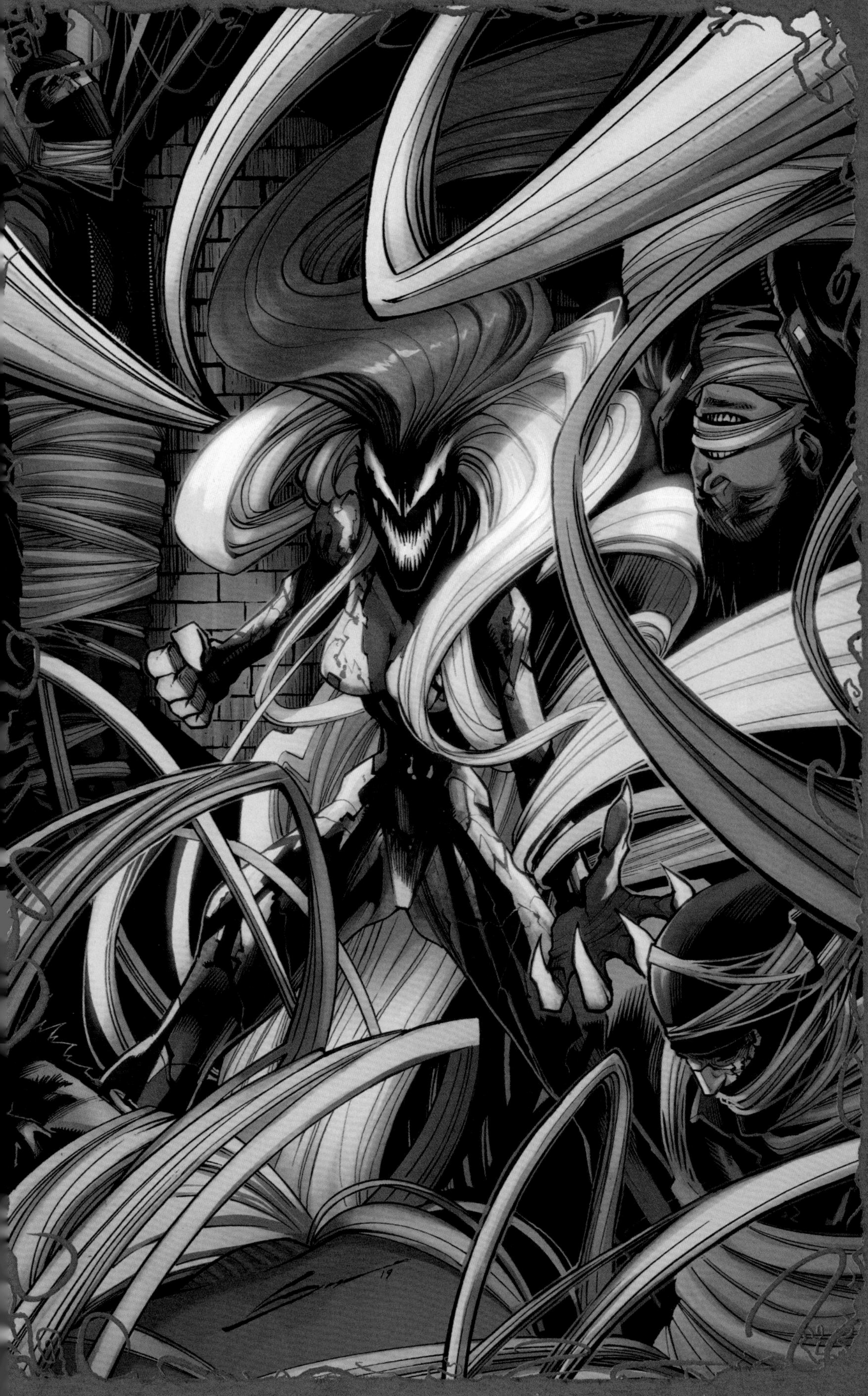

SCREAM 1

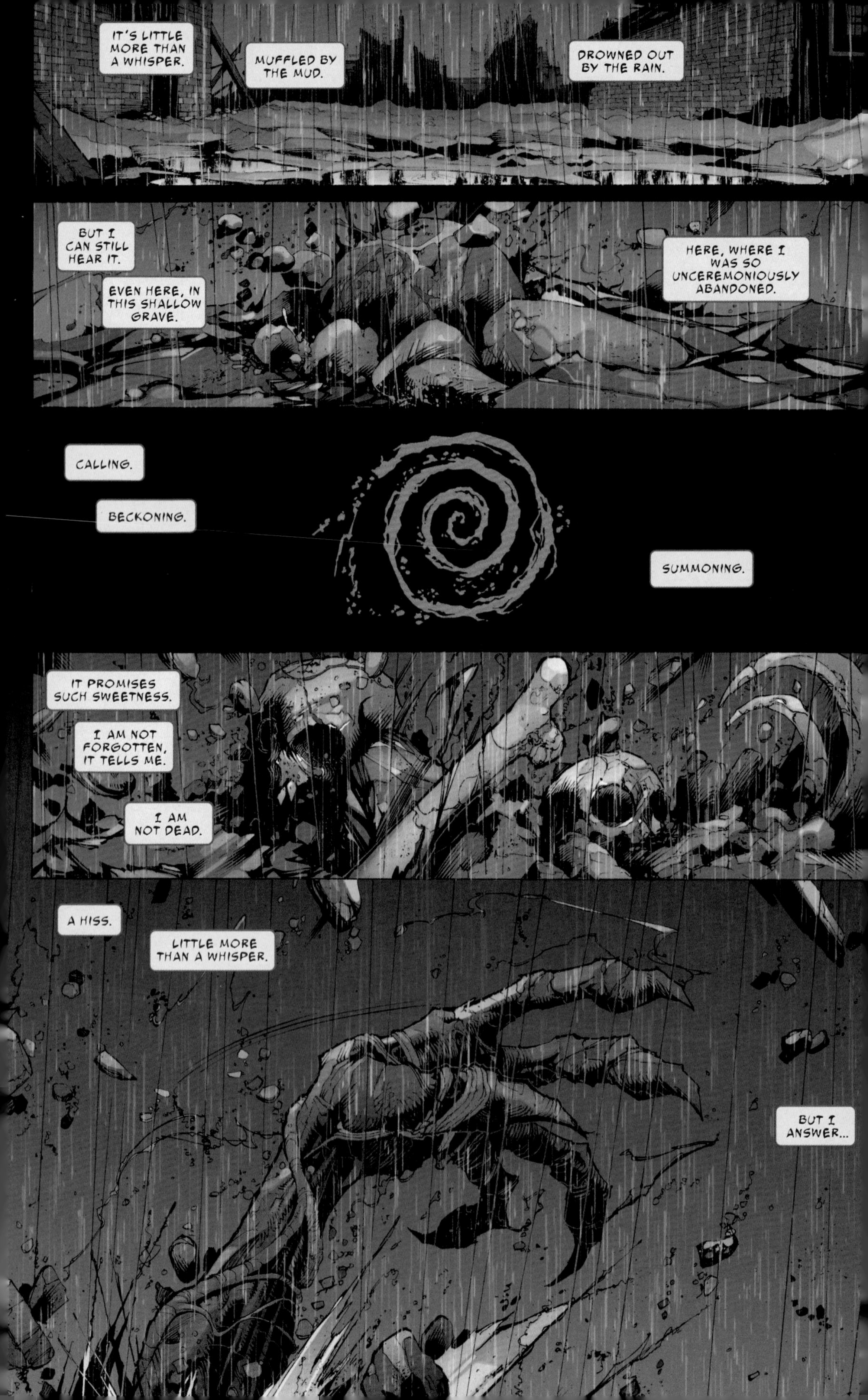
IT'S LITTLE MORE THAN A WHISPER.
MUFFLED BY THE MUD.
DROWNED OUT BY THE RAIN.
BUT I CAN STILL HEAR IT.
EVEN HERE, IN THIS SHALLOW GRAVE.
HERE, WHERE I WAS SO UNCEREMONIOUSLY ABANDONED.
CALLING.
BECKONING.
SUMMONING.
IT PROMISES SUCH SWEETNESS.
I AM NOT FORGOTTEN, IT TELLS ME.
I AM NOT DEAD.
A HISS.
LITTLE MORE THAN A WHISPER.
BUT I ANSWER...

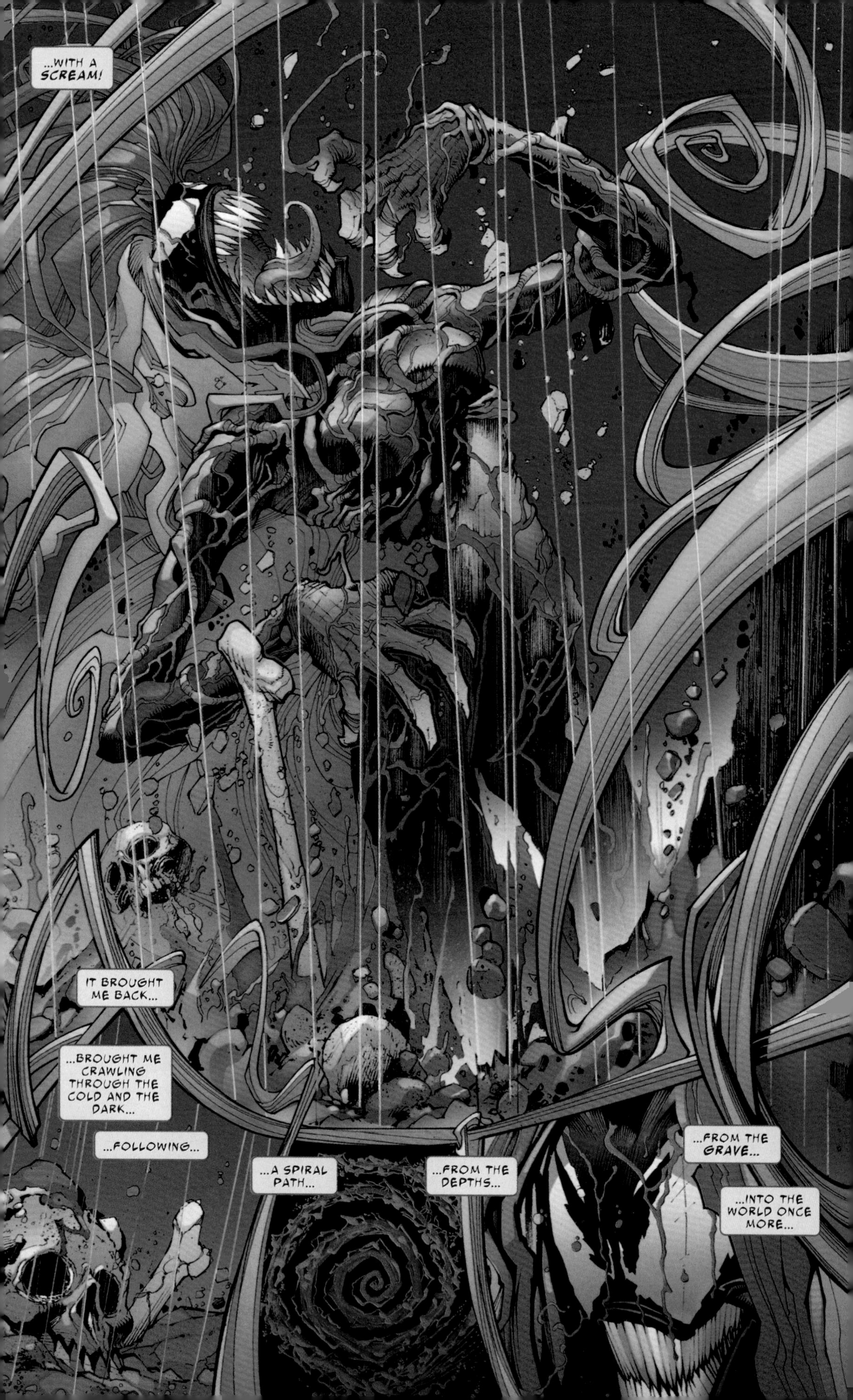
...WITH A SCREAM!
IT BROUGHT ME BACK...
...BROUGHT ME CRAWLING THROUGH THE COLD AND THE DARK...
...FOLLOWING...
...A SPIRAL PATH...
...FROM THE DEPTHS...
...FROM THE GRAVE...
...INTO THE WORLD ONCE MORE...

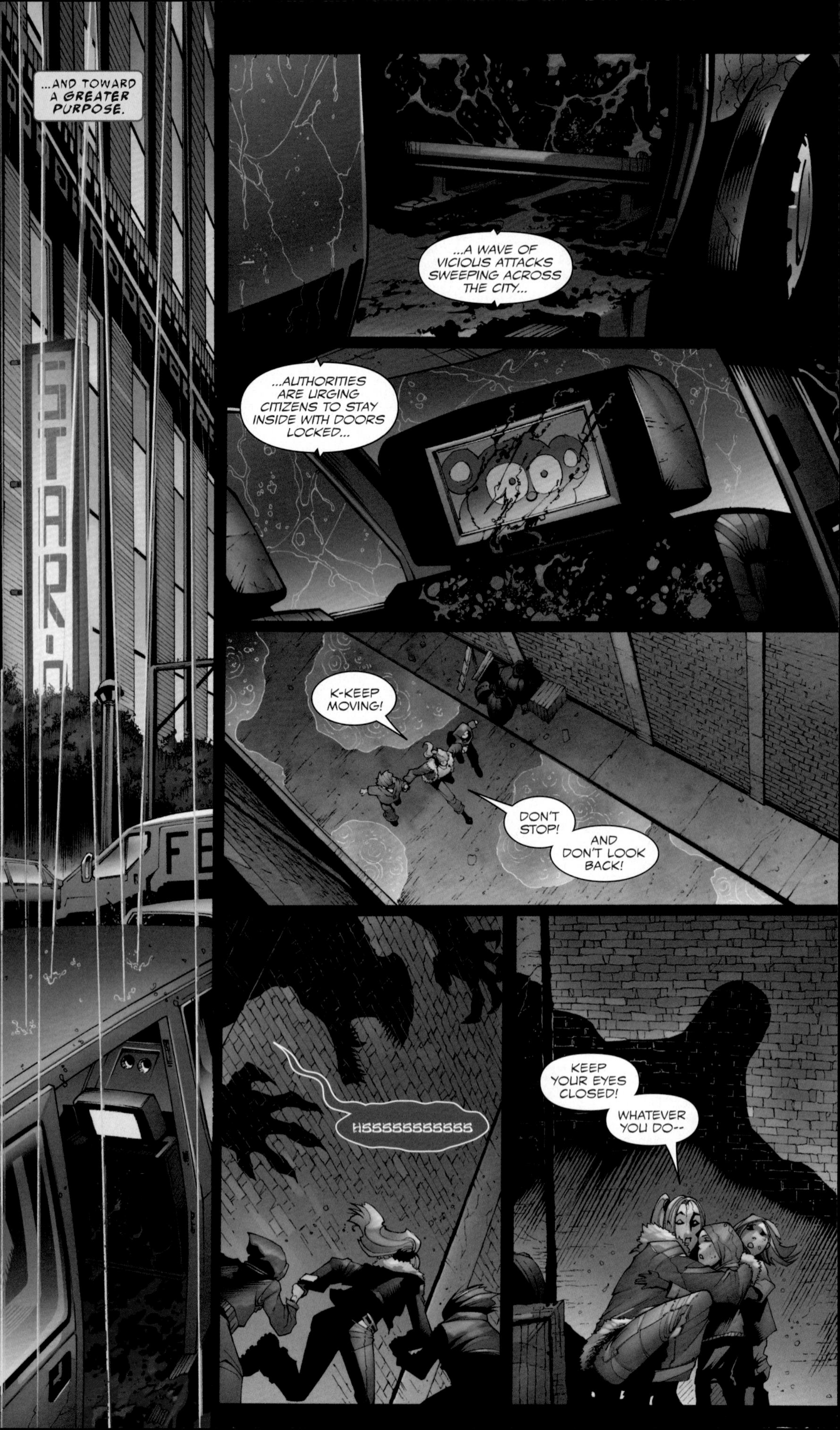
...AND TOWARD A GREATER PURPOSE.
STAR-C
FE
...A WAVE OF VICIOUS ATTACKS SWEEPING ACROSS THE CITY...
...AUTHORITIES ARE URGING CITIZENS TO STAY INSIDE WITH DOORS LOCKED...
K-KEEP MOVING!
DON'T STOP!
AND DON'T LOOK BACK!
HSSSSSSSSSSS
KEEP YOUR EYES CLOSED!
WHATEVER YOU DO--

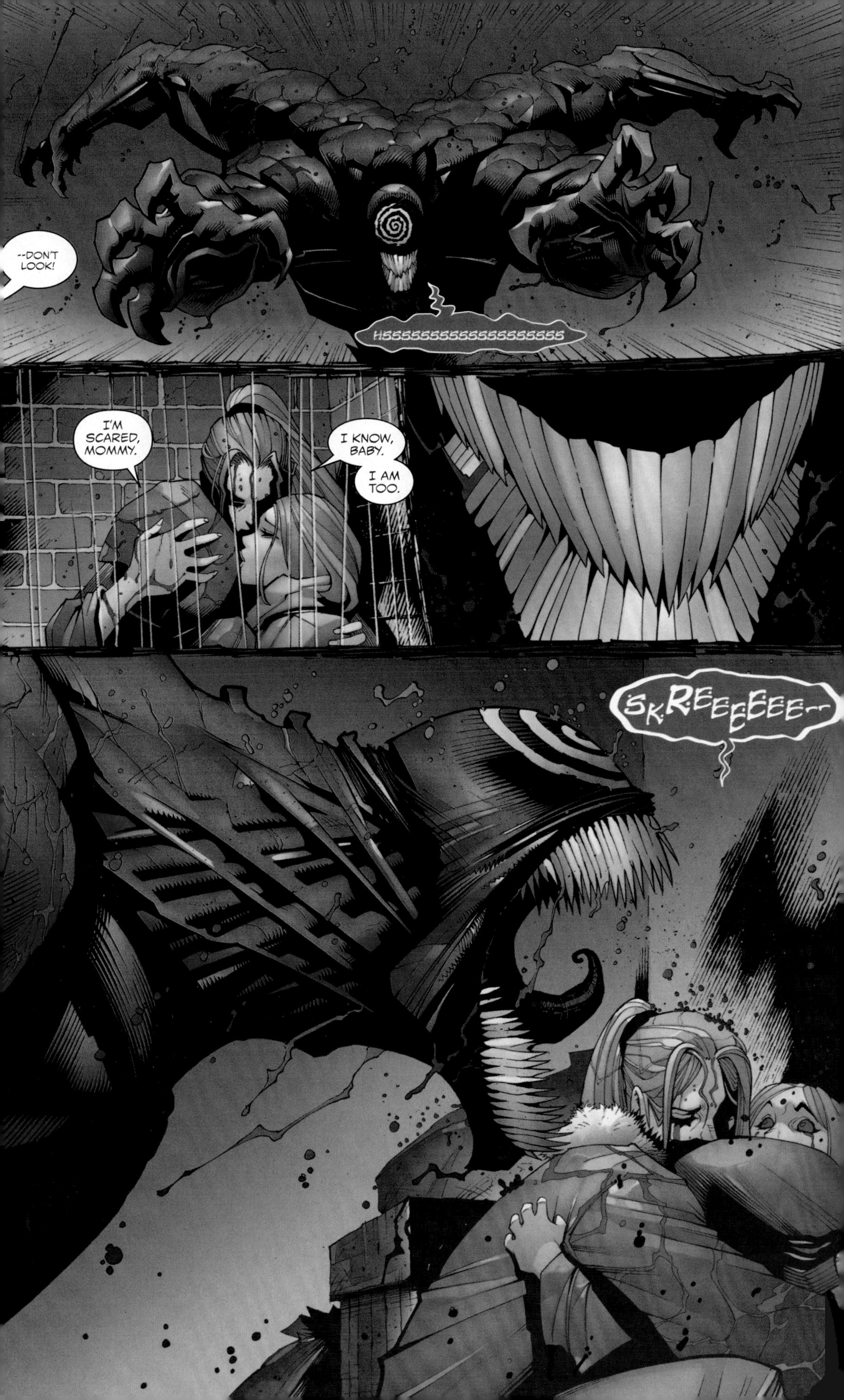
--DON'T LOOK!
HSSSSSSSSSSSSSSSSSSSS
I'M SCARED, MOMMY.
I KNOW, BABY.
I AM TOO.
SKREEEEEEE--

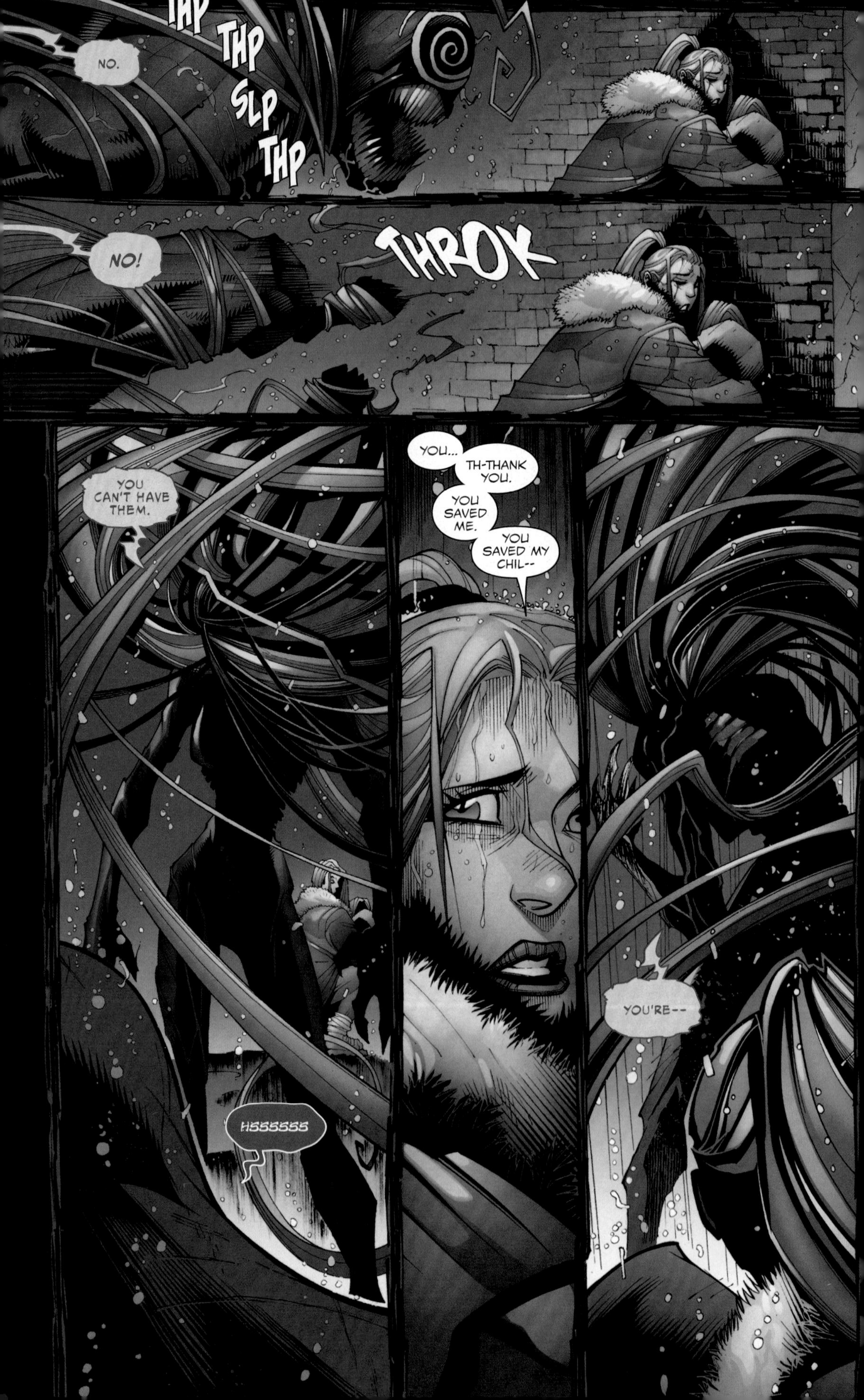
THP
THP
SLP
THP
NO.
NO!
THROK
YOU CAN'T HAVE THEM.
HSSSSSS
YOU...
TH-THANK YOU.
YOU SAVED ME.
YOU SAVED MY CHIL--
YOU'RE--

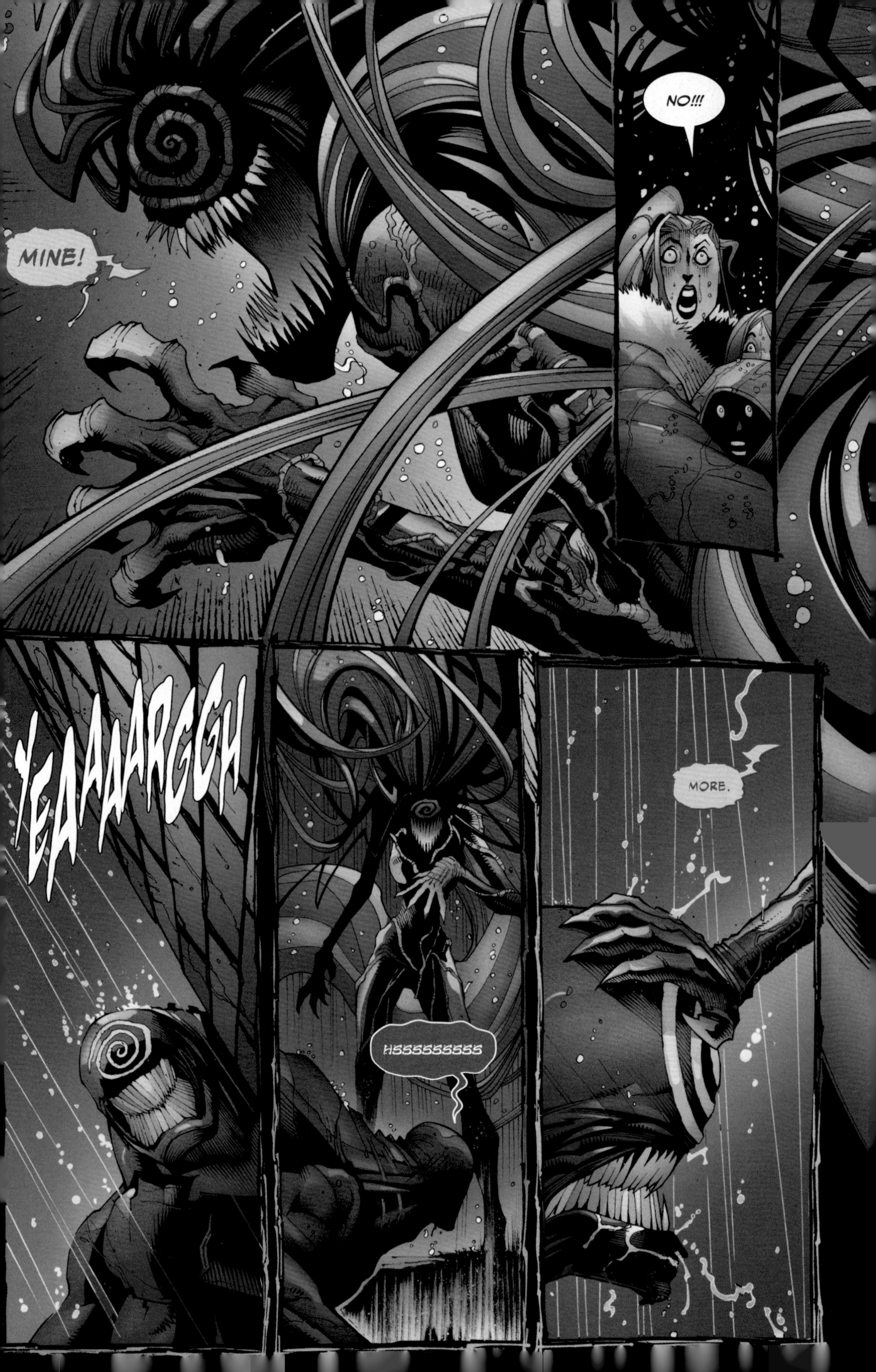
MINE!
NO!!!
YEAAAARGGH
HSSSSSSSSS
MORE.

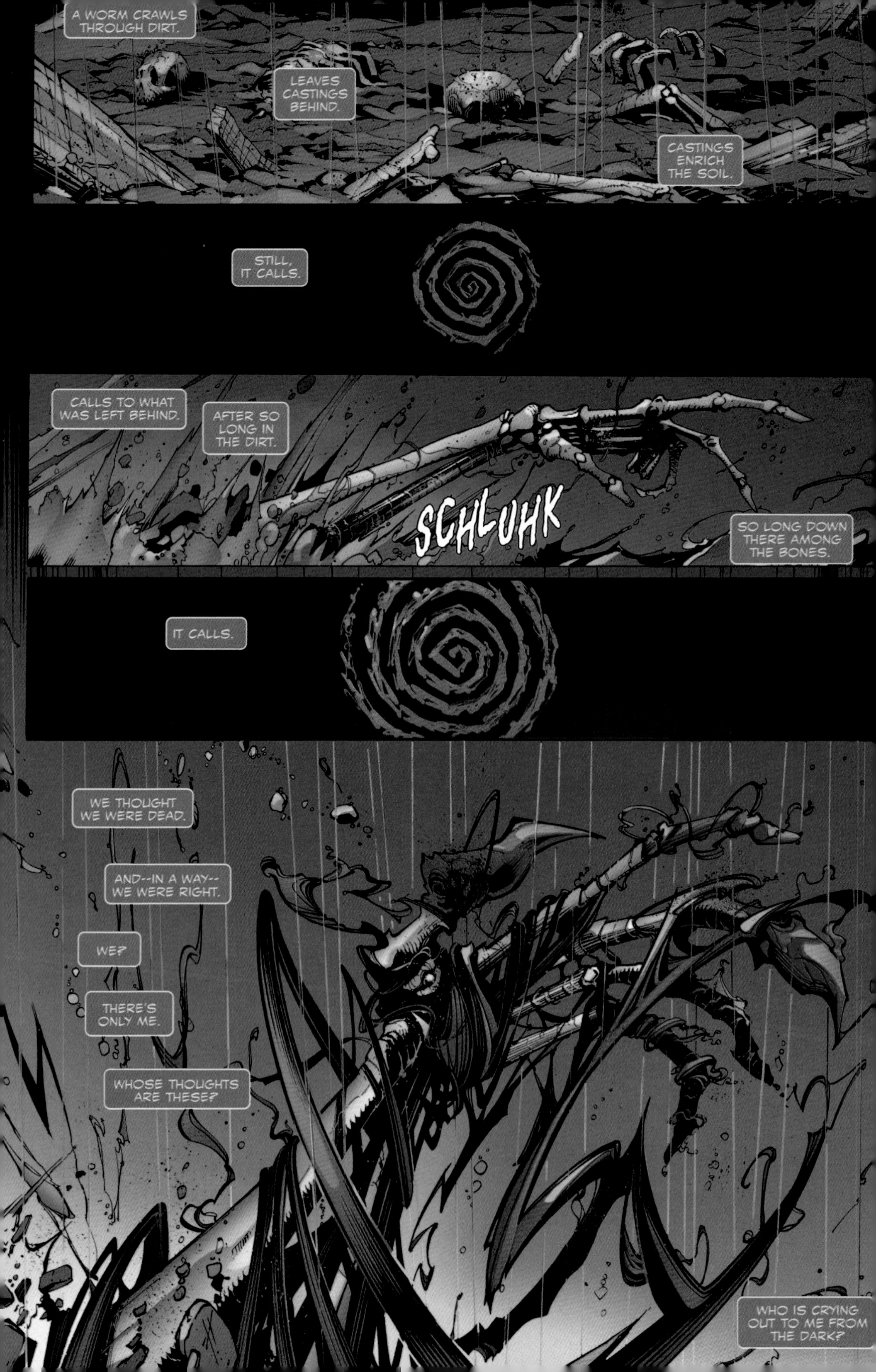
A WORM CRAWLS THROUGH DIRT.
LEAVES CASTINGS BEHIND.
CASTINGS ENRICH THE SOIL.
STILL, IT CALLS.
CALLS TO WHAT WAS LEFT BEHIND.
AFTER SO LONG IN THE DIRT.
SCHLUHK
SO LONG DOWN THERE AMONG THE BONES.
IT CALLS.
WE THOUGHT WE WERE DEAD.
AND--IN A WAY--WE WERE RIGHT.
WE?
THERE'S ONLY ME.
WHOSE THOUGHTS ARE THESE?
WHO IS CRYING OUT TO ME FROM THE DARK?

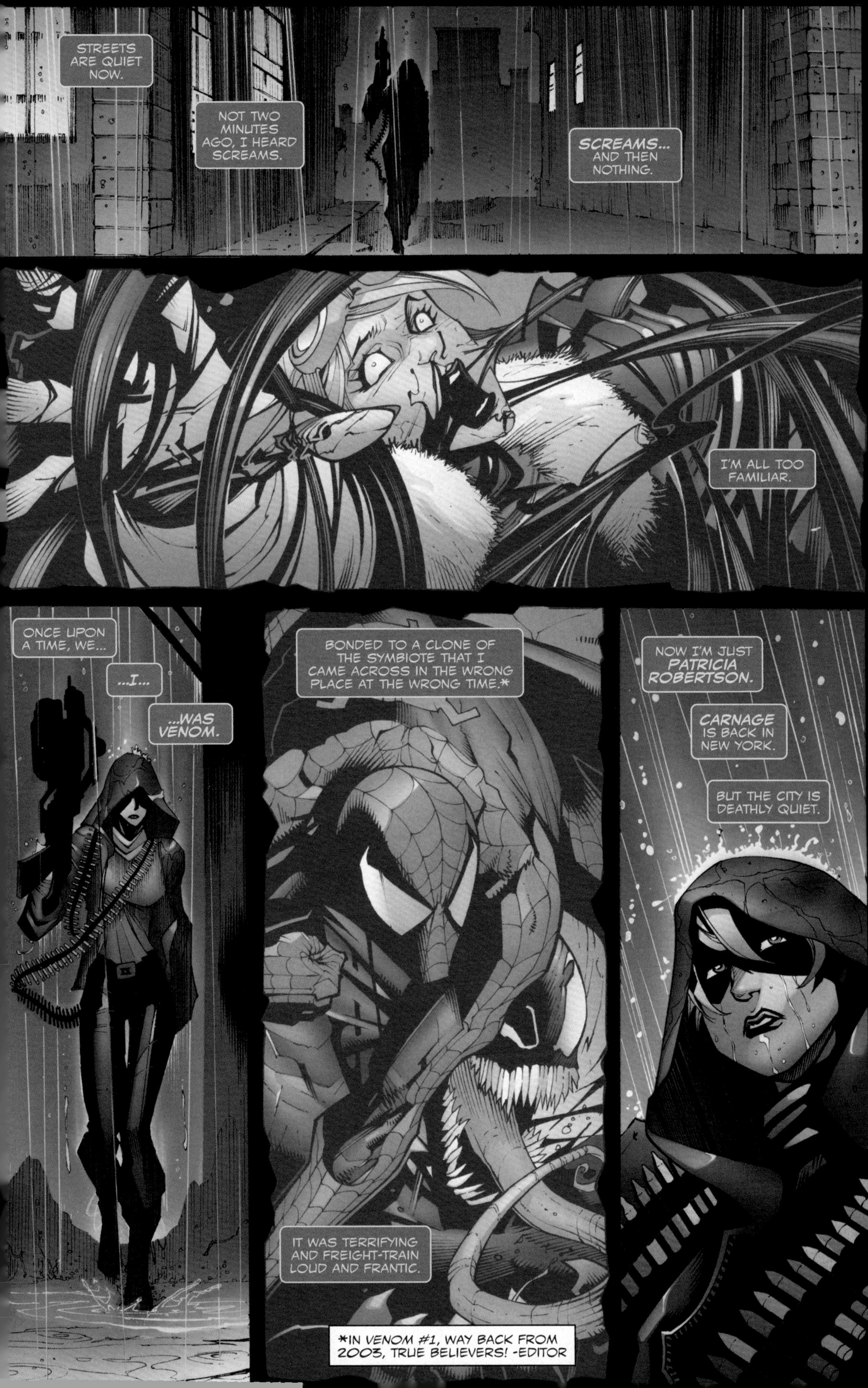
STREETS ARE QUIET NOW.
NOT TWO MINUTES AGO, I HEARD SCREAMS.
SCREAMS... AND THEN NOTHING.
I'M ALL TOO FAMILIAR.
ONCE UPON A TIME, WE...
...I...
...WAS VENOM.
BONDED TO A CLONE OF THE SYMBIOTE THAT I CAME ACROSS IN THE WRONG PLACE AT THE WRONG TIME.*
IT WAS TERRIFYING AND FREIGHT-TRAIN LOUD AND FRANTIC.
*IN VENOM #1, WAY BACK FROM 2003, TRUE BELIEVERS! -EDITOR
NOW I'M JUST PATRICIA ROBERTSON.
CARNAGE IS BACK IN NEW YORK.
BUT THE CITY IS DEATHLY QUIET.

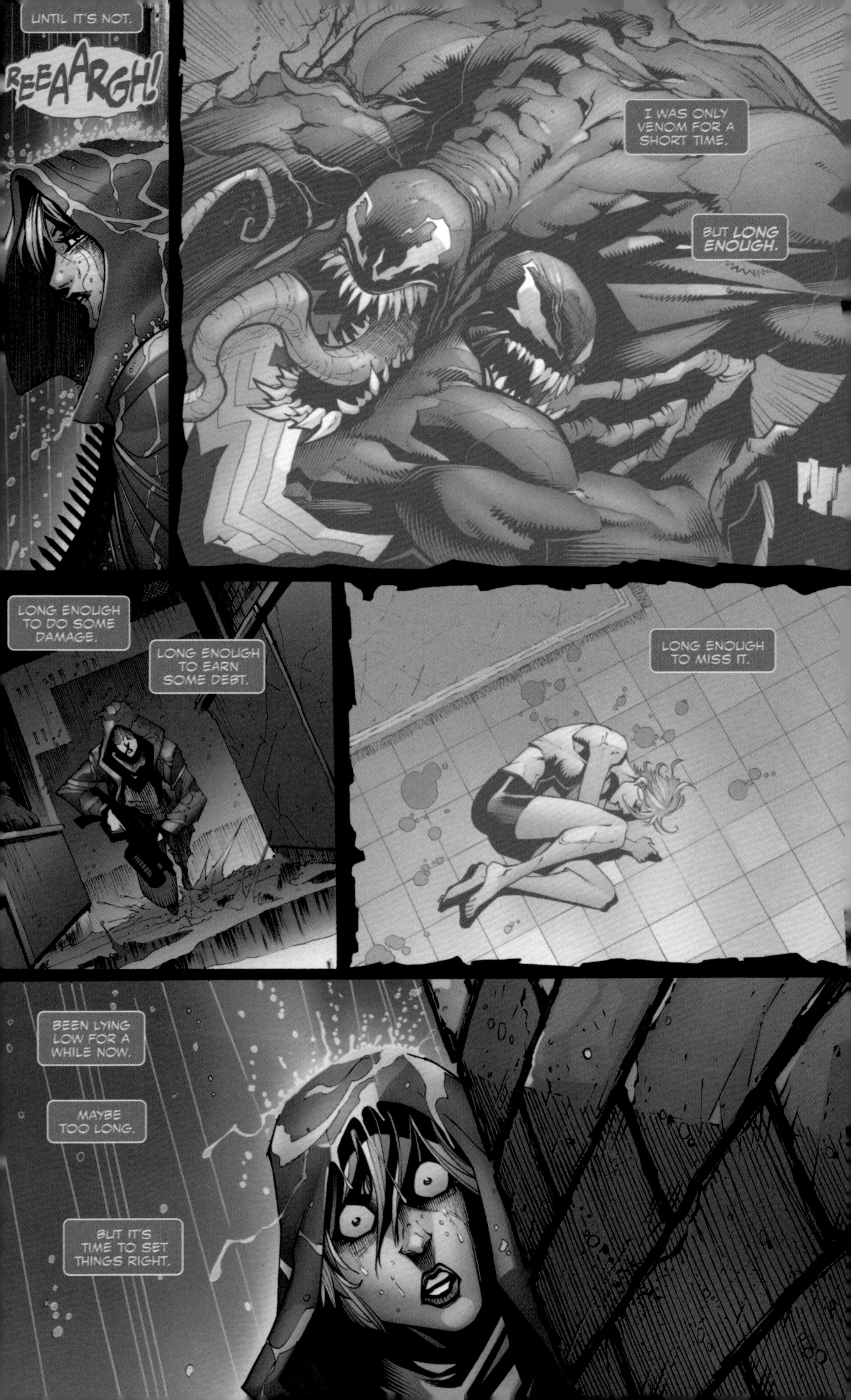
UNTIL IT'S NOT.
REEAARGH!
I WAS ONLY VENOM FOR A SHORT TIME.
BUT LONG ENOUGH.
LONG ENOUGH TO DO SOME DAMAGE.
LONG ENOUGH TO EARN SOME DEBT.
LONG ENOUGH TO MISS IT.
BEEN LYING LOW FOR A WHILE NOW.
MAYBE TOO LONG.
BUT IT'S TIME TO SET THINGS RIGHT.

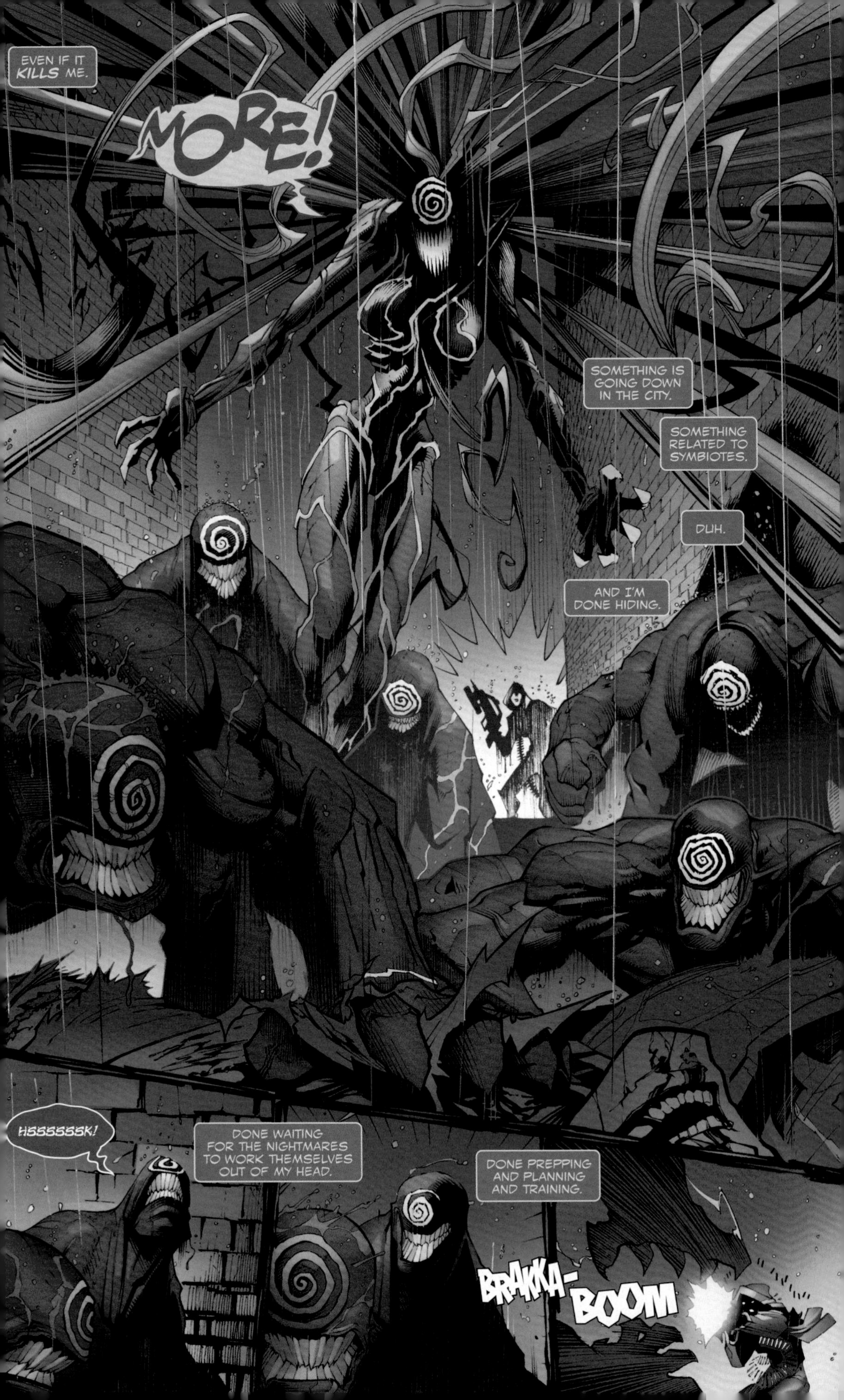
EVEN IF IT KILLS ME.
MORE!
SOMETHING IS GOING DOWN IN THE CITY.
SOMETHING RELATED TO SYMBIOTES.
DUH.
AND I'M DONE HIDING.
HSSSSSSK!
DONE WAITING FOR THE NIGHTMARES TO WORK THEMSELVES OUT OF MY HEAD.
DONE PREPPING AND PLANNING AND TRAINING.
BRAKKA-BOOM

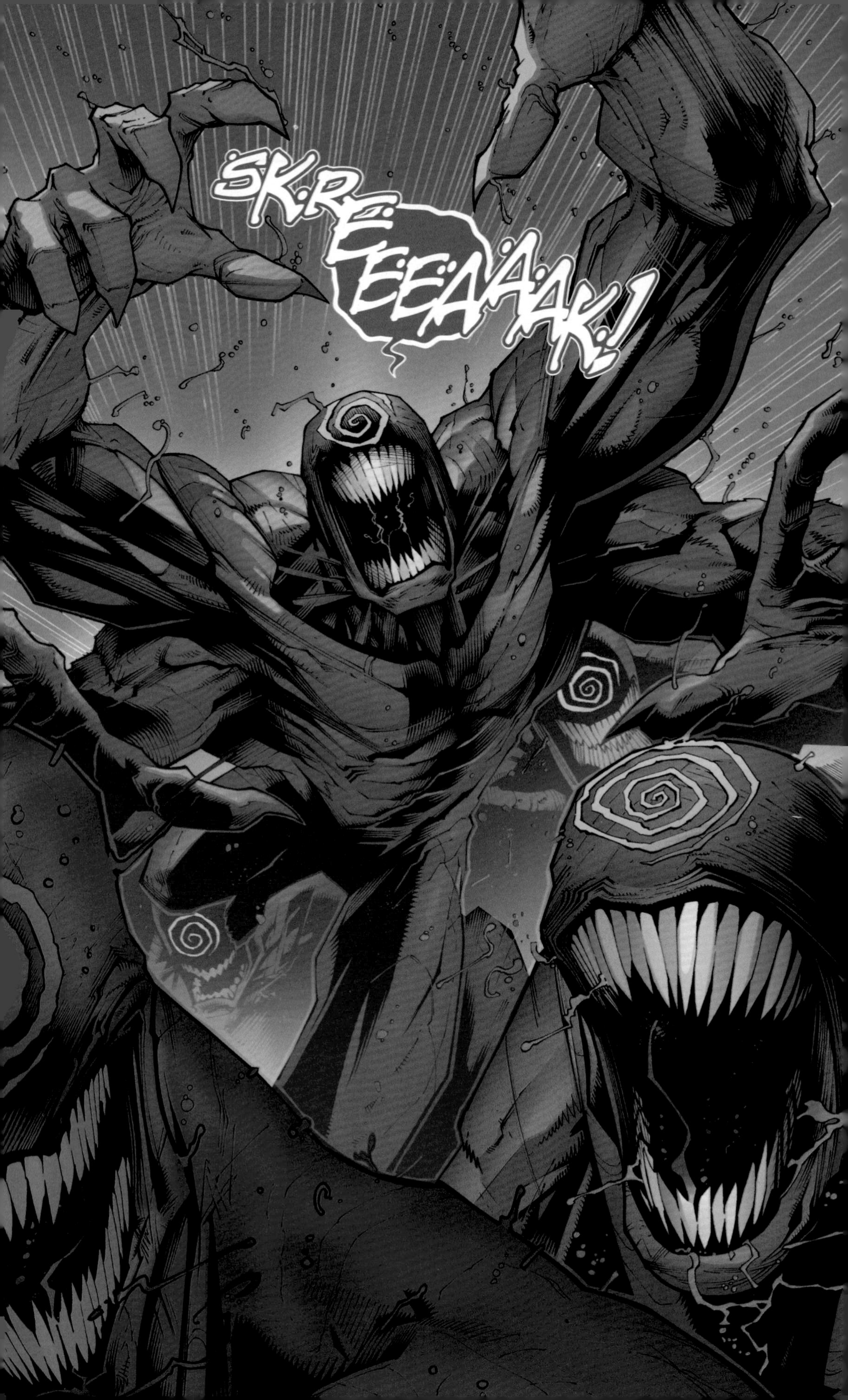
SKREEEAAAK!

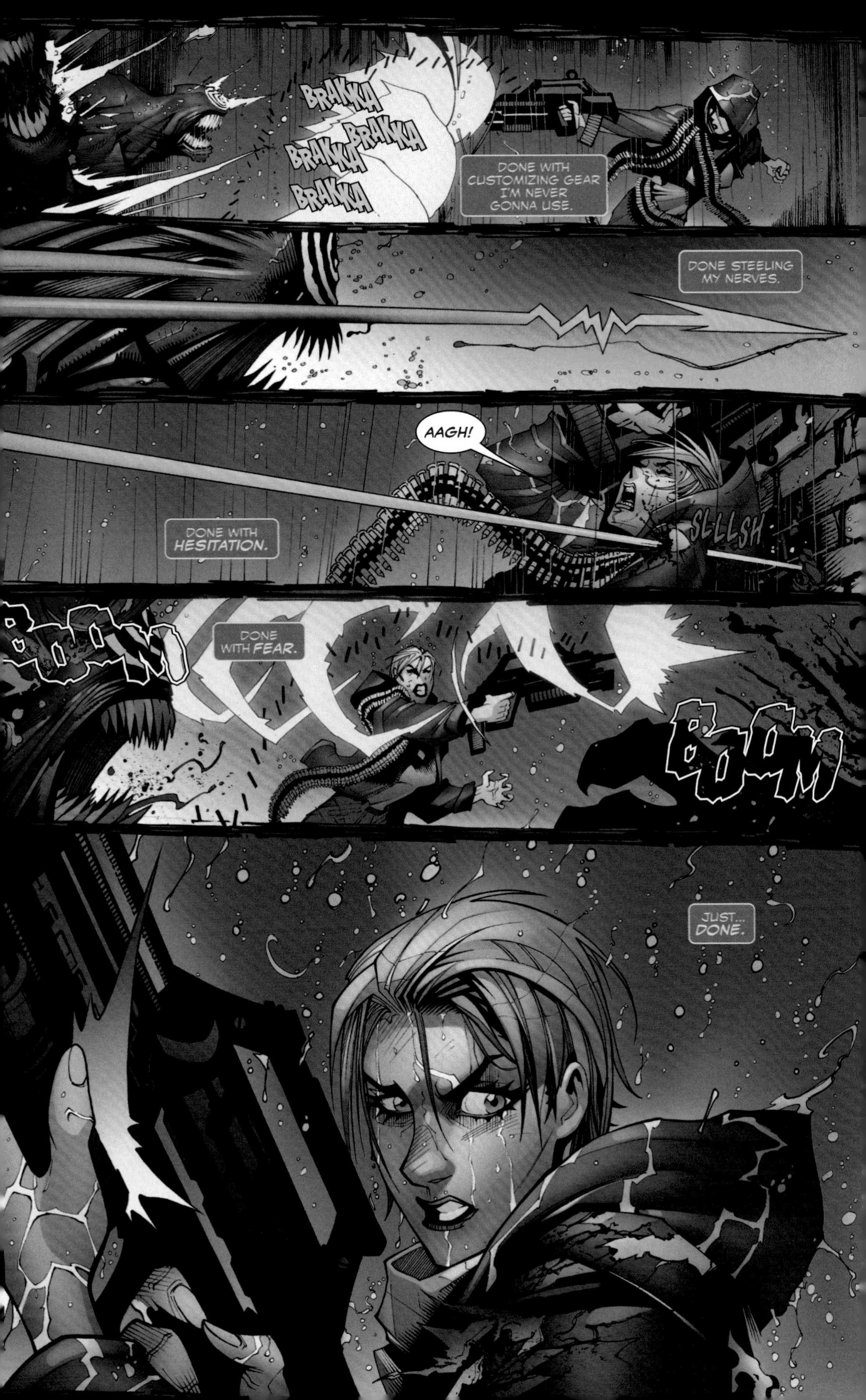
BRAKKA
BRAKKA
BRAKKA
BRAKKA
DONE WITH CUSTOMIZING GEAR I'M NEVER GONNA USE.
DONE STEELING MY NERVES.
AAGH!
DONE WITH HESITATION.
SLLLSH
BOOM
DONE WITH FEAR.
BOOM
JUST... DONE.

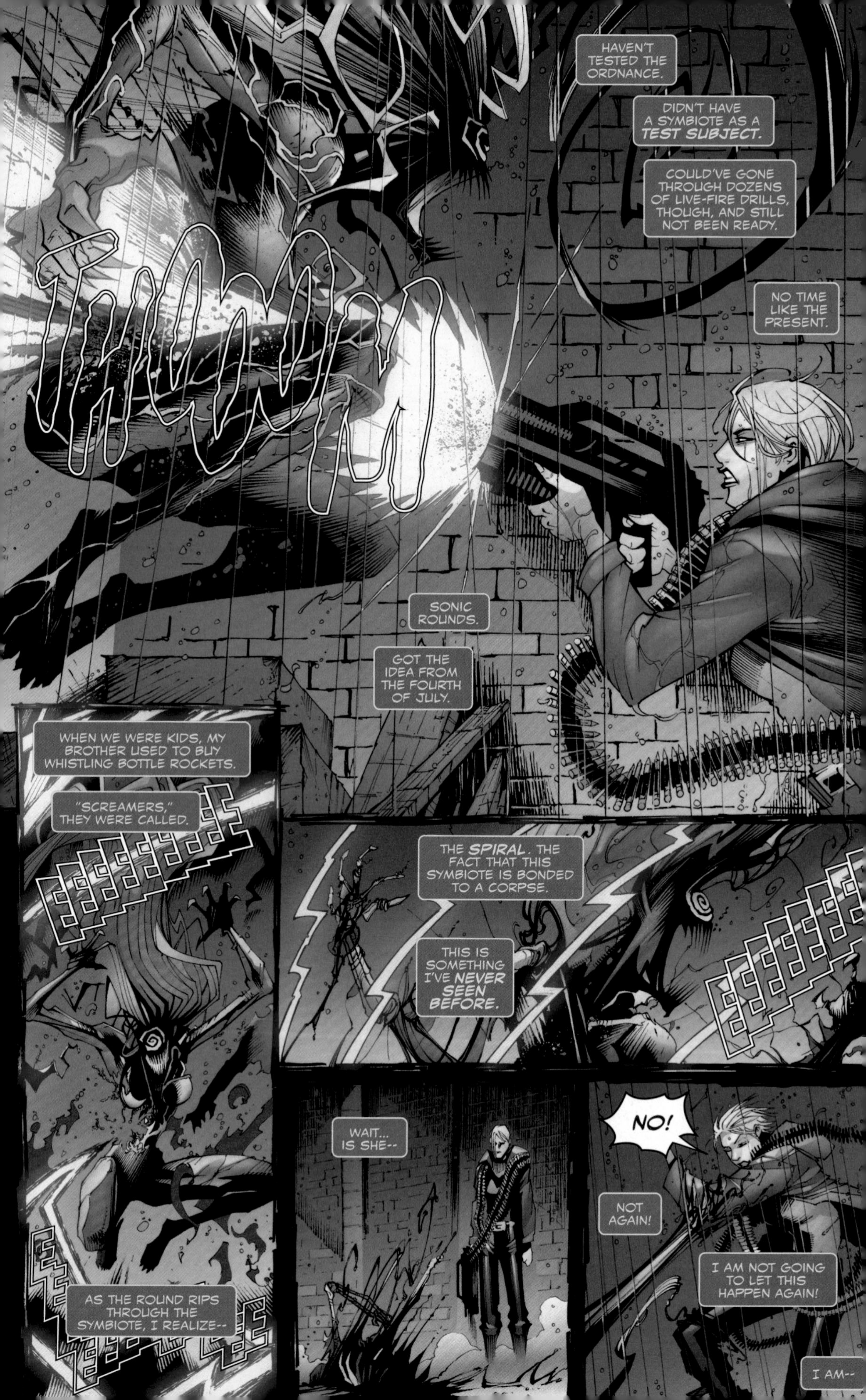
HAVEN'T TESTED THE ORDNANCE.
DIDN'T HAVE A SYMBIOTE AS A **TEST SUBJECT.**
COULD'VE GONE THROUGH DOZENS OF LIVE-FIRE DRILLS, THOUGH, AND STILL NOT BEEN READY.
NO TIME LIKE THE PRESENT.
SONIC ROUNDS.
GOT THE IDEA FROM THE FOURTH OF JULY.
WHEN WE WERE KIDS, MY BROTHER USED TO BUY WHISTLING BOTTLE ROCKETS.
"SCREAMERS," THEY WERE CALLED.
AS THE ROUND RIPS THROUGH THE SYMBIOTE, I REALIZE--
THE **SPIRAL**. THE FACT THAT THIS SYMBIOTE IS BONDED TO A CORPSE.
THIS IS SOMETHING I'VE **NEVER SEEN BEFORE.**
WAIT... IS SHE--
NO!
NOT AGAIN!
I AM NOT GOING TO LET THIS HAPPEN AGAIN!
I AM--

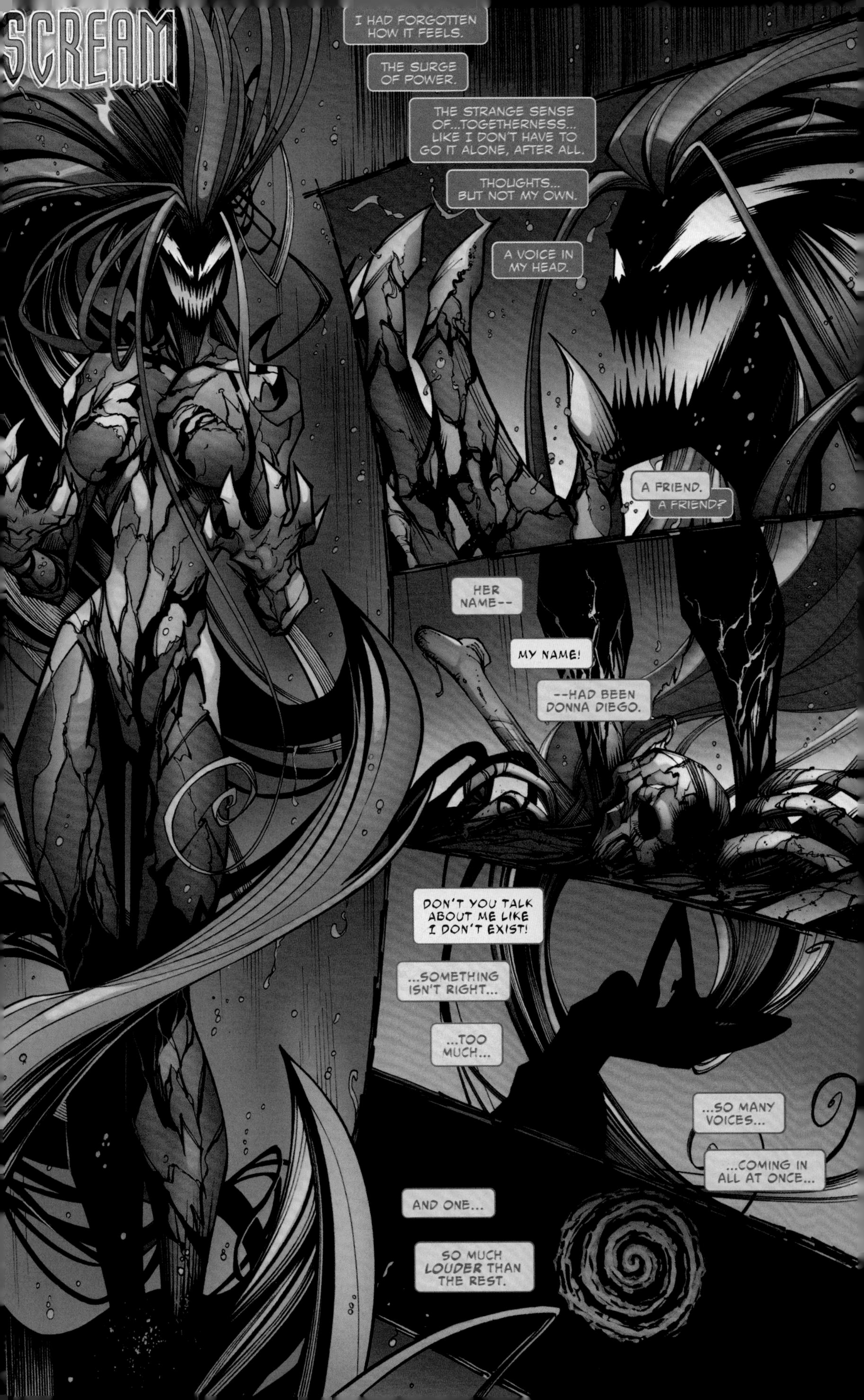
SCREAM
I HAD FORGOTTEN HOW IT FEELS.
THE SURGE OF POWER.
THE STRANGE SENSE OF...TOGETHERNESS... LIKE I DON'T HAVE TO GO IT ALONE, AFTER ALL.
THOUGHTS... BUT NOT MY OWN.
A VOICE IN MY HEAD.
A FRIEND.
A FRIEND?
HER NAME--
MY NAME!
--HAD BEEN DONNA DIEGO.
DON'T YOU TALK ABOUT ME LIKE I DON'T EXIST!
...SOMETHING ISN'T RIGHT...
...TOO MUCH...
...SO MANY VOICES...
...COMING IN ALL AT ONCE...
AND ONE...
SO MUCH LOUDER THAN THE REST.

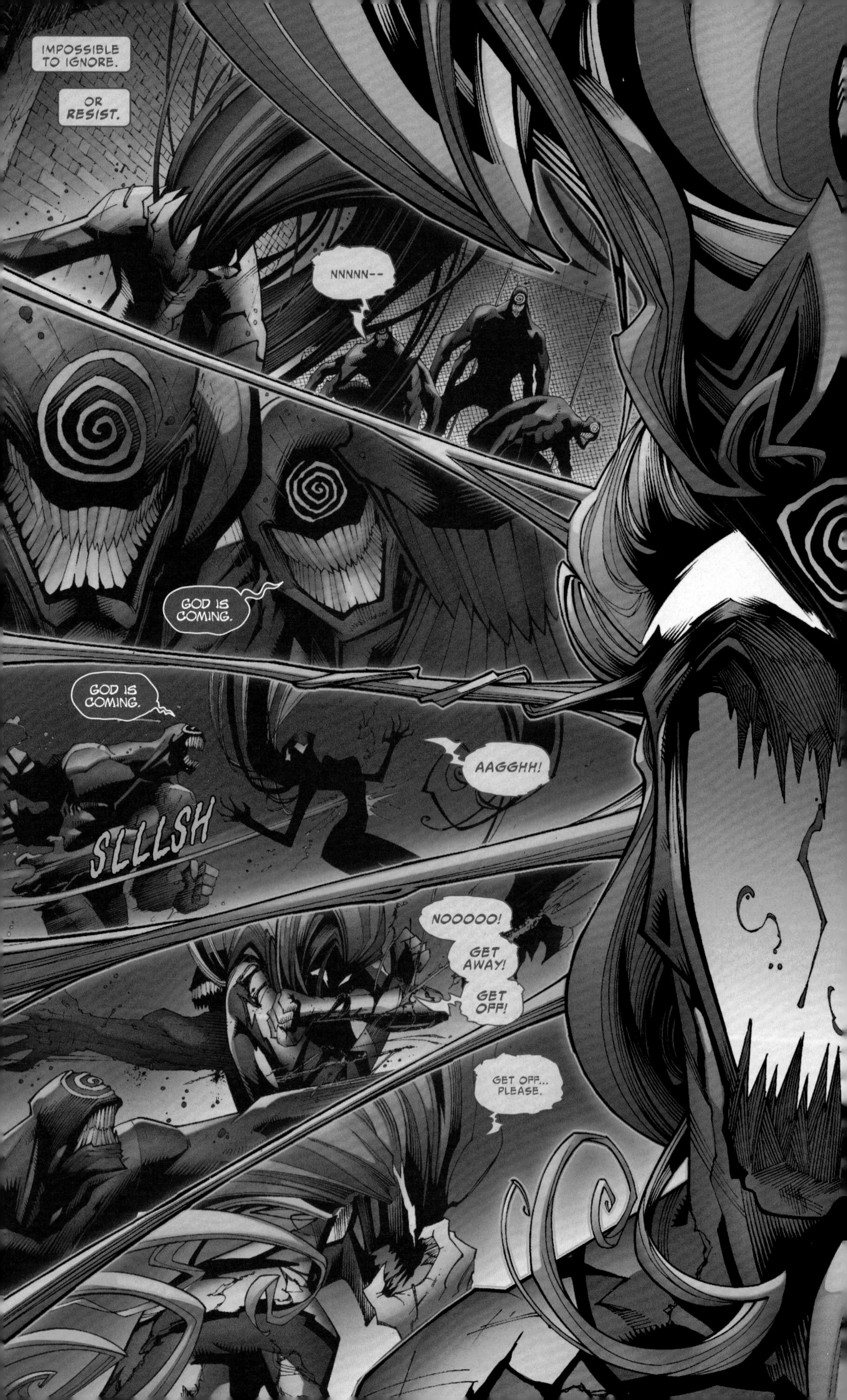
IMPOSSIBLE TO IGNORE.
OR RESIST.
NNNNN--
GOD IS COMING.
GOD IS COMING.
AAGGHH!
SLLLSH
NOOOOO!
GET AWAY!
GET OFF!
GET OFF... PLEASE.

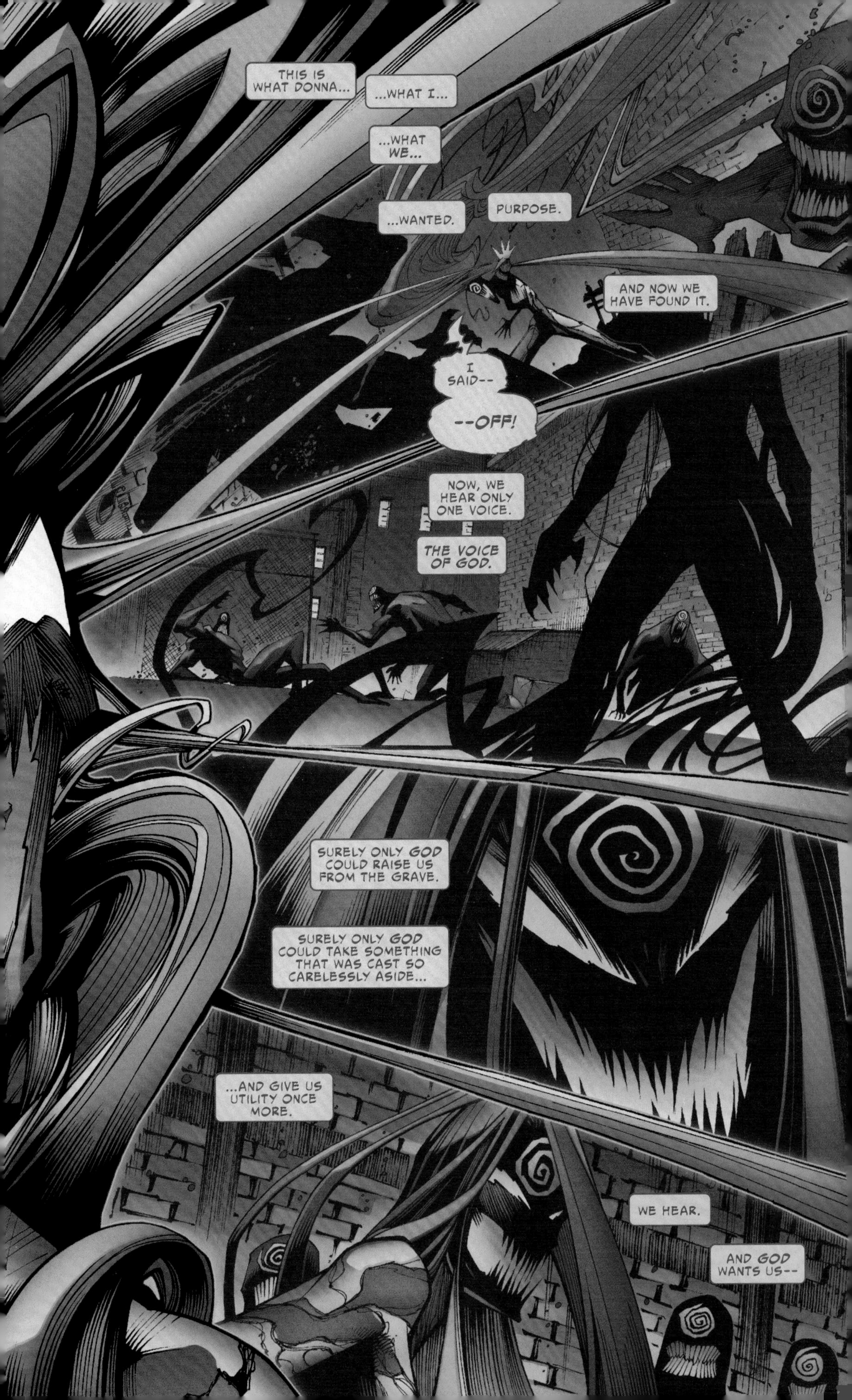
THIS IS WHAT DONNA...
...WHAT I...
...WHAT WE...
...WANTED.
PURPOSE.
AND NOW WE HAVE FOUND IT.
I SAID--
--OFF!
NOW, WE HEAR ONLY ONE VOICE.
THE VOICE OF GOD.
SURELY ONLY GOD COULD RAISE US FROM THE GRAVE.
SURELY ONLY GOD COULD TAKE SOMETHING THAT WAS CAST SO CARELESSLY ASIDE...
...AND GIVE US UTILITY ONCE MORE.
WE HEAR.
AND GOD WANTS US--

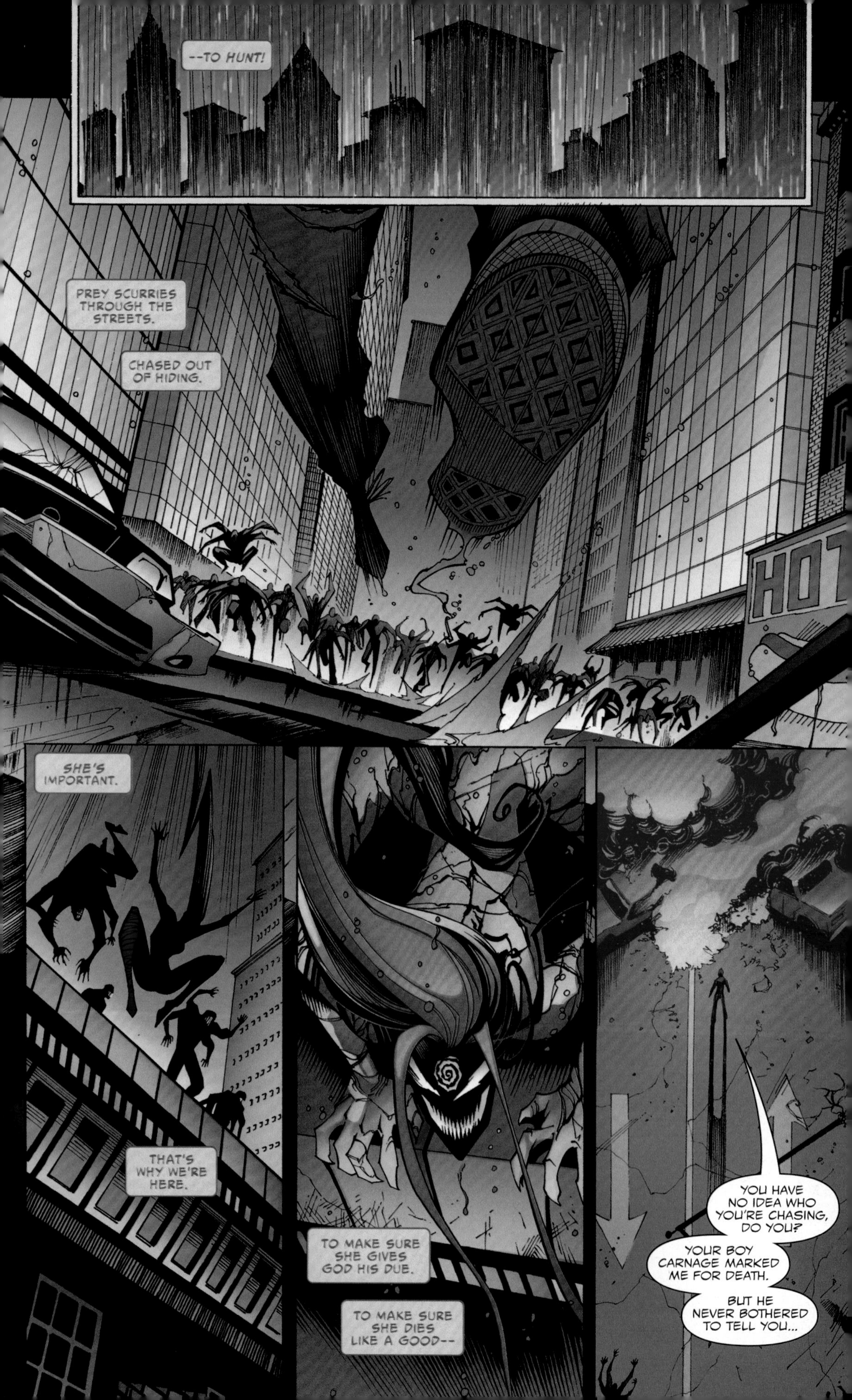
--TO HUNT!
PREY SCURRIES THROUGH THE STREETS.
CHASED OUT OF HIDING.
HOT
SHE'S IMPORTANT.
THAT'S WHY WE'RE HERE.
TO MAKE SURE SHE GIVES GOD HIS DUE.
TO MAKE SURE SHE DIES LIKE A GOOD--
YOU HAVE NO IDEA WHO YOU'RE CHASING, DO YOU?
YOUR BOY CARNAGE MARKED ME FOR DEATH.
BUT HE NEVER BOTHERED TO TELL YOU...

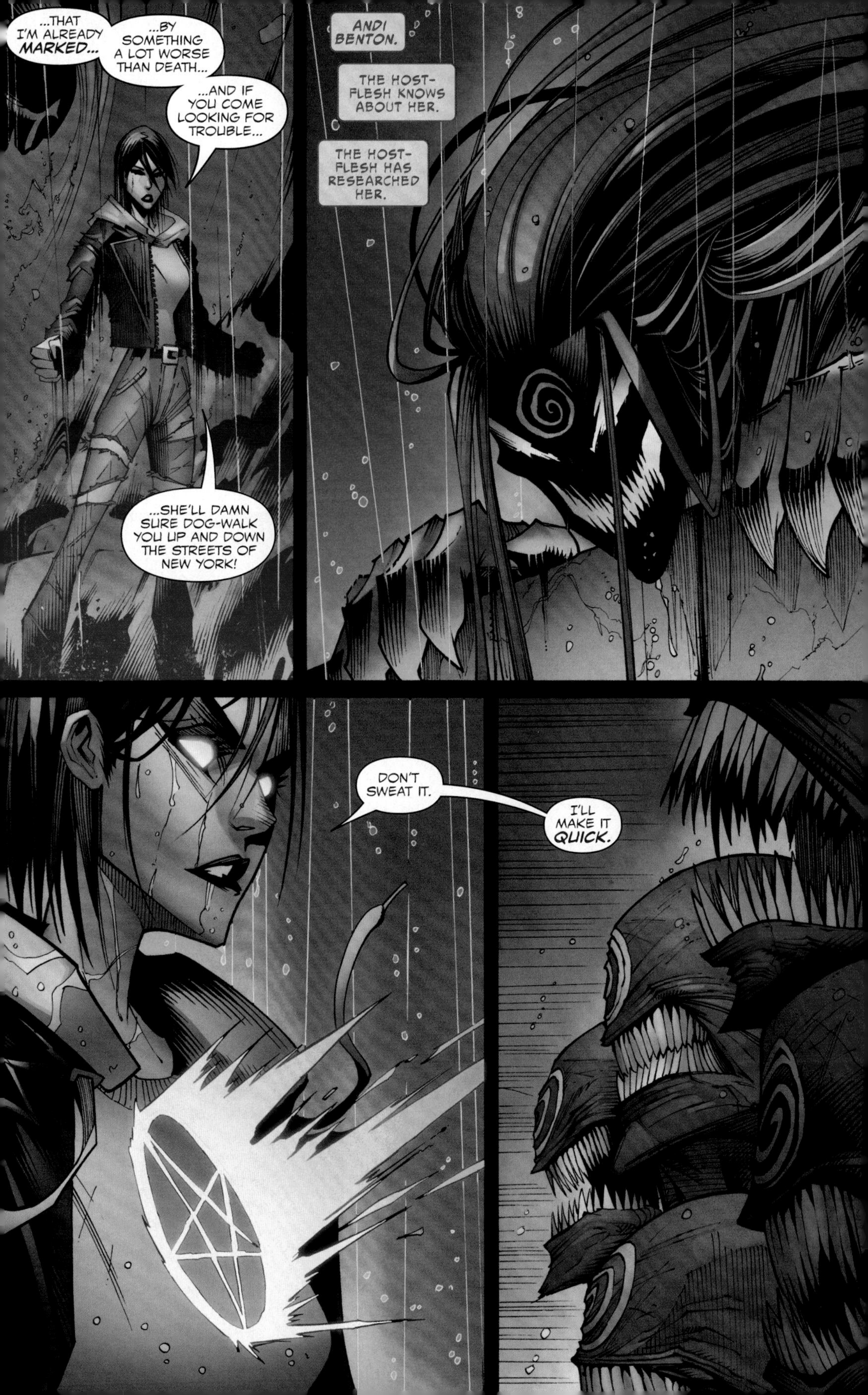
...THAT I'M ALREADY **MARKED...**
...BY SOMETHING A LOT WORSE THAN DEATH...
...AND IF YOU COME LOOKING FOR TROUBLE...
...SHE'LL DAMN SURE DOG-WALK YOU UP AND DOWN THE STREETS OF NEW YORK!
ANDI BENTON.
THE HOST-FLESH KNOWS ABOUT HER.
THE HOST-FLESH HAS RESEARCHED HER.
DON'T SWEAT IT.
I'LL MAKE IT **QUICK.**

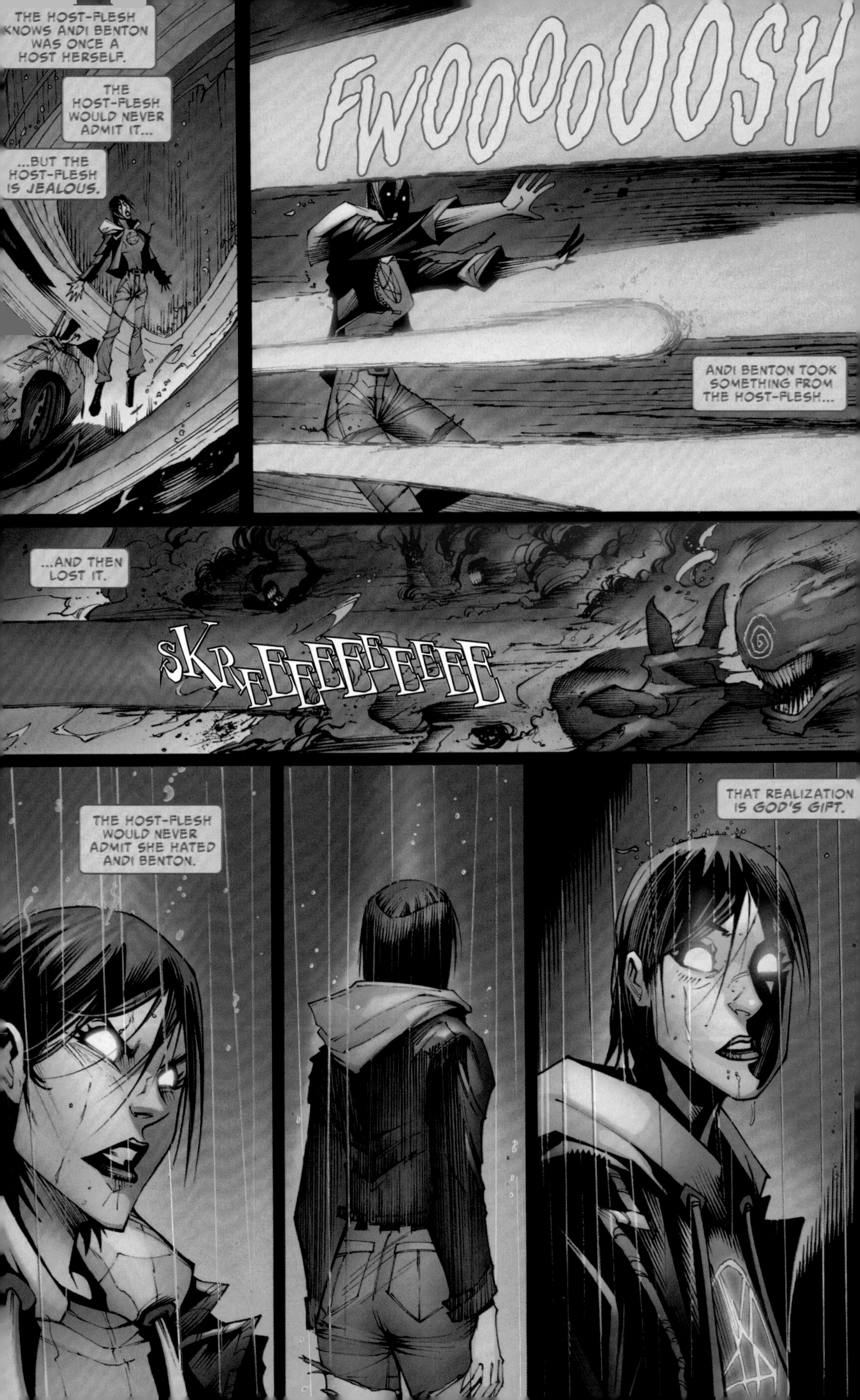
THE HOST-FLESH KNOWS ANDI BENTON WAS ONCE A HOST HERSELF.
THE HOST-FLESH WOULD NEVER ADMIT IT...
...BUT THE HOST-FLESH IS JEALOUS.
FWOOOOOOOSH
ANDI BENTON TOOK SOMETHING FROM THE HOST-FLESH...
...AND THEN LOST IT.
SKREEEEEEEEEE
THE HOST-FLESH WOULD NEVER ADMIT SHE HATED ANDI BENTON.
THAT REALIZATION IS GOD'S GIFT.

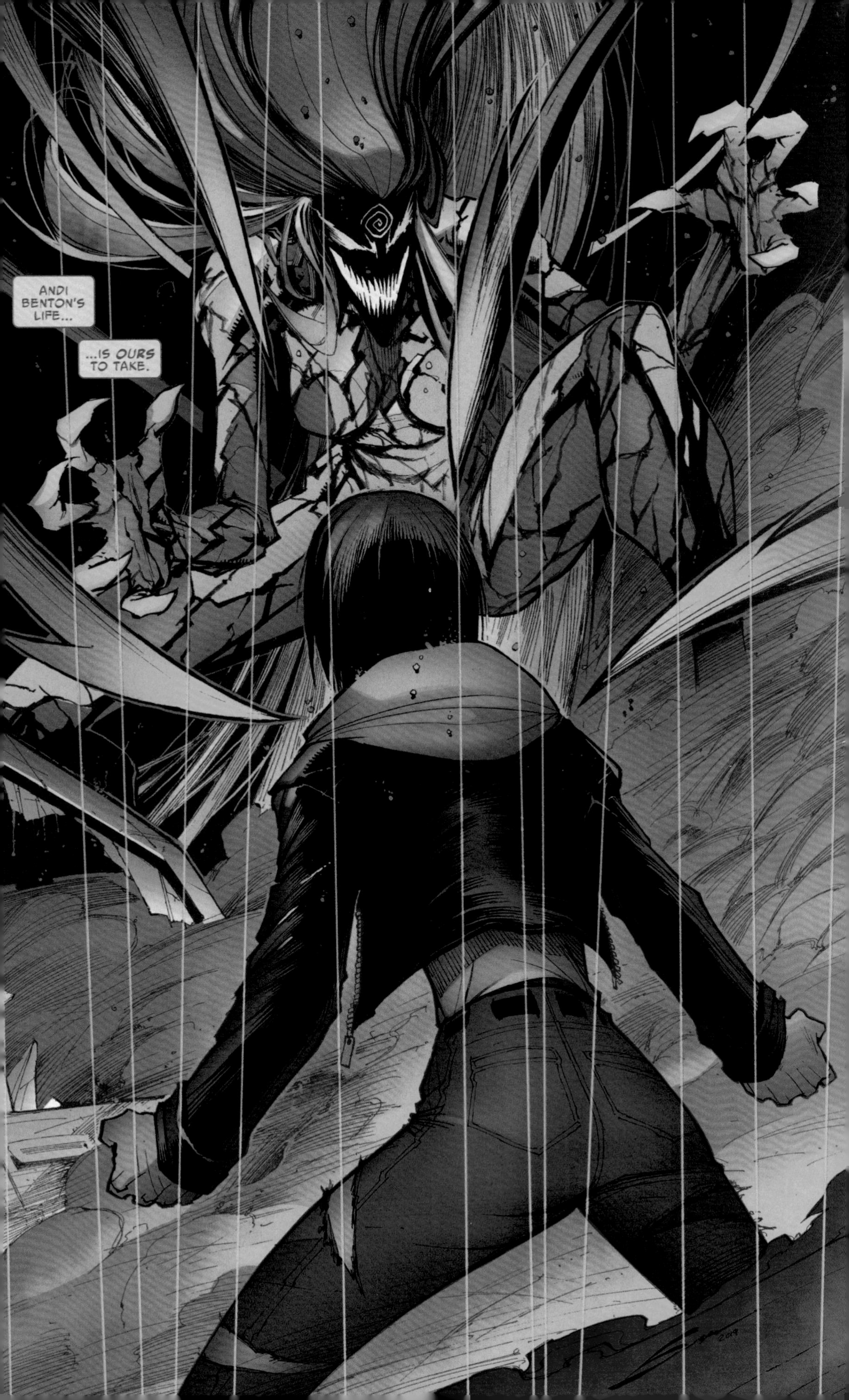
ANDI BENTON'S LIFE...
...IS *OURS* TO TAKE.

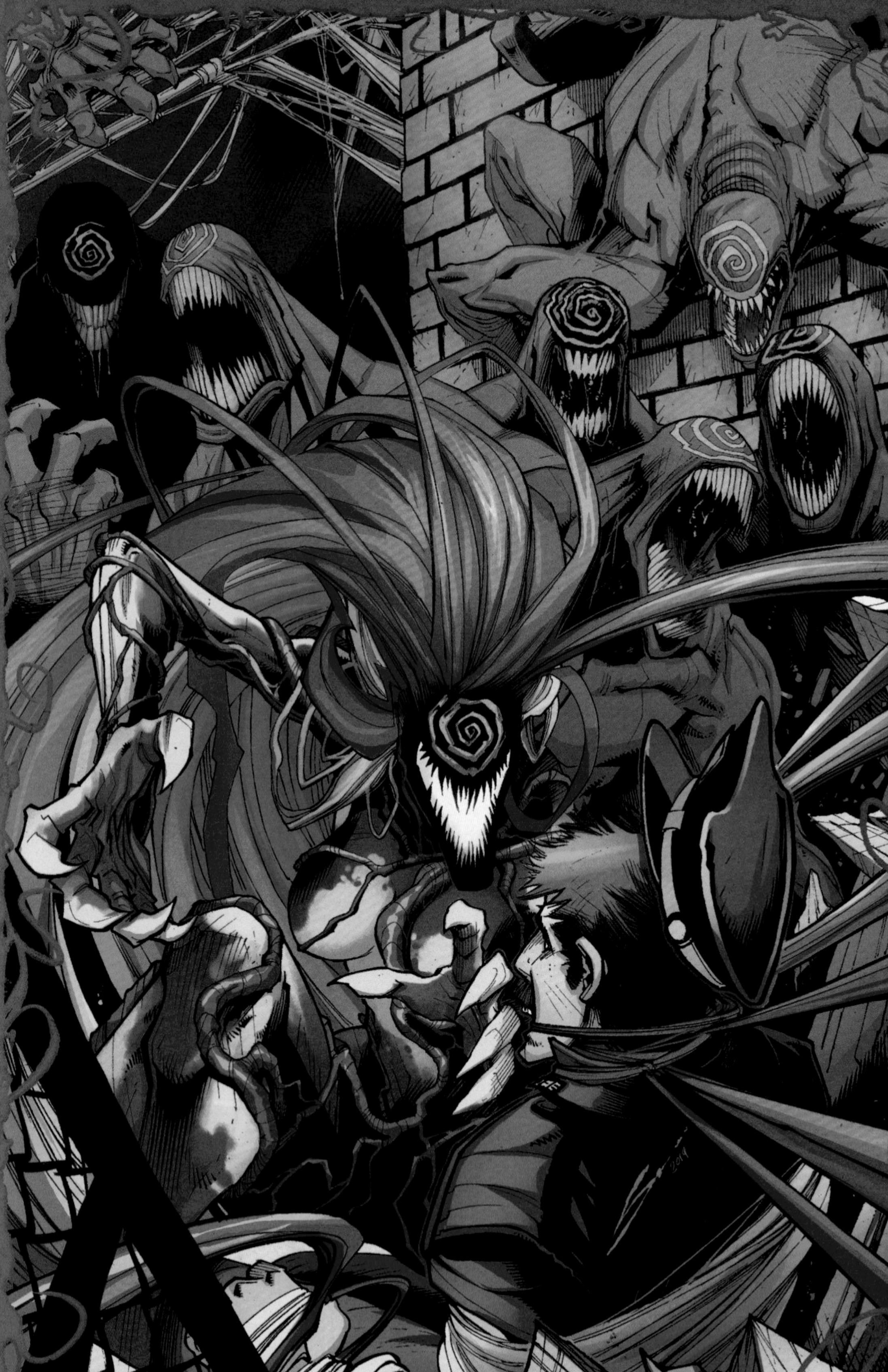

SCREAM 2

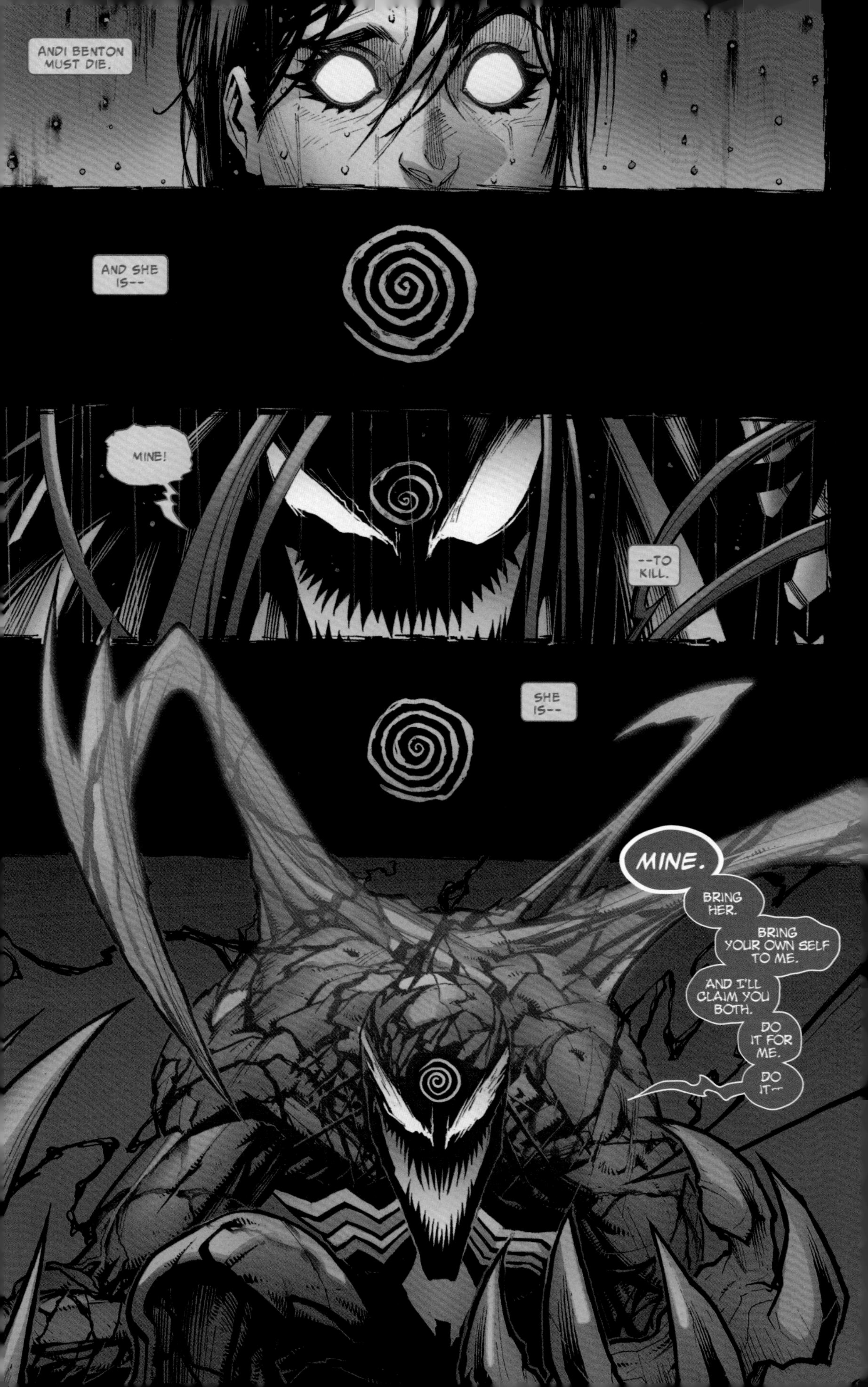
ANDI BENTON MUST DIE.
AND SHE IS--
MINE!
--TO KILL.
SHE IS--
MINE.
BRING HER.
BRING YOUR OWN SELF TO ME.
AND I'LL CLAIM YOU BOTH.
DO IT FOR ME.
DO IT--

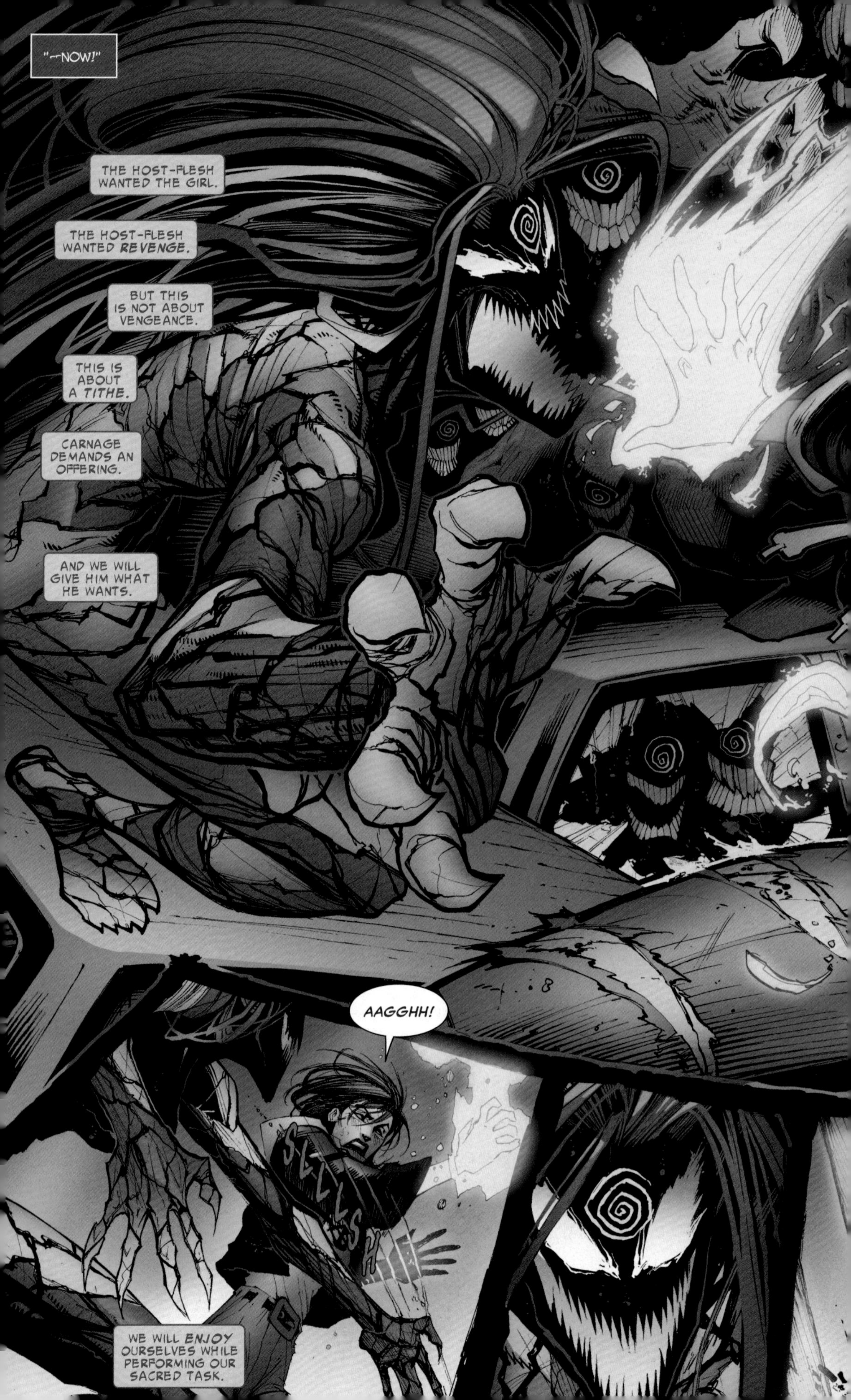
"—NOW!"
THE HOST-FLESH WANTED THE GIRL.
THE HOST-FLESH WANTED REVENGE.
BUT THIS IS NOT ABOUT VENGEANCE.
THIS IS ABOUT A TITHE.
CARNAGE DEMANDS AN OFFERING.
AND WE WILL GIVE HIM WHAT HE WANTS.
AAGGHH!
SLLLSH
WE WILL ENJOY OURSELVES WHILE PERFORMING OUR SACRED TASK.

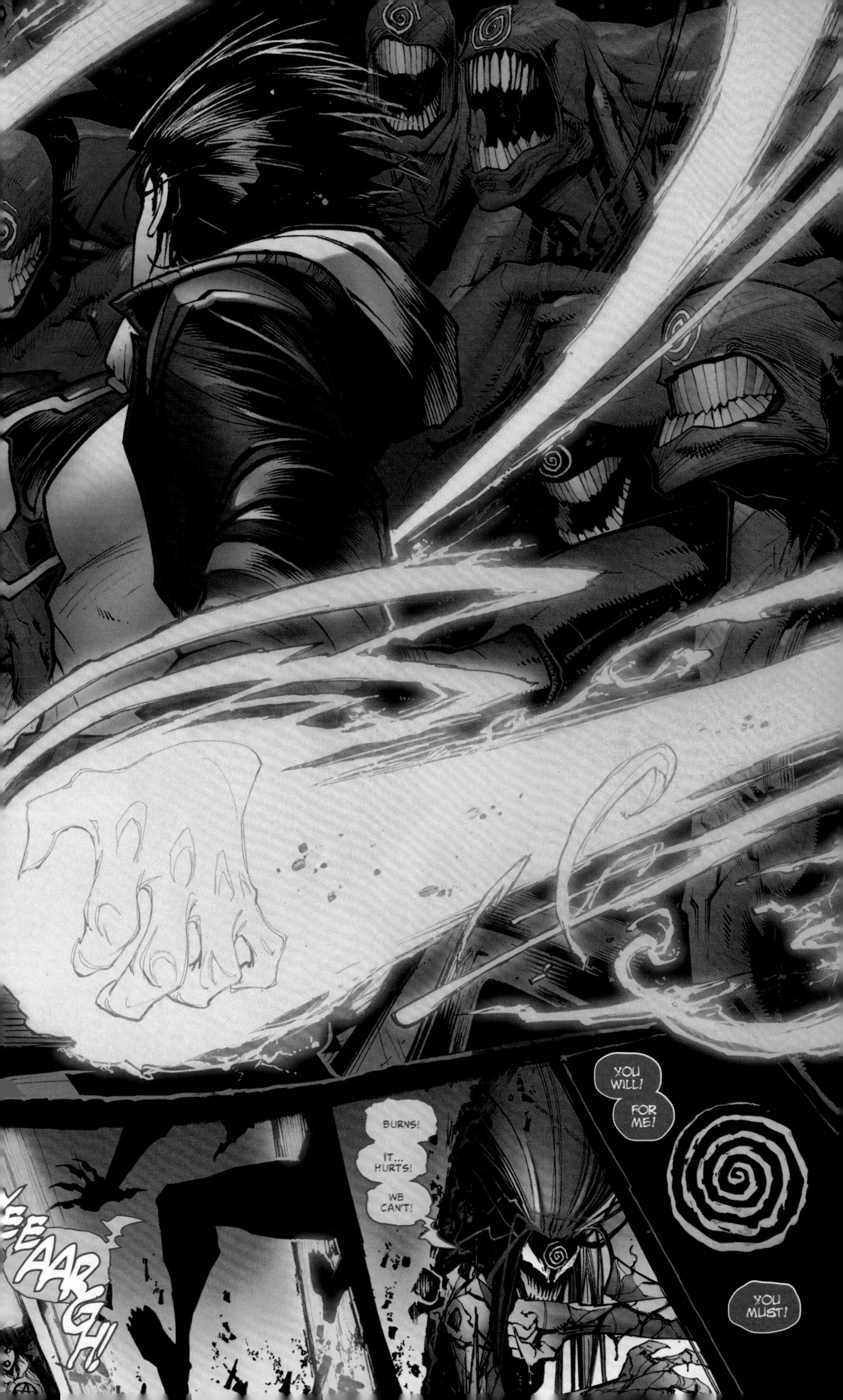

EEAARGH!
BURNS!
IT... HURTS!
WE CAN'T!
YOU WILL!
FOR ME!
YOU MUST!

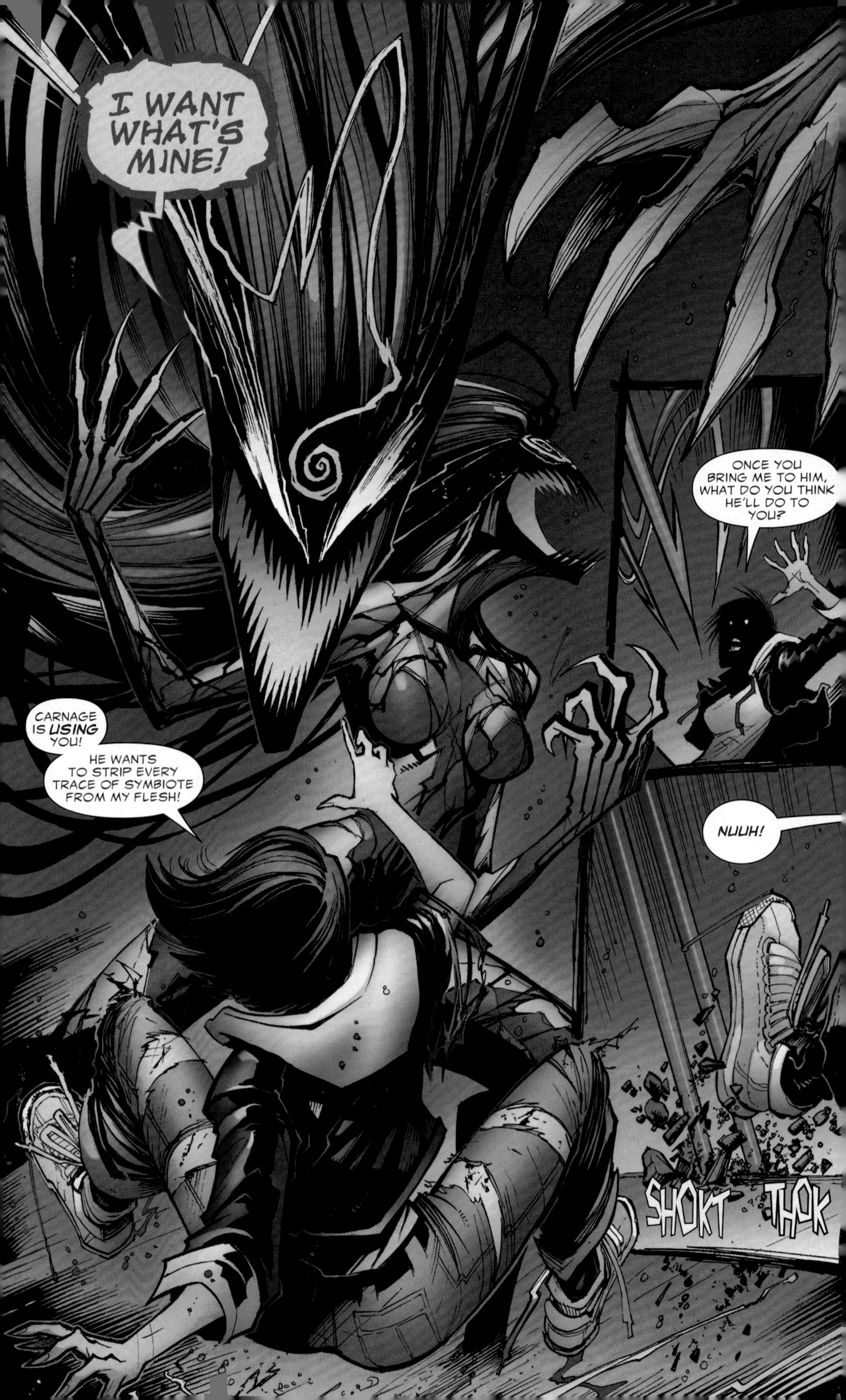
I WANT WHAT'S MINE!
CARNAGE IS USING YOU!
HE WANTS TO STRIP EVERY TRACE OF SYMBIOTE FROM MY FLESH!
ONCE YOU BRING ME TO HIM, WHAT DO YOU THINK HE'LL DO TO YOU?
NUUH!
SHOKT
THOK

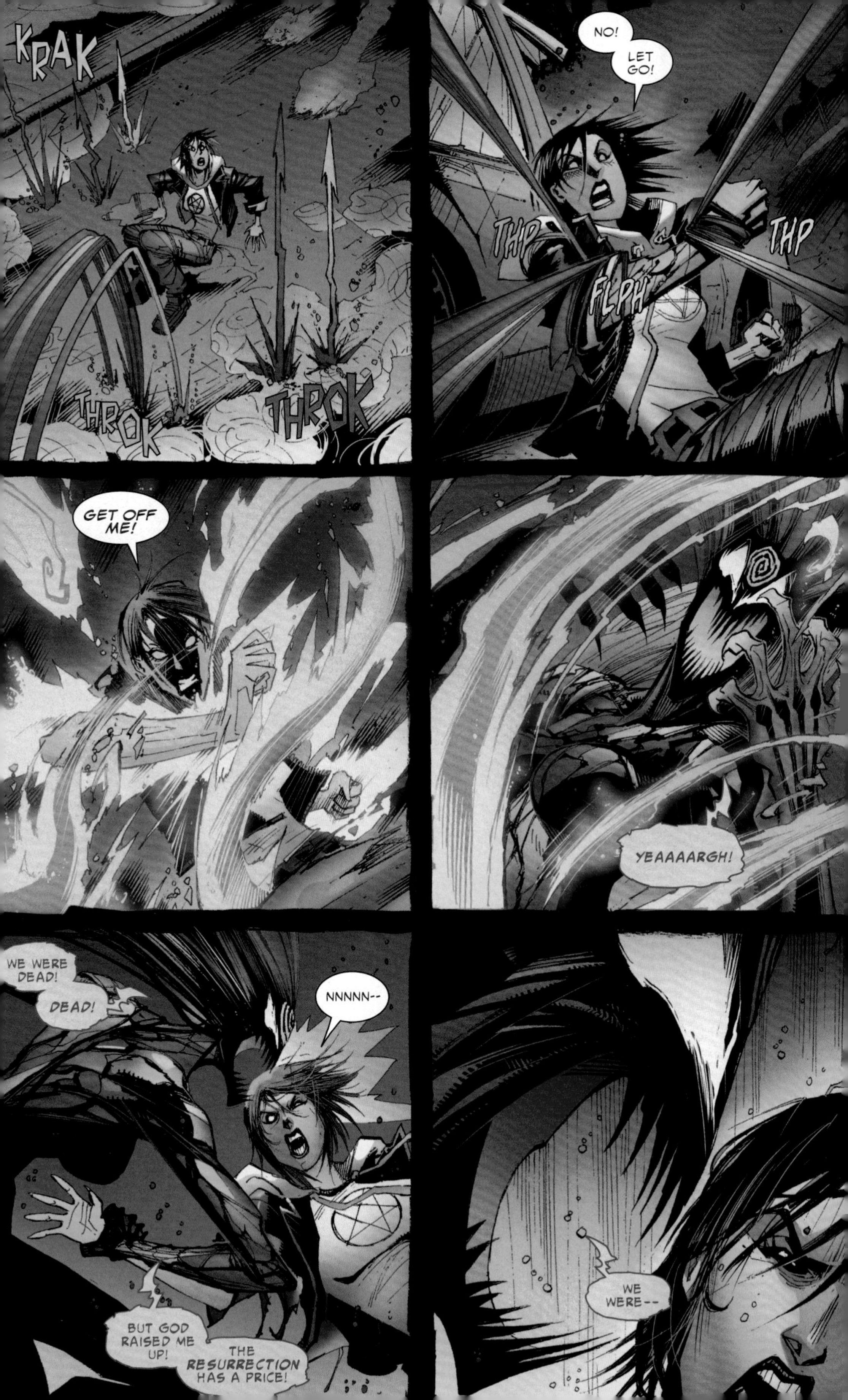
KRAK
THROK
THROK
NO!
LET GO!
THP
THP
FLPH
GET OFF ME!
YEAAAARGH!
WE WERE DEAD!
DEAD!
NNNNN--
BUT GOD RAISED ME UP!
THE RESURRECTION HAS A PRICE!
WE WERE--

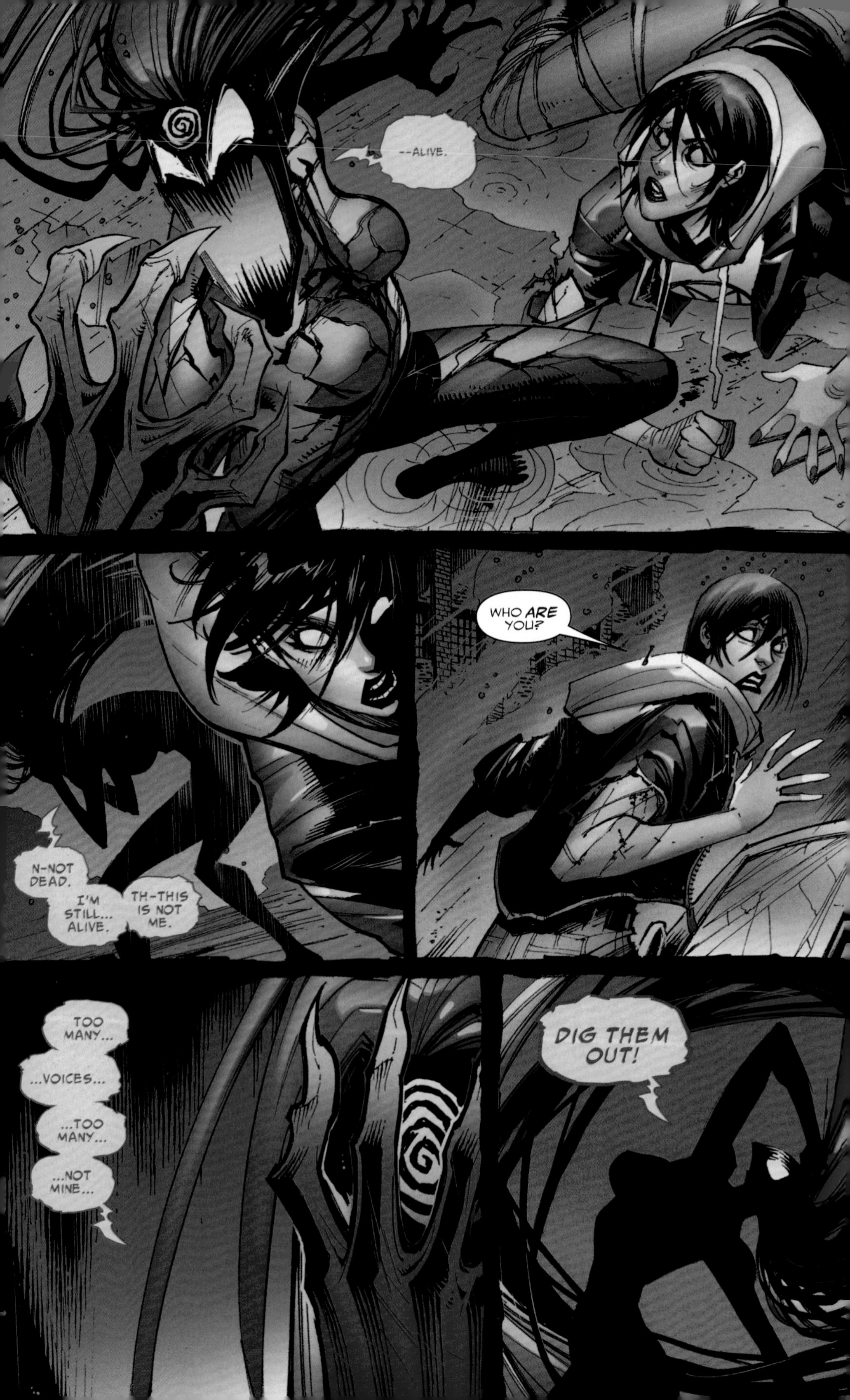
--ALIVE.
N-NOT DEAD.
I'M STILL... ALIVE.
TH-THIS IS NOT ME.
WHO ARE YOU?
TOO MANY...
...VOICES...
...TOO MANY...
...NOT MINE...
DIG THEM OUT!

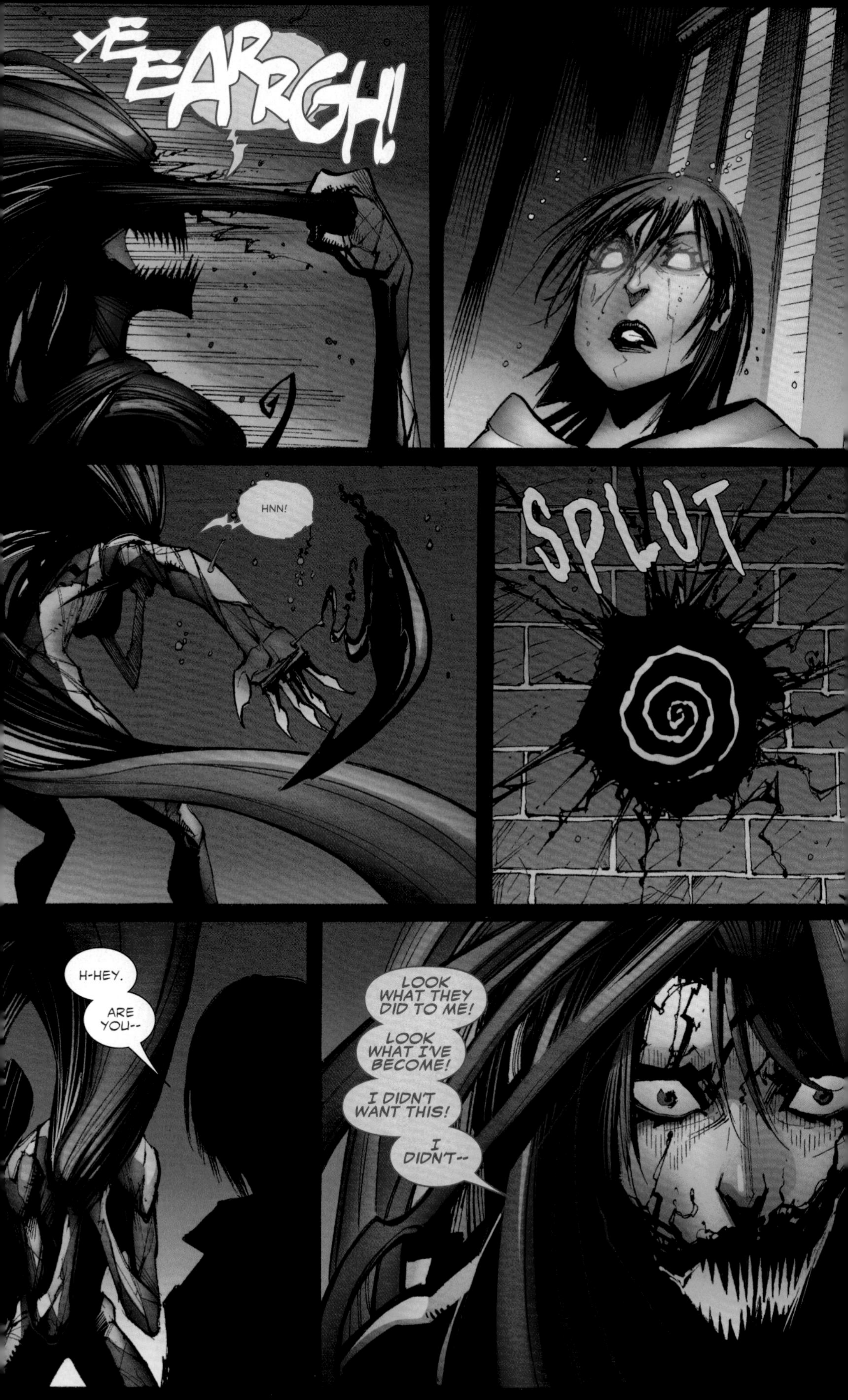
YEEARRGH!
HNN!
SPLUT
H-HEY.
ARE YOU--
LOOK WHAT THEY DID TO ME!
LOOK WHAT I'VE BECOME!
I DIDN'T WANT THIS!
I DIDN'T--

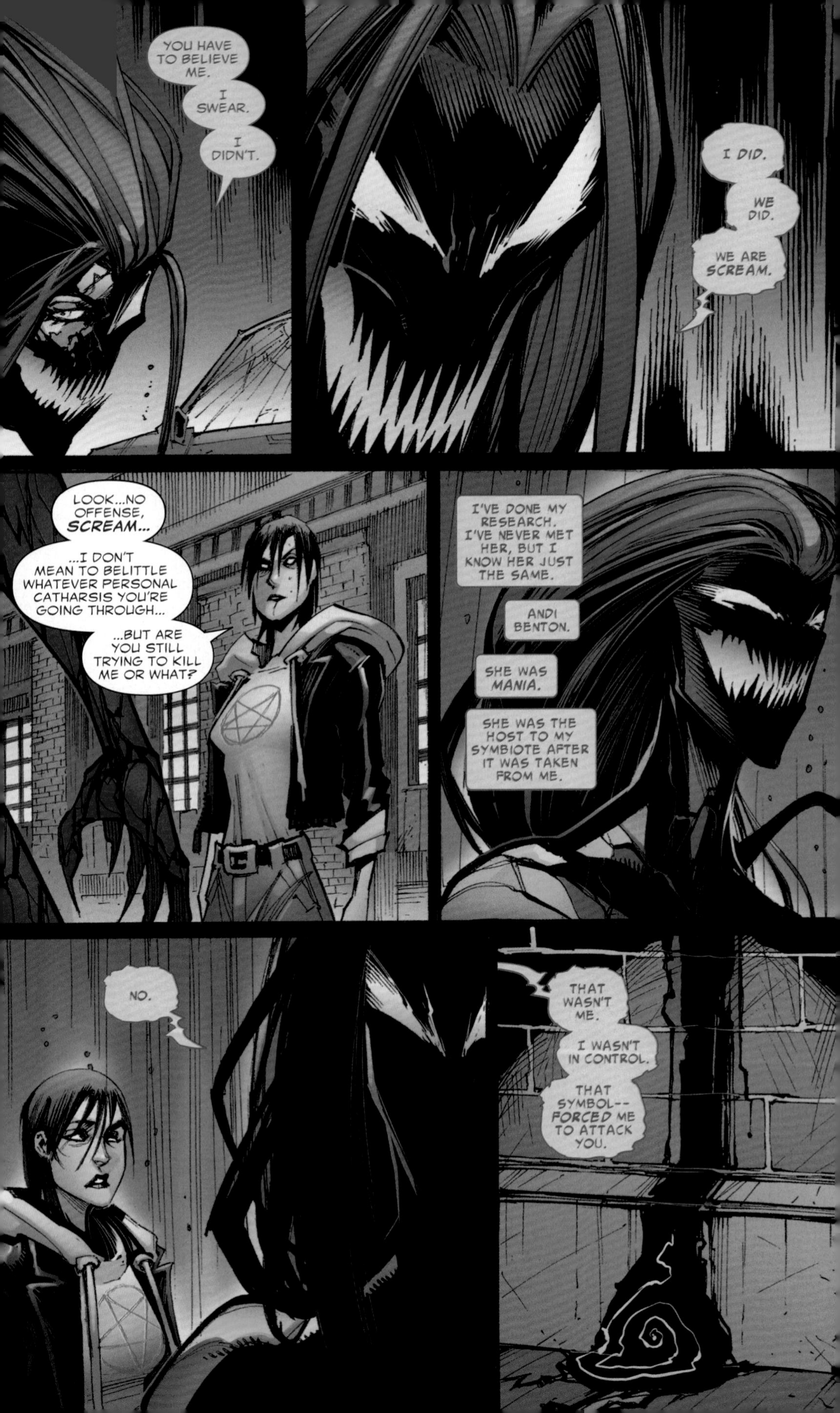

YOU HAVE TO BELIEVE ME.
I SWEAR.
I DIDN'T.
I DID.
WE DID.
WE ARE SCREAM.
LOOK...NO OFFENSE, SCREAM...
...I DON'T MEAN TO BELITTLE WHATEVER PERSONAL CATHARSIS YOU'RE GOING THROUGH...
...BUT ARE YOU STILL TRYING TO KILL ME OR WHAT?
I'VE DONE MY RESEARCH. I'VE NEVER MET HER, BUT I KNOW HER JUST THE SAME.
ANDI BENTON.
SHE WAS MANIA.
SHE WAS THE HOST TO MY SYMBIOTE AFTER IT WAS TAKEN FROM ME.
NO.
THAT WASN'T ME.
I WASN'T IN CONTROL.
THAT SYMBOL-- FORCED ME TO ATTACK YOU.

YEAH. THAT TRACKS.

WELL--

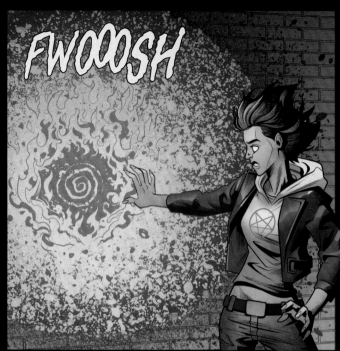

FWOOOSH

I DON'T KNOW IF THAT WILL DO ANY GOOD.

THE SPIRAL WASN'T JUST THERE ON THE WALL.

IT'S PART OF ME.

IT MIGHT APPEAR AGAIN.

THEN WE'D BEST HOPE YOU CAN FIGHT IT OFF AGAIN.

EITHER THAT OR I CAN ROAST YOU WHERE YOU STAND.

WHAT'S HAPPENING?

TO ME... TO THE CITY.

WHY IS THIS HAPPENING?

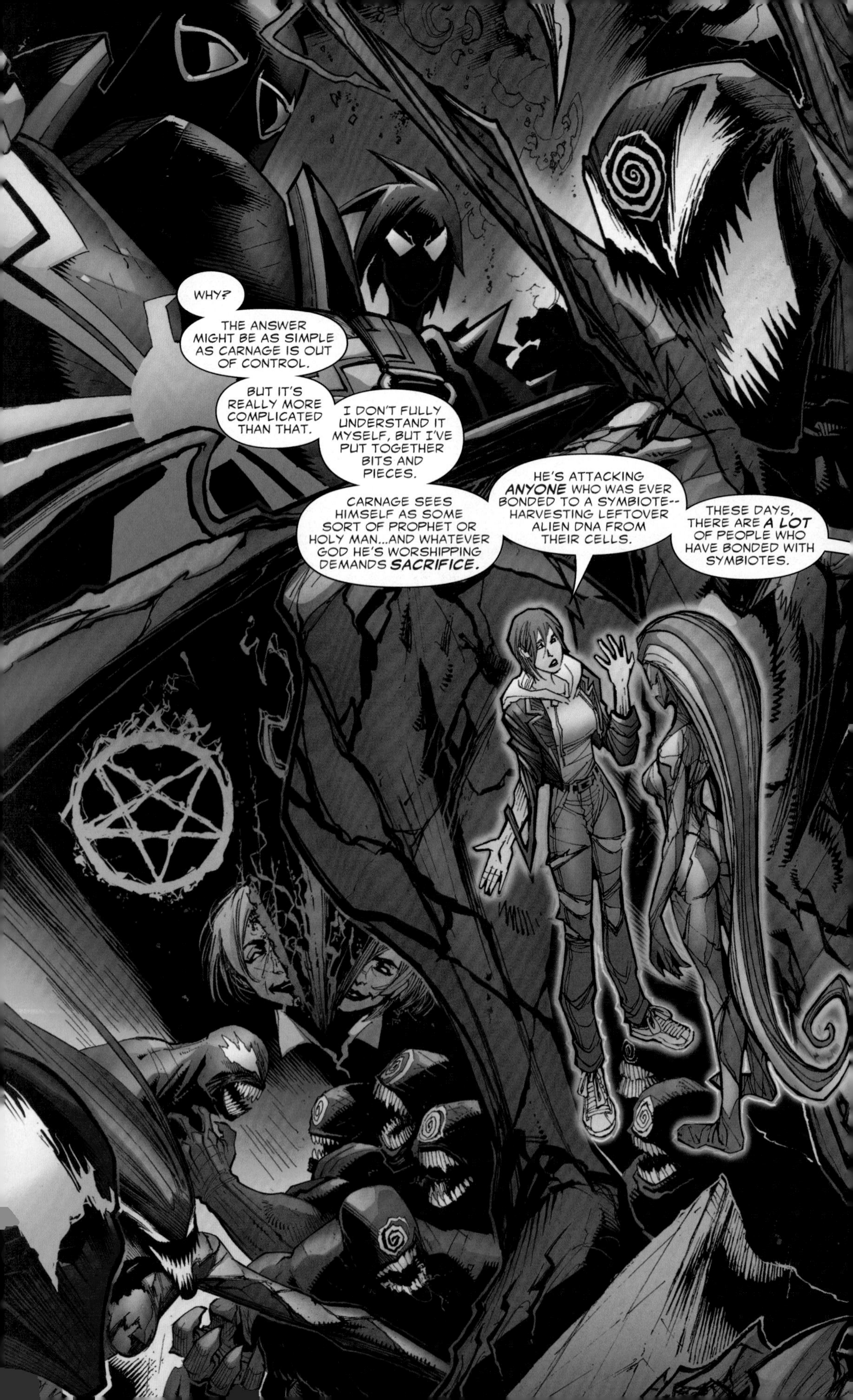
WHY?
THE ANSWER MIGHT BE AS SIMPLE AS CARNAGE IS OUT OF CONTROL.
BUT IT'S REALLY MORE COMPLICATED THAN THAT.
I DON'T FULLY UNDERSTAND IT MYSELF, BUT I'VE PUT TOGETHER BITS AND PIECES.
CARNAGE SEES HIMSELF AS SOME SORT OF PROPHET OR HOLY MAN...AND WHATEVER GOD HE'S WORSHIPPING DEMANDS **SACRIFICE.**
HE'S ATTACKING **ANYONE** WHO WAS EVER BONDED TO A SYMBIOTE-- HARVESTING LEFTOVER ALIEN DNA FROM THEIR CELLS.
THESE DAYS, THERE ARE **A LOT** OF PEOPLE WHO HAVE BONDED WITH SYMBIOTES.

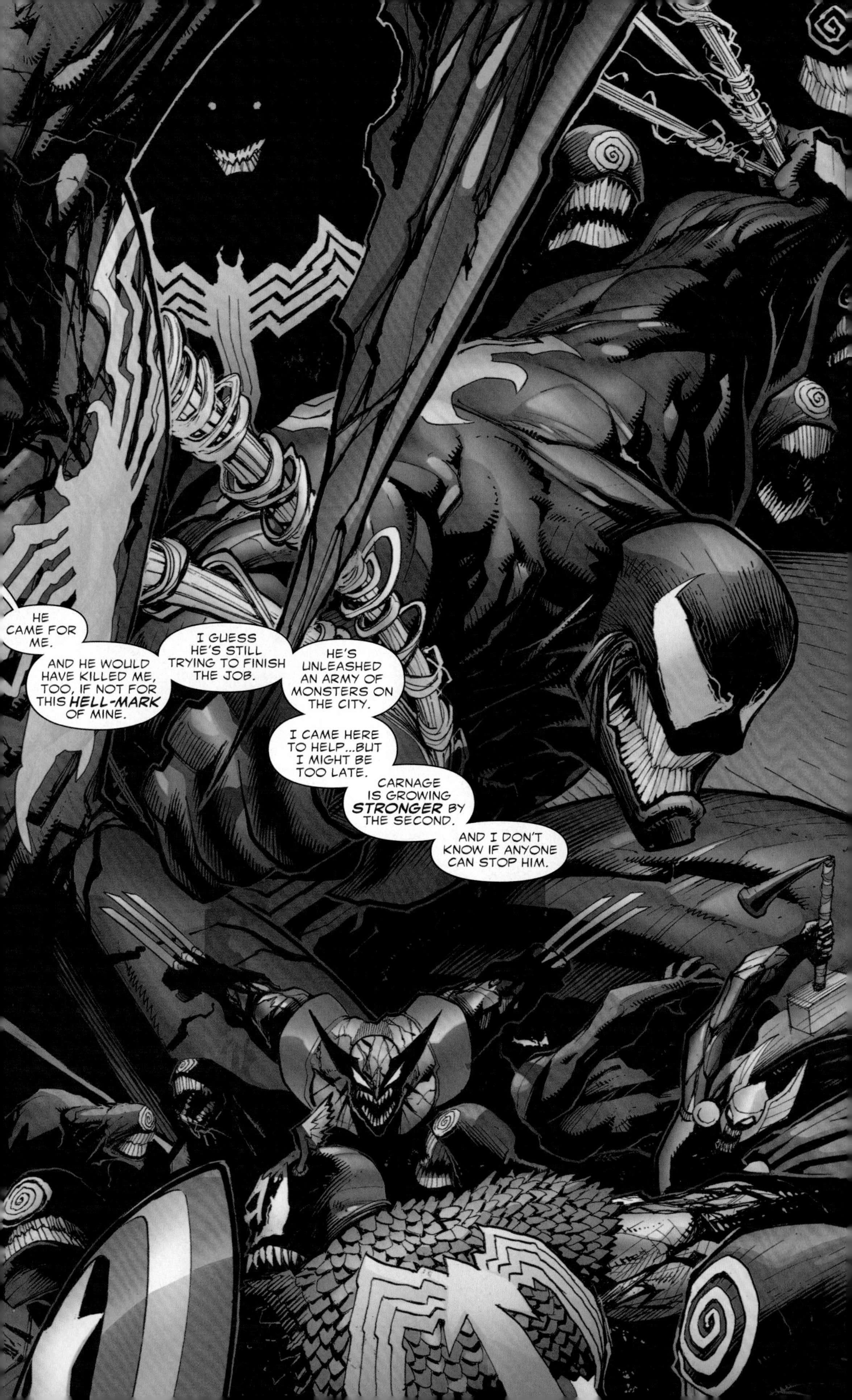
HE CAME FOR ME.
AND HE WOULD HAVE KILLED ME, TOO, IF NOT FOR THIS HELL-MARK OF MINE.
I GUESS HE'S STILL TRYING TO FINISH THE JOB.
HE'S UNLEASHED AN ARMY OF MONSTERS ON THE CITY.
I CAME HERE TO HELP...BUT I MIGHT BE TOO LATE.
CARNAGE IS GROWING STRONGER BY THE SECOND.
AND I DON'T KNOW IF ANYONE CAN STOP HIM.

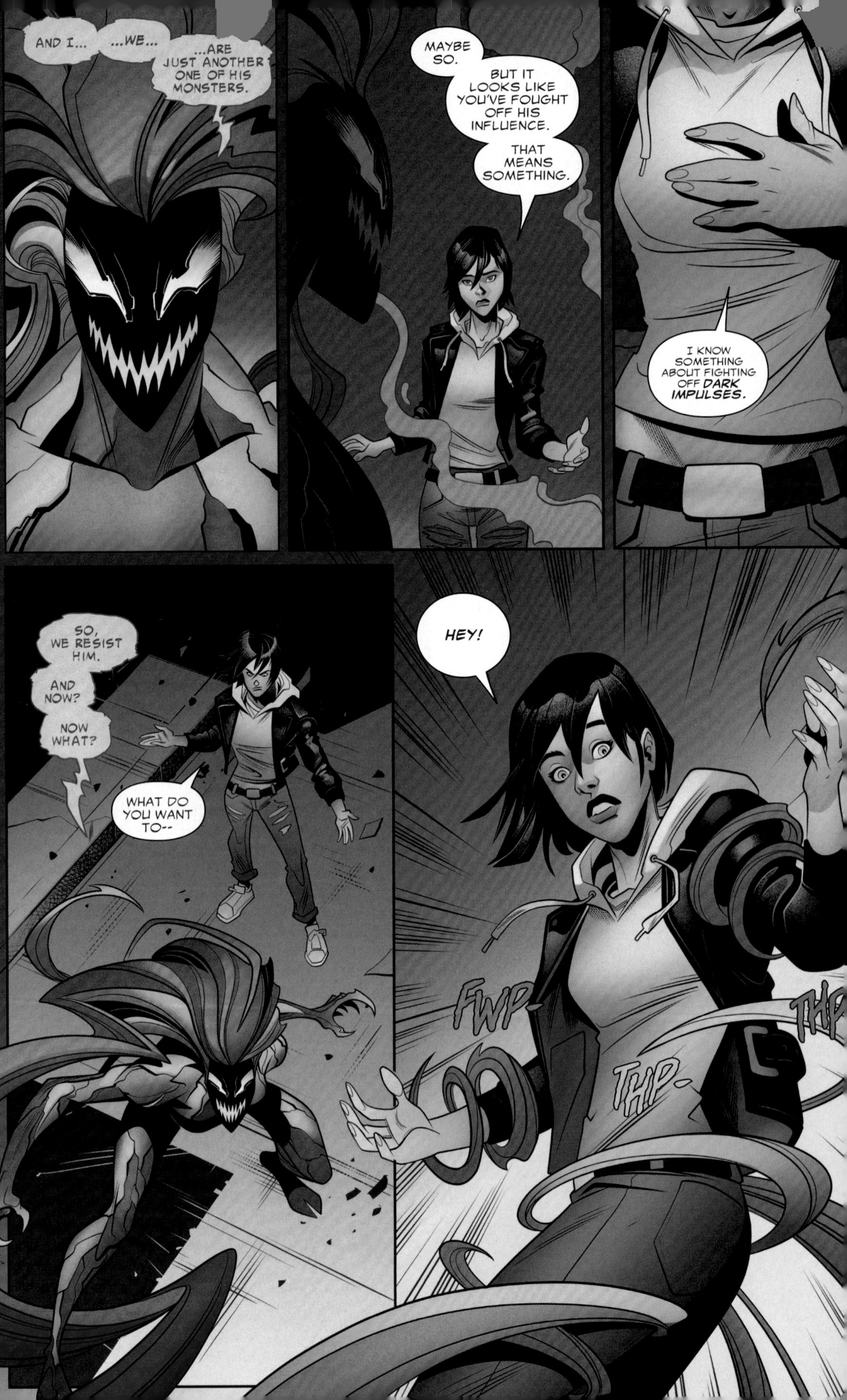
AND I...
...WE...
...ARE JUST ANOTHER ONE OF HIS MONSTERS.
MAYBE SO.
BUT IT LOOKS LIKE YOU'VE FOUGHT OFF HIS INFLUENCE.
THAT MEANS SOMETHING.
I KNOW SOMETHING ABOUT FIGHTING OFF DARK IMPULSES.
SO, WE RESIST HIM.
AND NOW?
NOW WHAT?
WHAT DO YOU WANT TO--
HEY!
FWP
THP-
THP

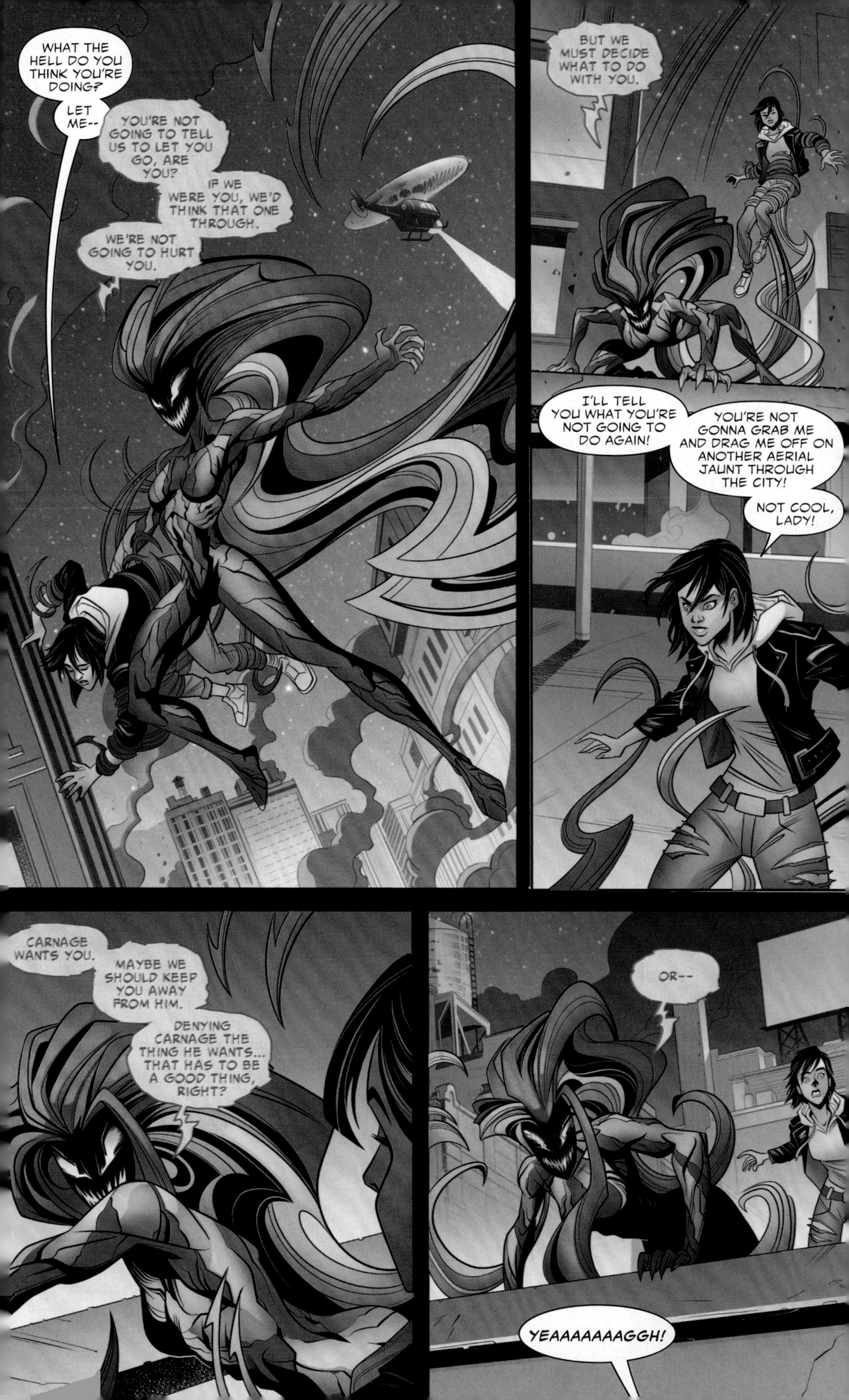
WHAT THE HELL DO YOU THINK YOU'RE DOING?
LET ME--
YOU'RE NOT GOING TO TELL US TO LET YOU GO, ARE YOU?
IF WE WERE YOU, WE'D THINK THAT ONE THROUGH.
WE'RE NOT GOING TO HURT YOU.
BUT WE MUST DECIDE WHAT TO DO WITH YOU.
I'LL TELL YOU WHAT YOU'RE NOT GOING TO DO AGAIN!
YOU'RE NOT GONNA GRAB ME AND DRAG ME OFF ON ANOTHER AERIAL JAUNT THROUGH THE CITY!
NOT COOL, LADY!
CARNAGE WANTS YOU.
MAYBE WE SHOULD KEEP YOU AWAY FROM HIM.
DENYING CARNAGE THE THING HE WANTS... THAT HAS TO BE A GOOD THING, RIGHT?
OR--
YEAAAAAAAGGH!

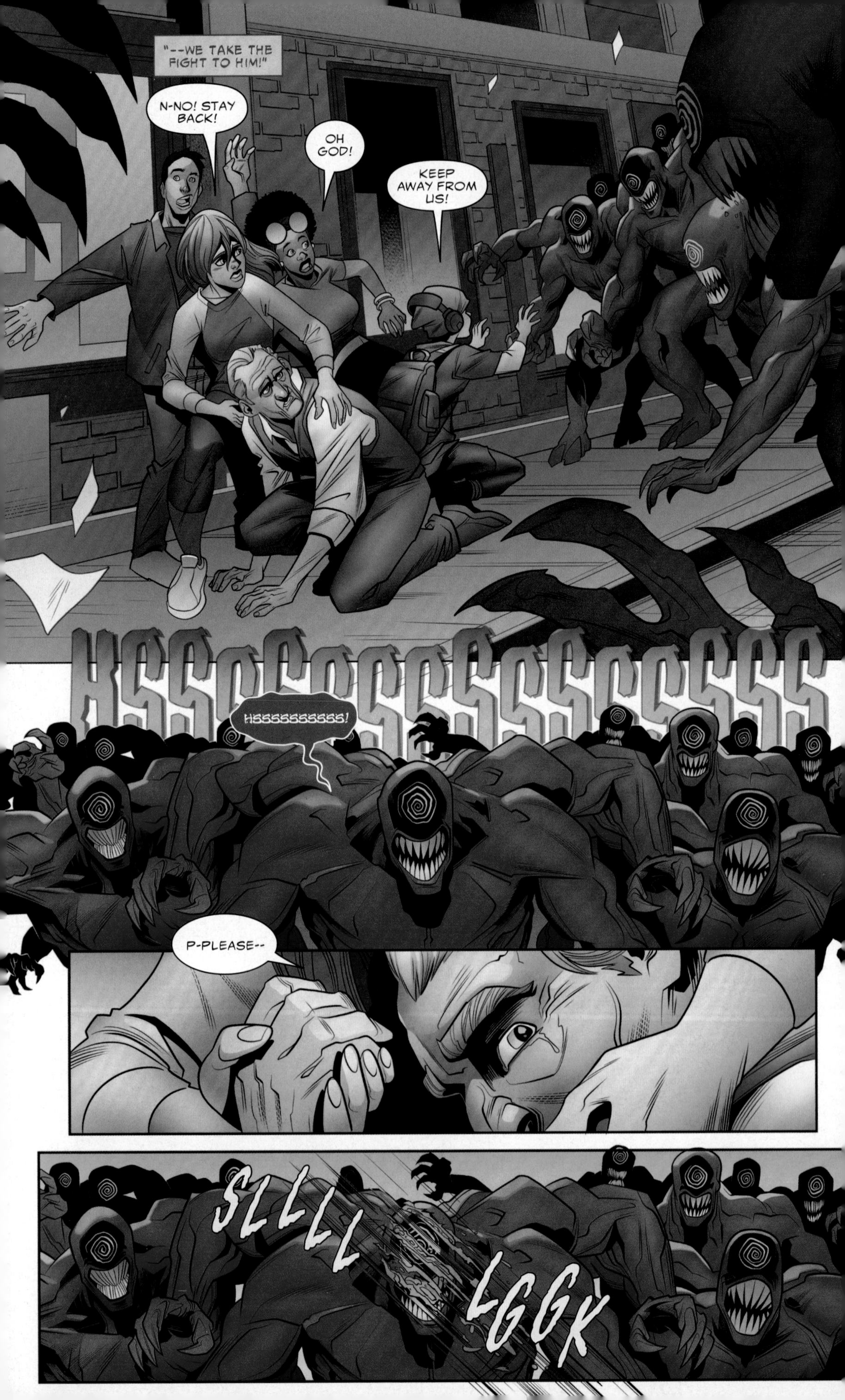
"--WE TAKE THE FIGHT TO HIM!"
N-NO! STAY BACK!
OH GOD!
KEEP AWAY FROM US!
HSSSSSSSSSSSSS
HSSSSSSSSSSS!
P-PLEASE--
SLLLL LGGK

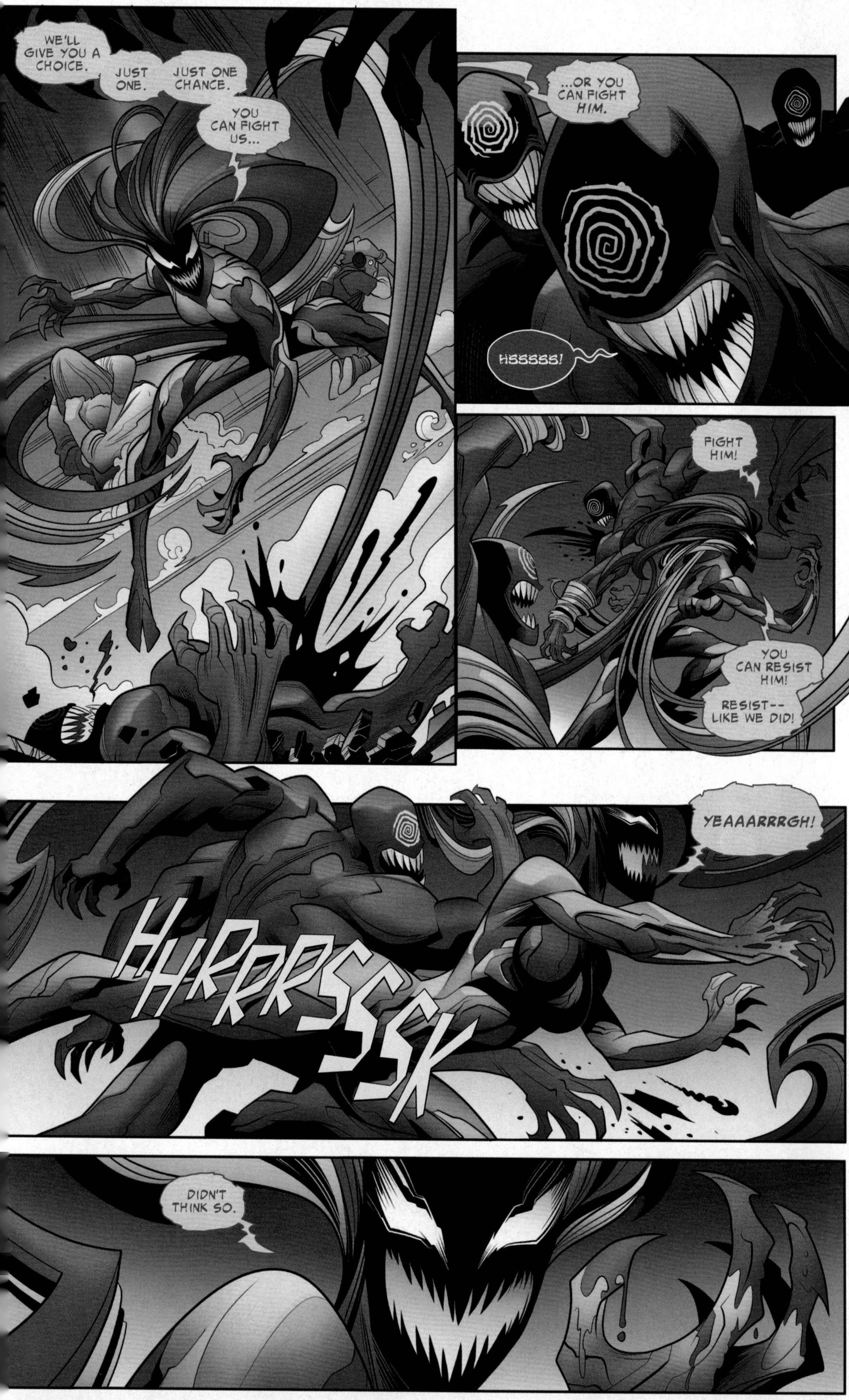
WE'LL GIVE YOU A CHOICE.
JUST ONE.
JUST ONE CHANCE.
YOU CAN FIGHT US...
...OR YOU CAN FIGHT HIM.
HSSSSS!
FIGHT HIM!
YOU CAN RESIST HIM!
RESIST--LIKE WE DID!
YEAAARRRGH!
HHRRRSSSK
DIDN'T THINK SO.

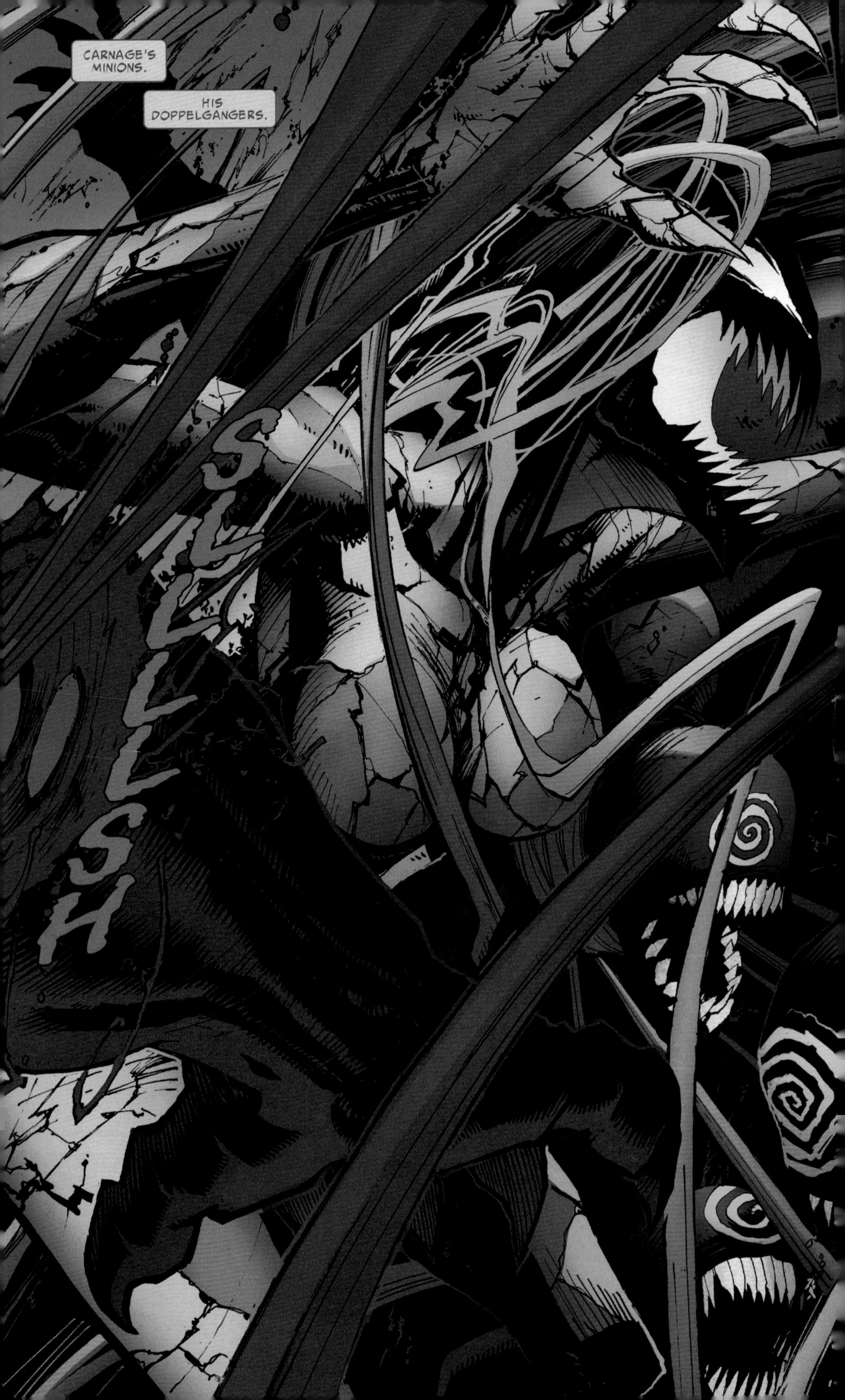
CARNAGE'S MINIONS.
HIS DOPPELGANGERS.
SLLLLSH

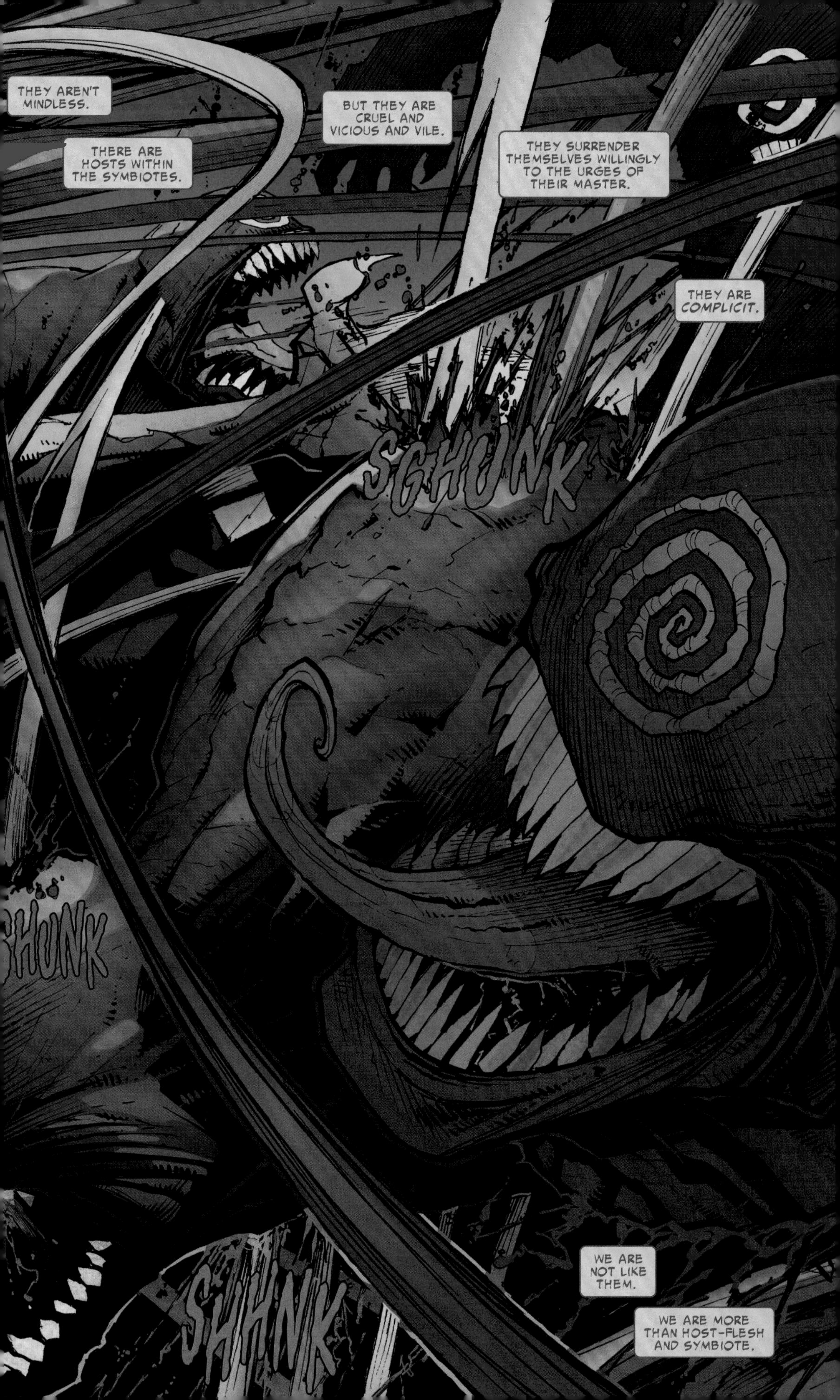
THEY AREN'T MINDLESS.
THERE ARE HOSTS WITHIN THE SYMBIOTES.
BUT THEY ARE CRUEL AND VICIOUS AND VILE.
THEY SURRENDER THEMSELVES WILLINGLY TO THE URGES OF THEIR MASTER.
THEY ARE COMPLICIT.
SCHUNK
SHUNK
SHHNK
WE ARE NOT LIKE THEM.
WE ARE MORE THAN HOST-FLESH AND SYMBIOTE.

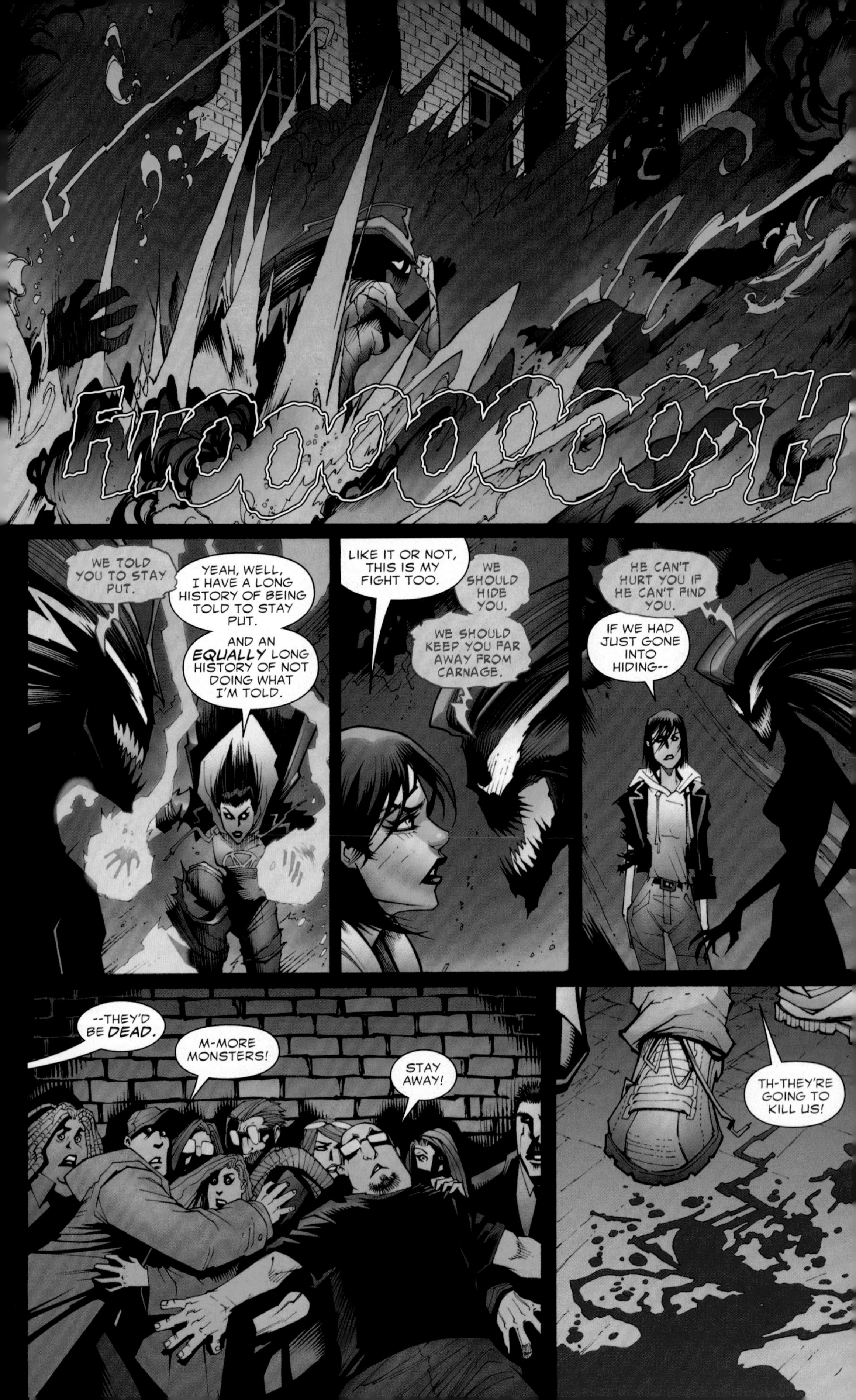
FWOOOOOOOSH
WE TOLD YOU TO STAY PUT.
YEAH, WELL, I HAVE A LONG HISTORY OF BEING TOLD TO STAY PUT.
AND AN EQUALLY LONG HISTORY OF NOT DOING WHAT I'M TOLD.
LIKE IT OR NOT, THIS IS MY FIGHT TOO.
WE SHOULD HIDE YOU.
WE SHOULD KEEP YOU FAR AWAY FROM CARNAGE.
HE CAN'T HURT YOU IF HE CAN'T FIND YOU.
IF WE HAD JUST GONE INTO HIDING--
--THEY'D BE DEAD.
M-MORE MONSTERS!
STAY AWAY!
TH-THEY'RE GOING TO KILL US!

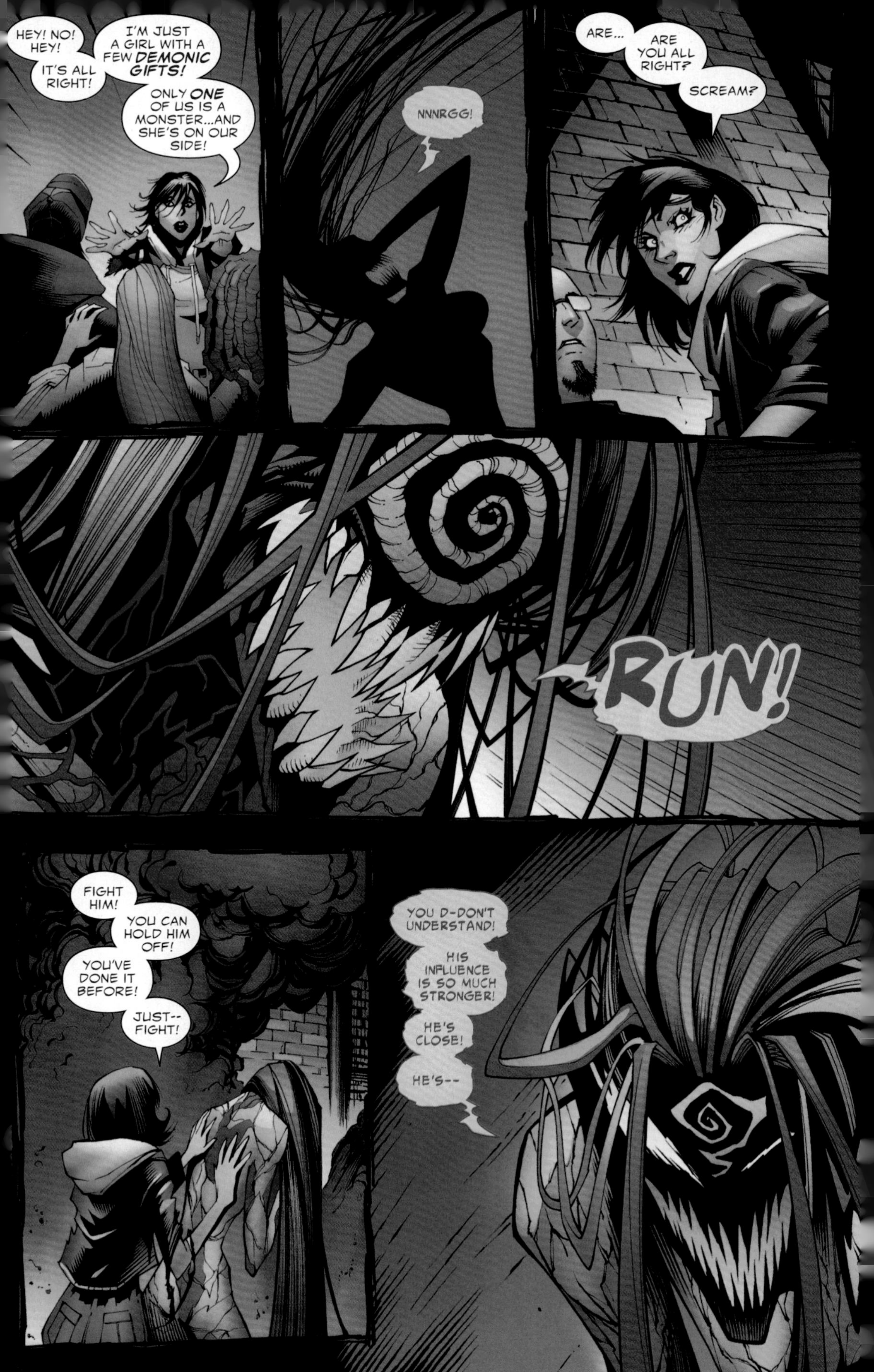
HEY! NO! HEY!
IT'S ALL RIGHT!
I'M JUST A GIRL WITH A FEW DEMONIC GIFTS!
ONLY ONE OF US IS A MONSTER...AND SHE'S ON OUR SIDE!
NNNRGG!
ARE...
ARE YOU ALL RIGHT?
SCREAM?
RUN!
FIGHT HIM!
YOU CAN HOLD HIM OFF!
YOU'VE DONE IT BEFORE!
JUST--FIGHT!
YOU D-DON'T UNDERSTAND!
HIS INFLUENCE IS SO MUCH STRONGER!
HE'S CLOSE!
HE'S--

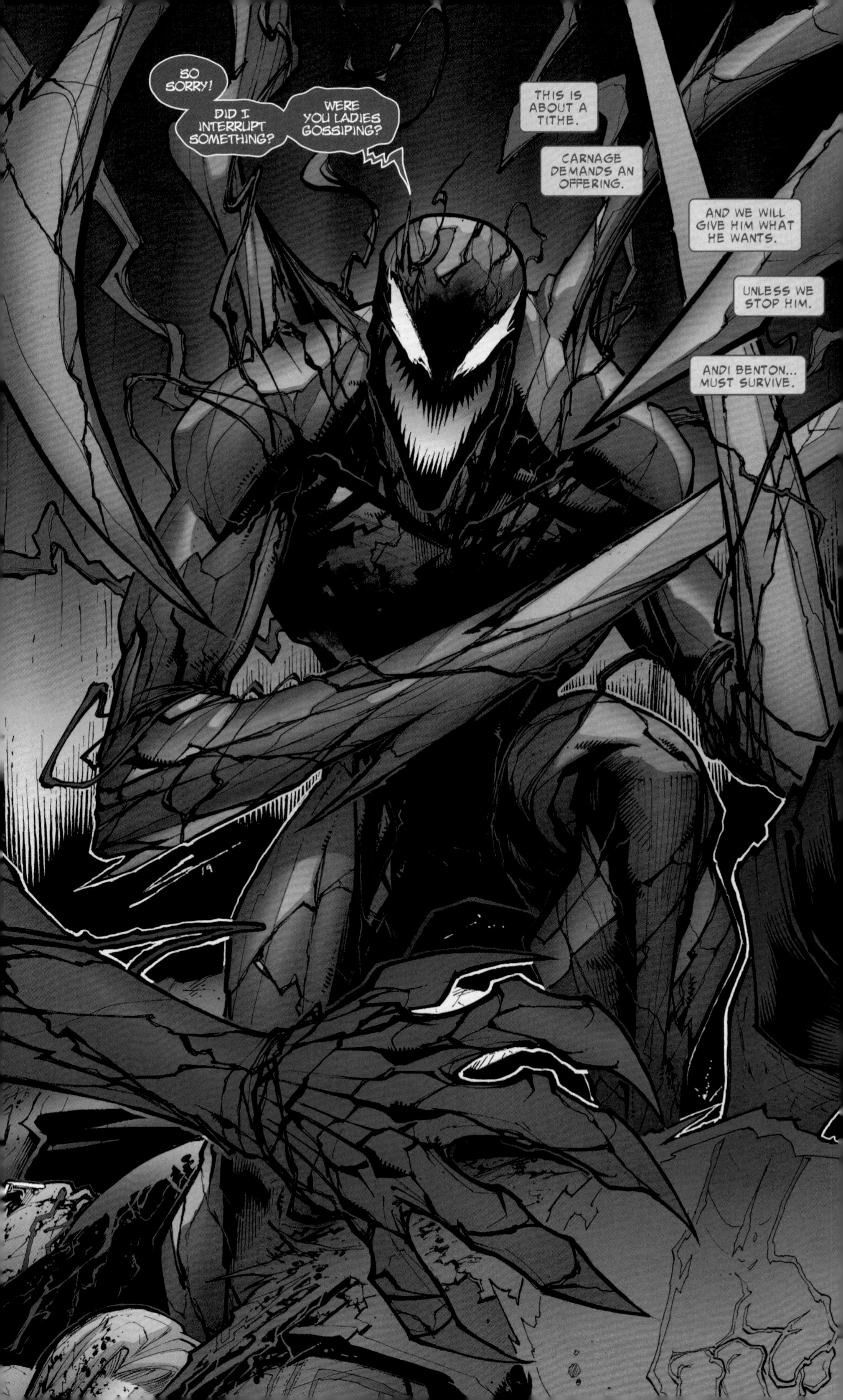
SO SORRY!
DID I INTERRUPT SOMETHING?
WERE YOU LADIES GOSSIPING?
THIS IS ABOUT A TITHE.
CARNAGE DEMANDS AN OFFERING.
AND WE WILL GIVE HIM WHAT HE WANTS.
UNLESS WE STOP HIM.
ANDI BENTON... MUST SURVIVE.

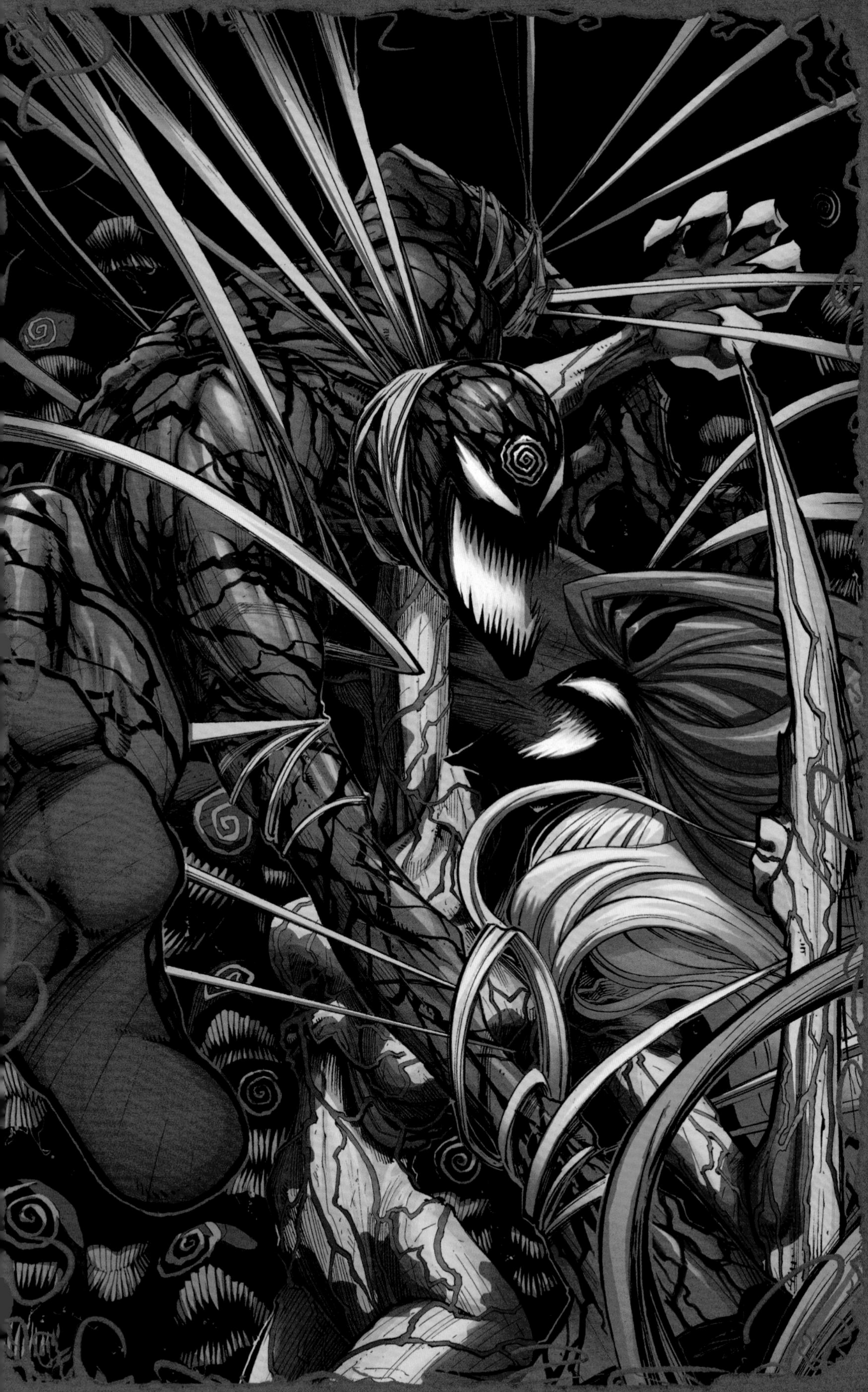

SCREAM 3

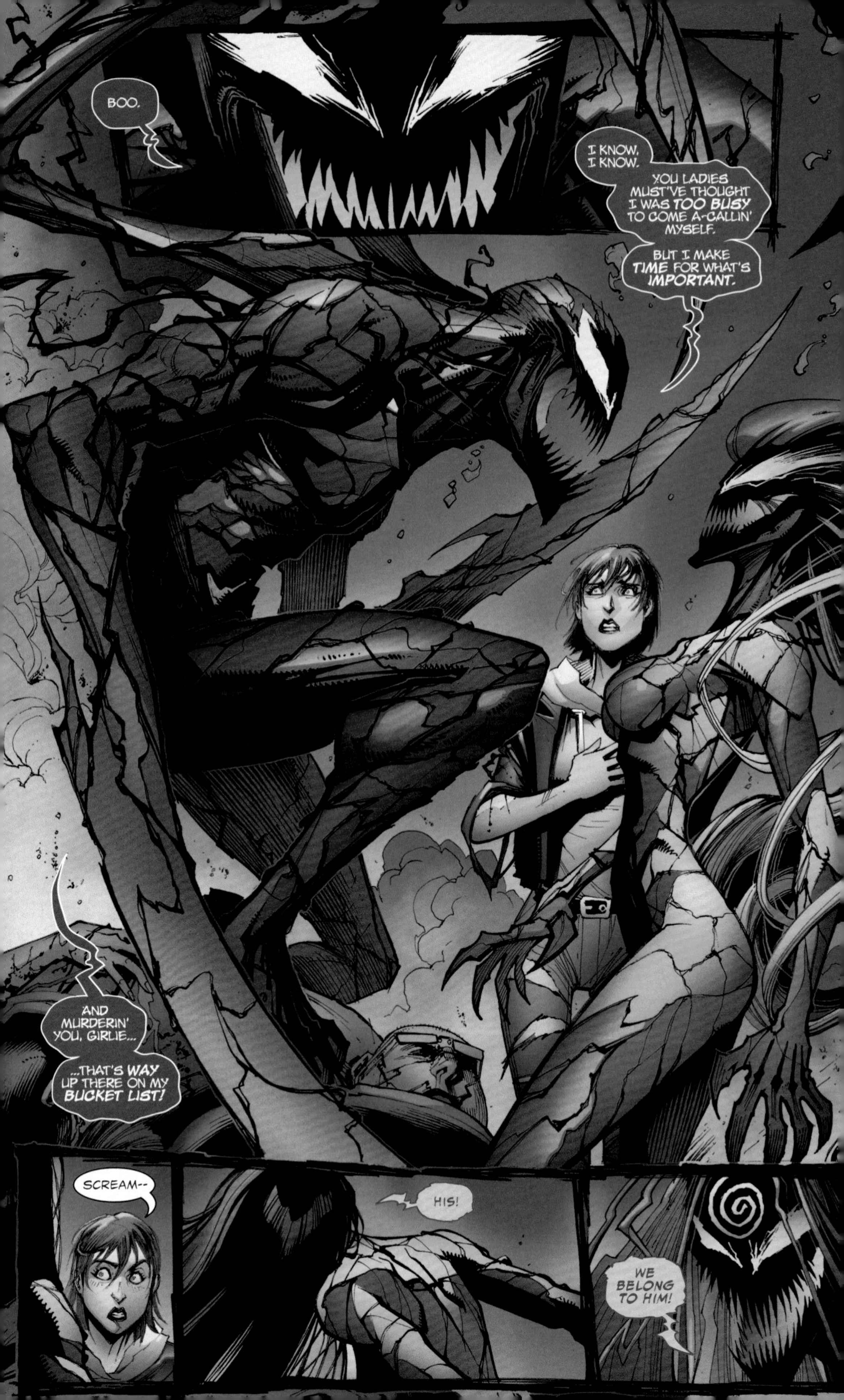
BOO.
I KNOW, I KNOW.
YOU LADIES MUST'VE THOUGHT I WAS TOO BUSY TO COME A-CALLIN' MYSELF.
BUT I MAKE TIME FOR WHAT'S IMPORTANT.
AND MURDERIN' YOU, GIRLIE...
...THAT'S WAY UP THERE ON MY BUCKET LIST!
SCREAM--
HIS!
WE BELONG TO HIM!

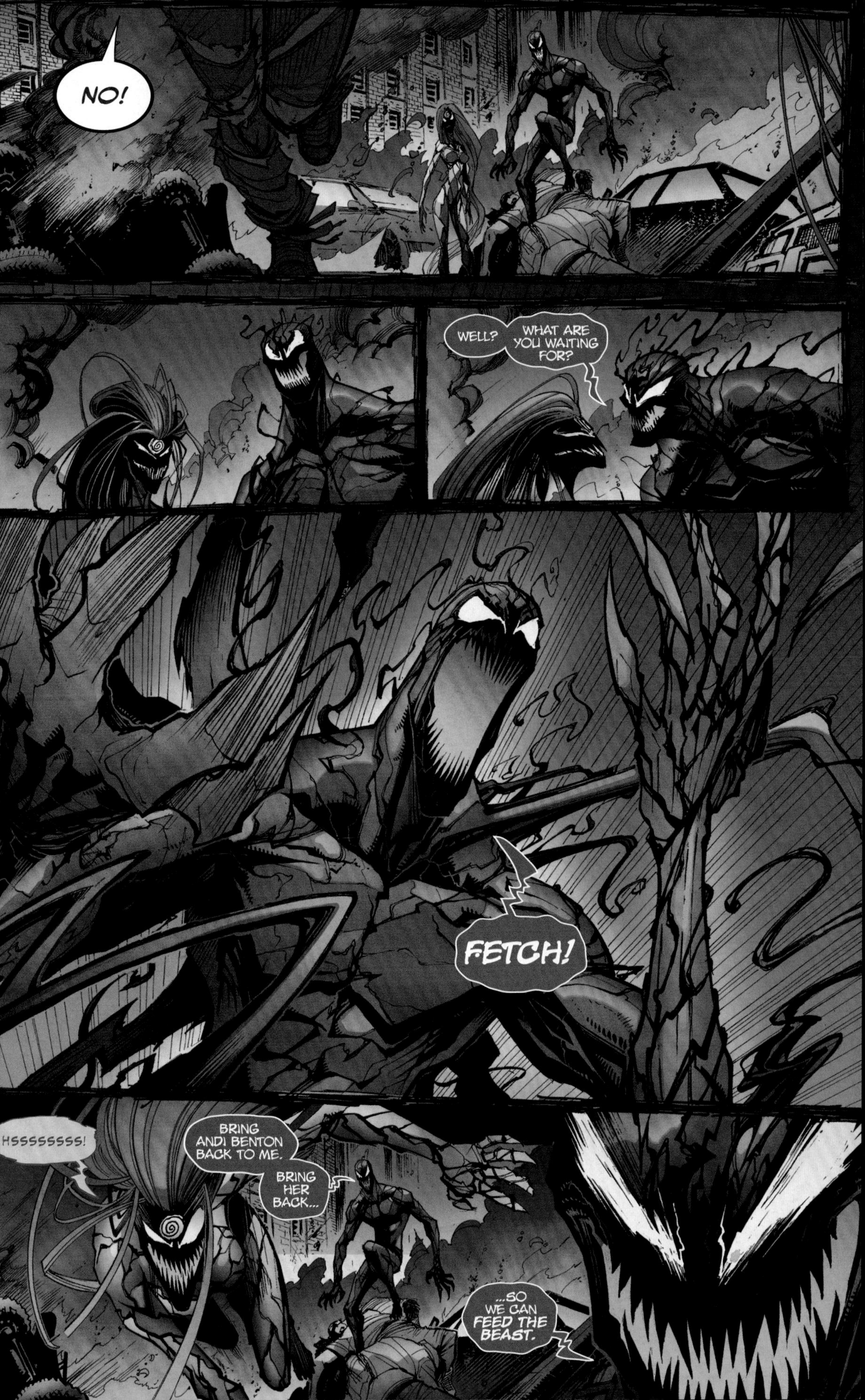
NO!
WELL?
WHAT ARE YOU WAITING FOR?
FETCH!
HSSSSSSSS!
BRING ANDI BENTON BACK TO ME.
BRING HER BACK...
...SO WE CAN FEED THE BEAST.

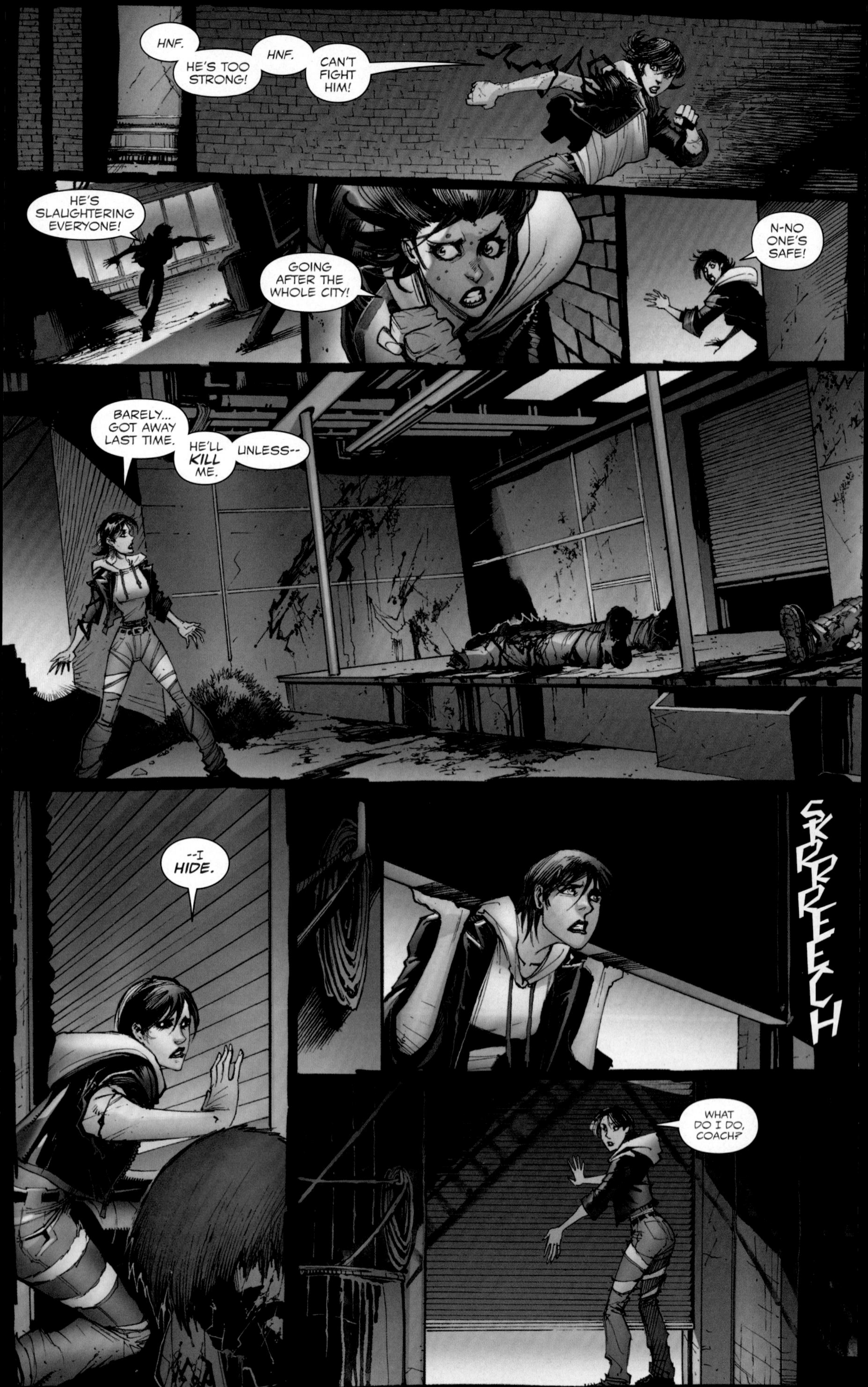
HNF.
HE'S TOO STRONG!
HNF.
CAN'T FIGHT HIM!
HE'S SLAUGHTERING EVERYONE!
GOING AFTER THE WHOLE CITY!
N-NO ONE'S SAFE!
BARELY... GOT AWAY LAST TIME.
HE'LL **KILL** ME.
UNLESS--
--I **HIDE.**
SKREEECH
WHAT DO I DO, COACH?

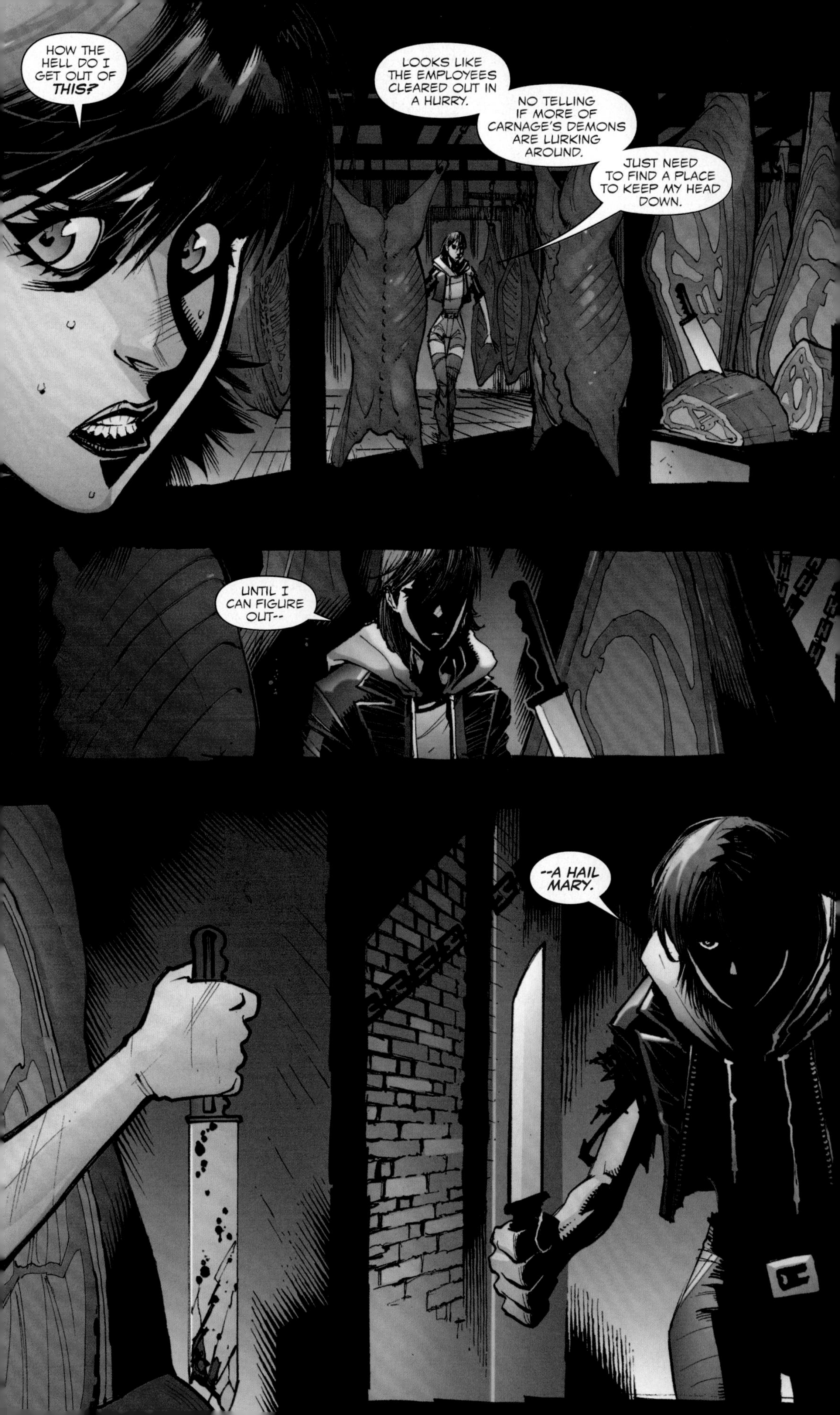

HOW THE HELL DO I GET OUT OF THIS?
LOOKS LIKE THE EMPLOYEES CLEARED OUT IN A HURRY.
NO TELLING IF MORE OF CARNAGE'S DEMONS ARE LURKING AROUND.
JUST NEED TO FIND A PLACE TO KEEP MY HEAD DOWN.
UNTIL I CAN FIGURE OUT--
--A HAIL MARY.

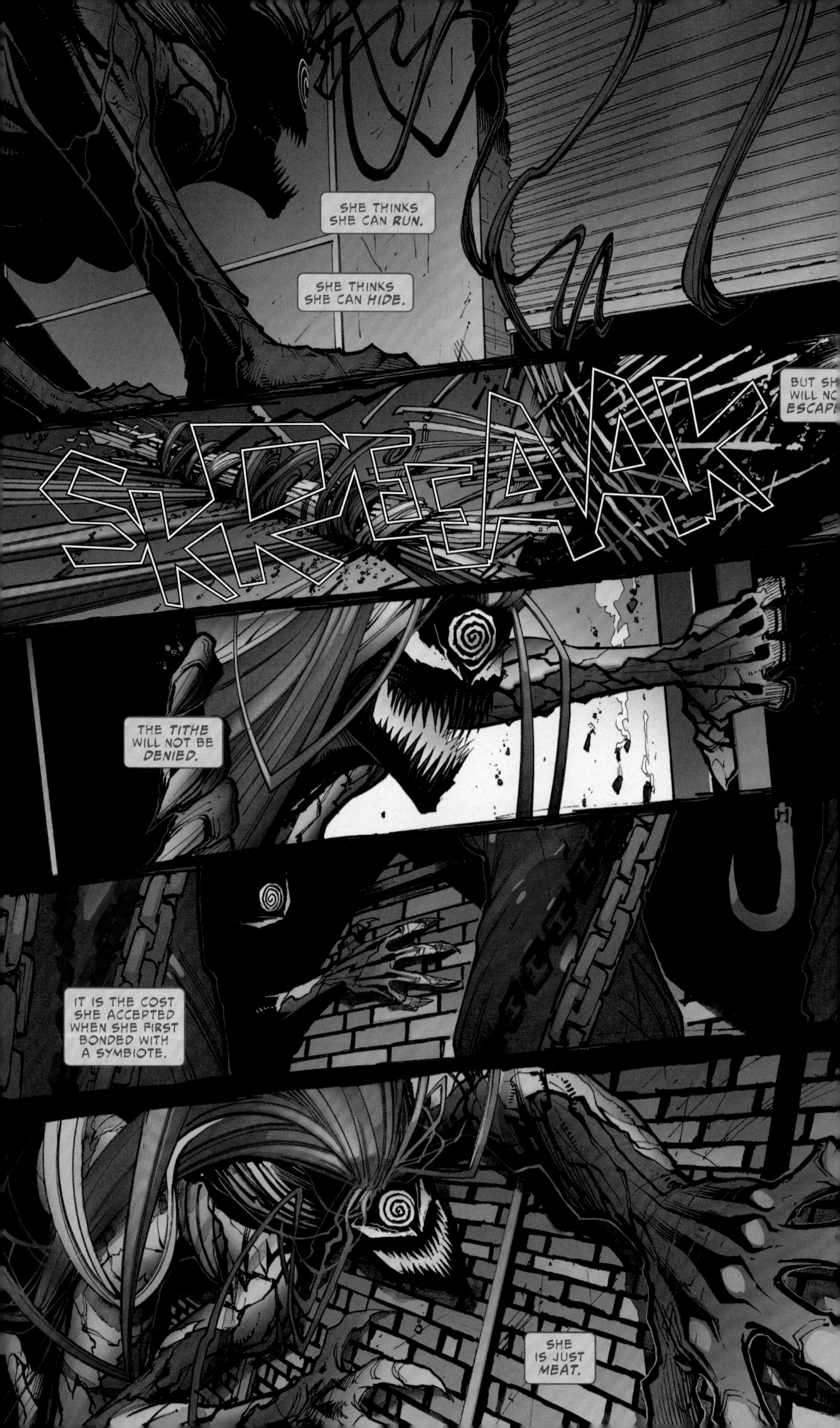
SHE THINKS SHE CAN RUN.
SHE THINKS SHE CAN HIDE.
SKREEAAK
BUT SH WILL NO ESCAP
THE TITHE WILL NOT BE DENIED.
IT IS THE COST SHE ACCEPTED WHEN SHE FIRST BONDED WITH A SYMBIOTE.
SHE IS JUST MEAT.

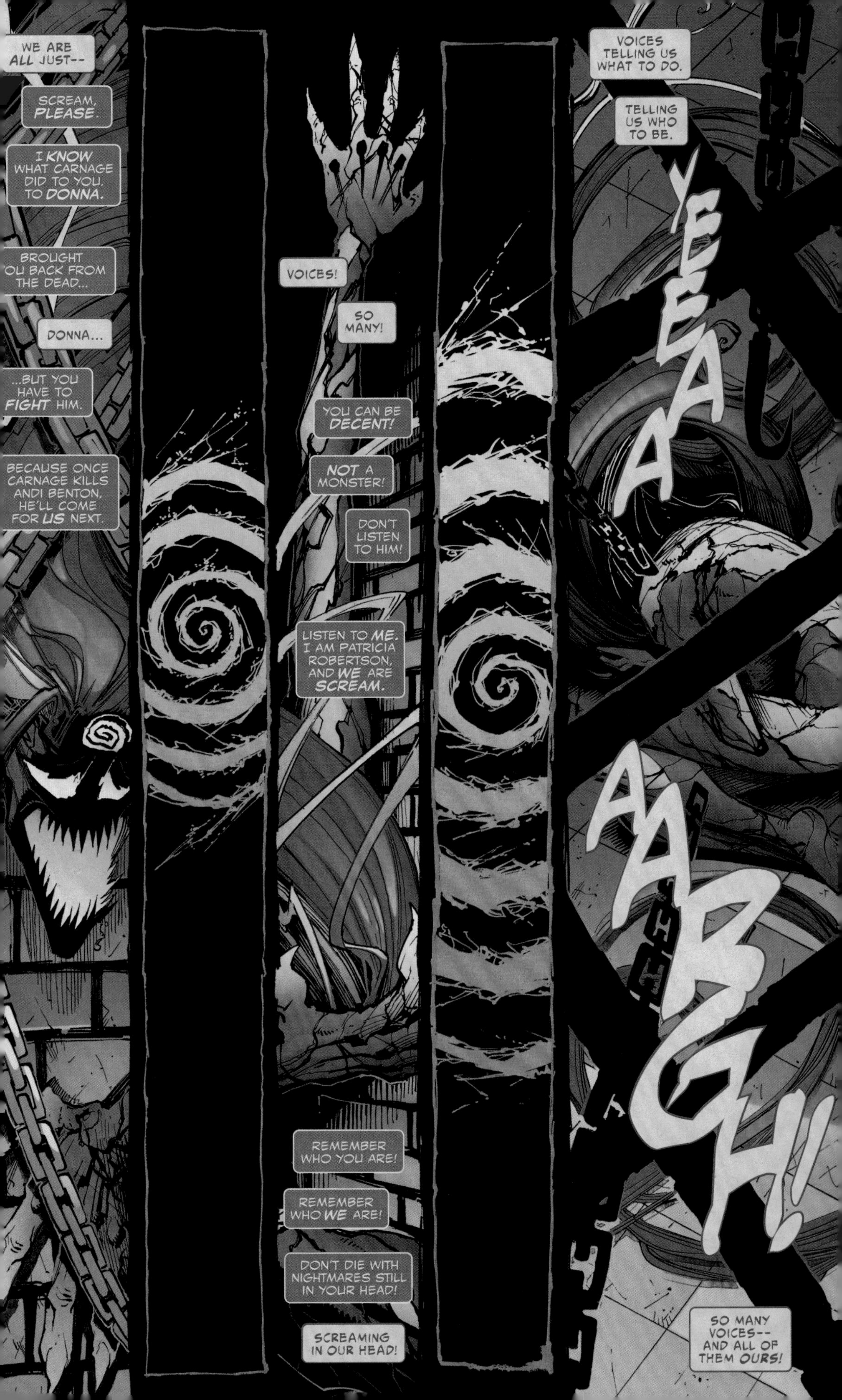

WE ARE ALL JUST--
SCREAM, PLEASE.
I KNOW WHAT CARNAGE DID TO YOU. TO DONNA.
BROUGHT YOU BACK FROM THE DEAD...
DONNA...
...BUT YOU HAVE TO FIGHT HIM.
BECAUSE ONCE CARNAGE KILLS ANDI BENTON, HE'LL COME FOR US NEXT.
VOICES!
SO MANY!
YOU CAN BE DECENT!
NOT A MONSTER!
DON'T LISTEN TO HIM!
LISTEN TO ME. I AM PATRICIA ROBERTSON, AND WE ARE SCREAM.
REMEMBER WHO YOU ARE!
REMEMBER WHO WE ARE!
DON'T DIE WITH NIGHTMARES STILL IN YOUR HEAD!
SCREAMING IN OUR HEAD!
VOICES TELLING US WHAT TO DO.
TELLING US WHO TO BE.
YEEAAA
AAAARGH!!
SO MANY VOICES-- AND ALL OF THEM OURS!

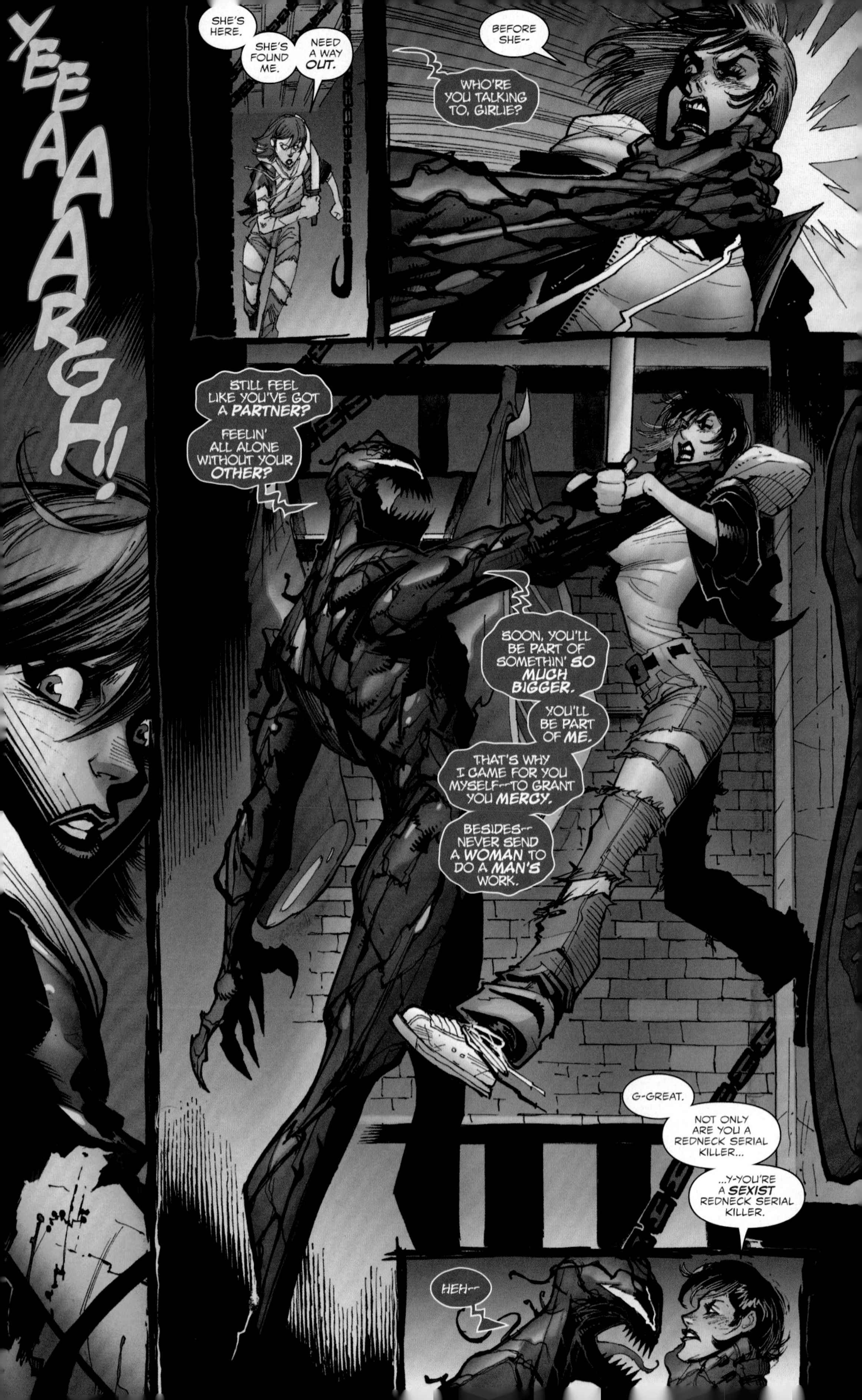
YEEAAAARGH!
SHE'S HERE.
SHE'S FOUND ME.
NEED A WAY OUT.
BEFORE SHE--
WHO'RE YOU TALKING TO, GIRLIE?
STILL FEEL LIKE YOU'VE GOT A PARTNER?
FEELIN' ALL ALONE WITHOUT YOUR OTHER?
SOON, YOU'LL BE PART OF SOMETHIN' SO MUCH BIGGER.
YOU'LL BE PART OF ME.
THAT'S WHY I CAME FOR YOU MYSELF--TO GRANT YOU MERCY.
BESIDES-- NEVER SEND A WOMAN TO DO A MAN'S WORK.
G-GREAT.
NOT ONLY ARE YOU A REDNECK SERIAL KILLER...
...Y-YOU'RE A SEXIST REDNECK SERIAL KILLER.
HEH--

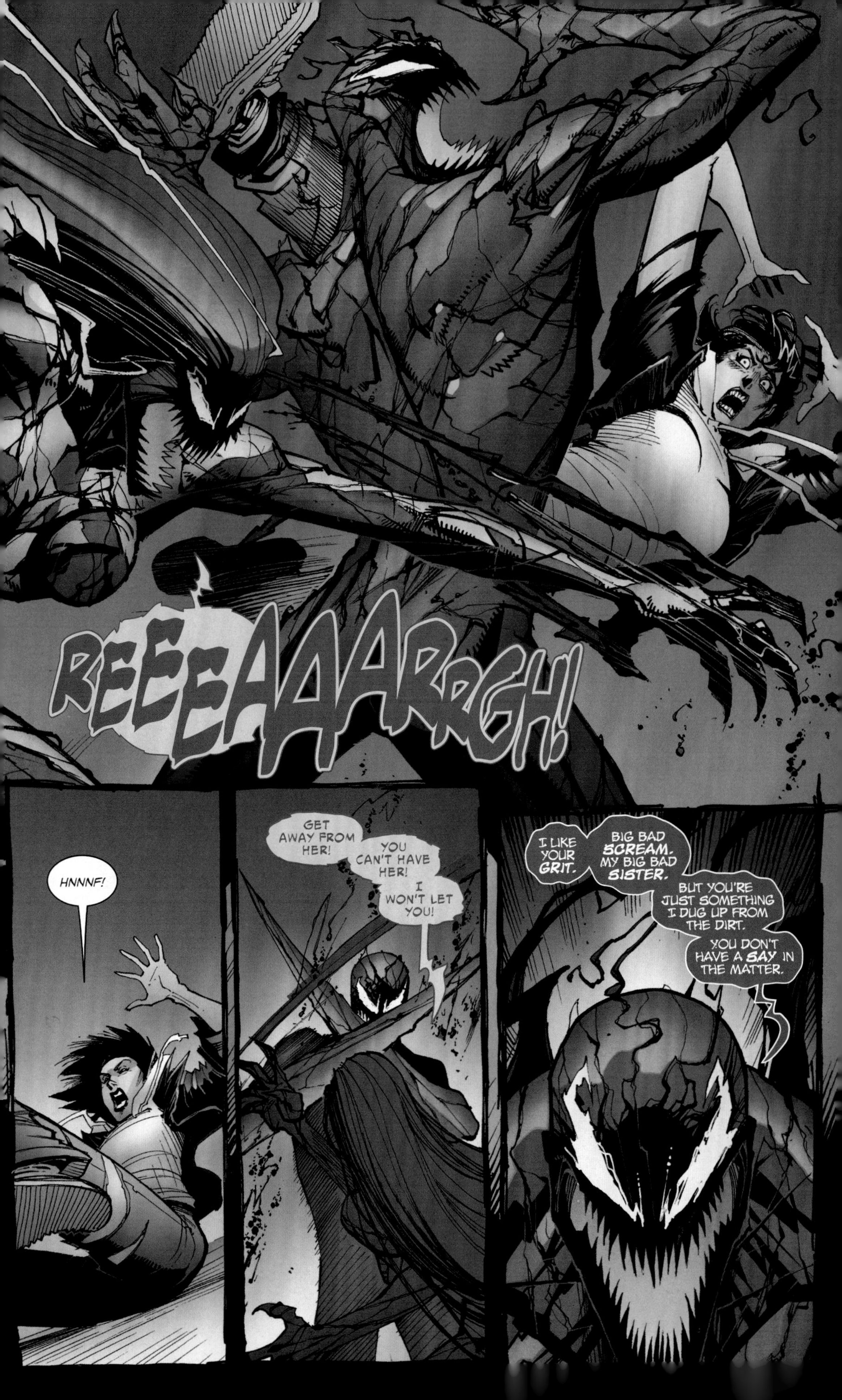
REEEAAARRGH!
HNNNF!
GET AWAY FROM HER!
YOU CAN'T HAVE HER!
I WON'T LET YOU!
I LIKE YOUR GRIT.
BIG BAD SCREAM. MY BIG BAD SISTER.
BUT YOU'RE JUST SOMETHING I DUG UP FROM THE DIRT.
YOU DON'T HAVE A SAY IN THE MATTER.

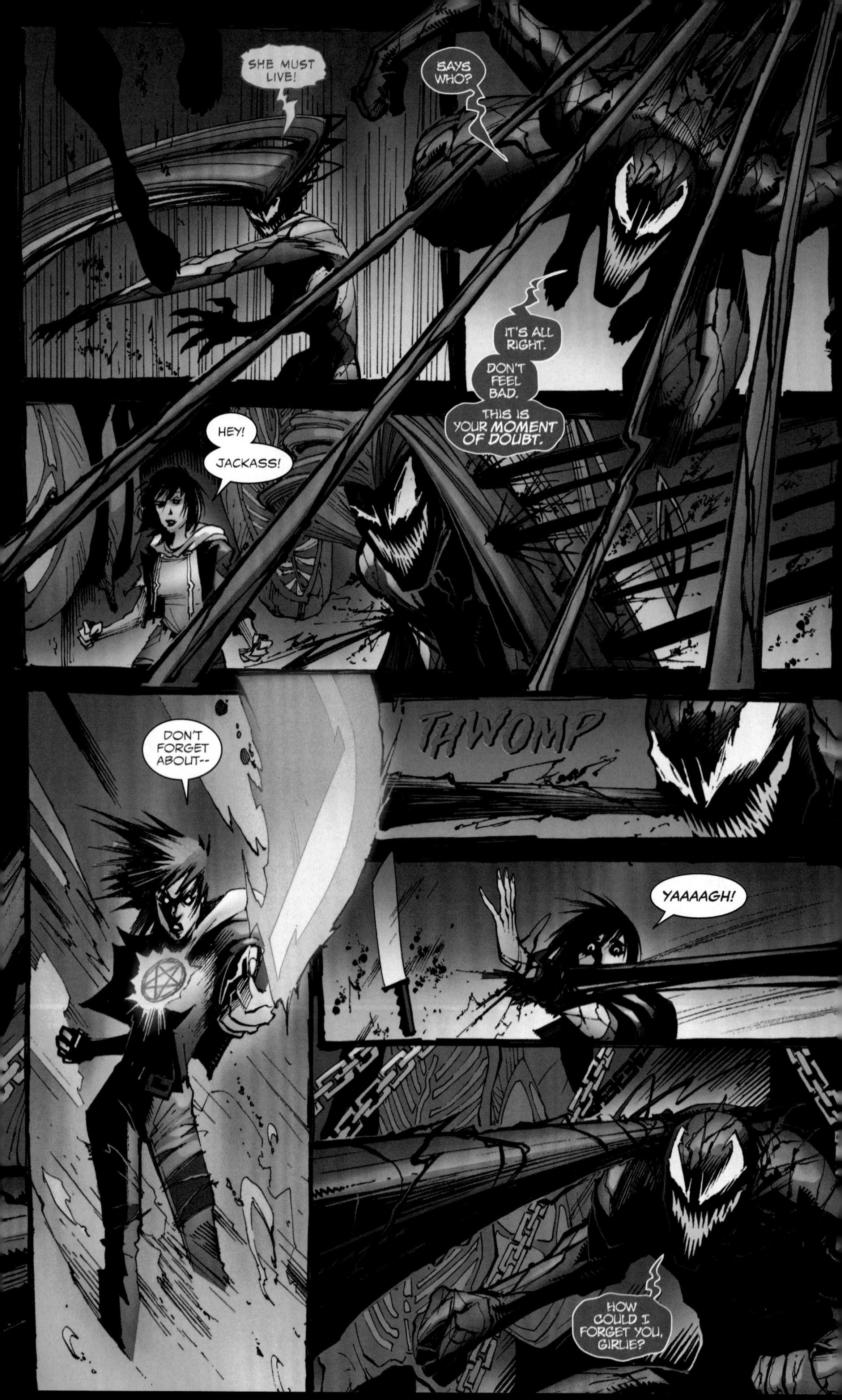

SHE MUST LIVE!
SAYS WHO?
IT'S ALL RIGHT.
DON'T FEEL BAD.
THIS IS YOUR MOMENT OF DOUBT.
HEY!
JACKASS!
DON'T FORGET ABOUT--
THWOMP
YAAAAGH!
HOW COULD I FORGET YOU, GIRLIE?

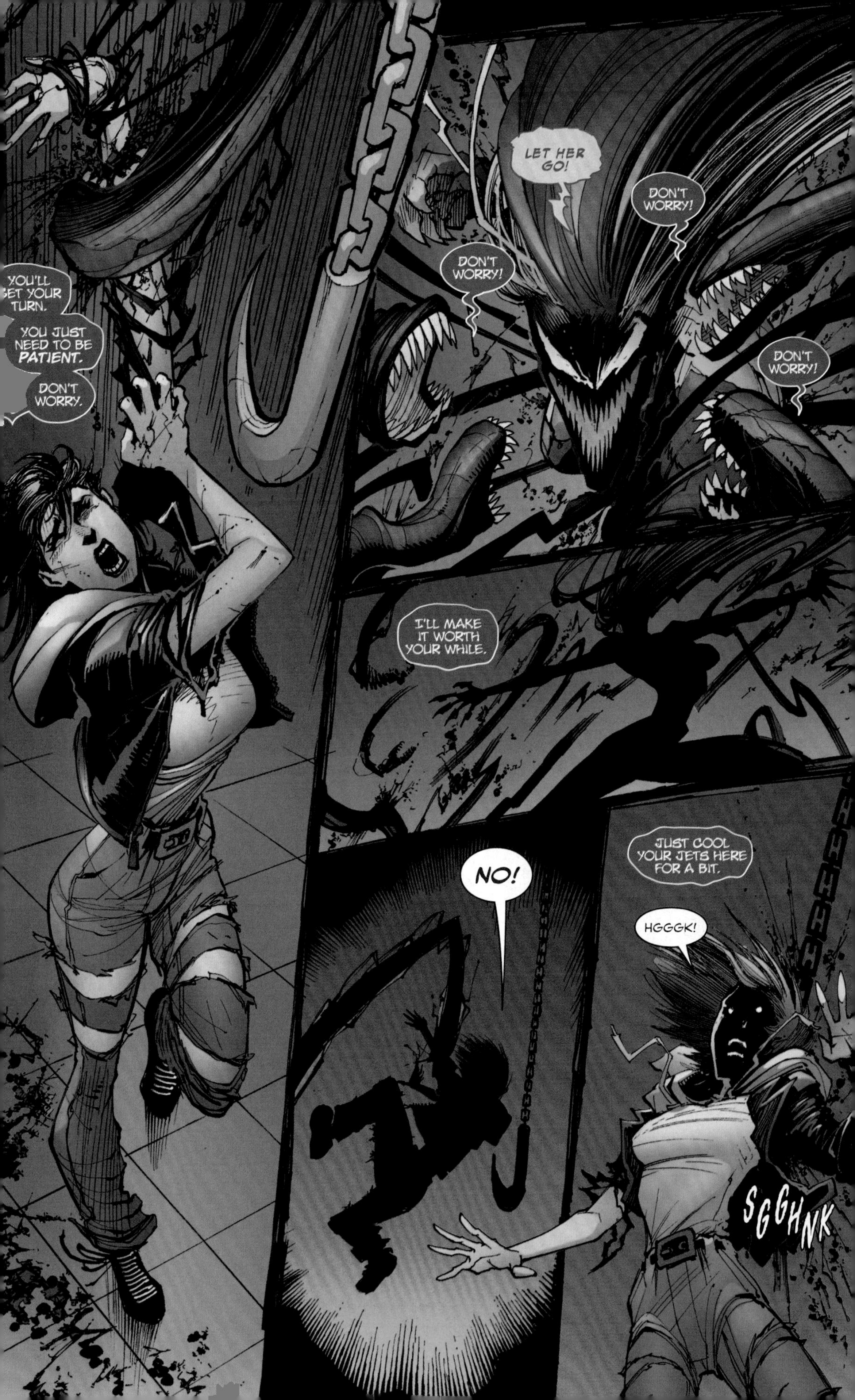
YOU'LL
GET YOUR
TURN.
YOU JUST
NEED TO BE
PATIENT.
DON'T
WORRY.
LET HER
GO!
DON'T
WORRY!
DON'T
WORRY!
DON'T
WORRY!
I'LL MAKE
IT WORTH
YOUR WHILE.
NO!
JUST COOL
YOUR JETS HERE
FOR A BIT.
HGGGK!
SGGHNK

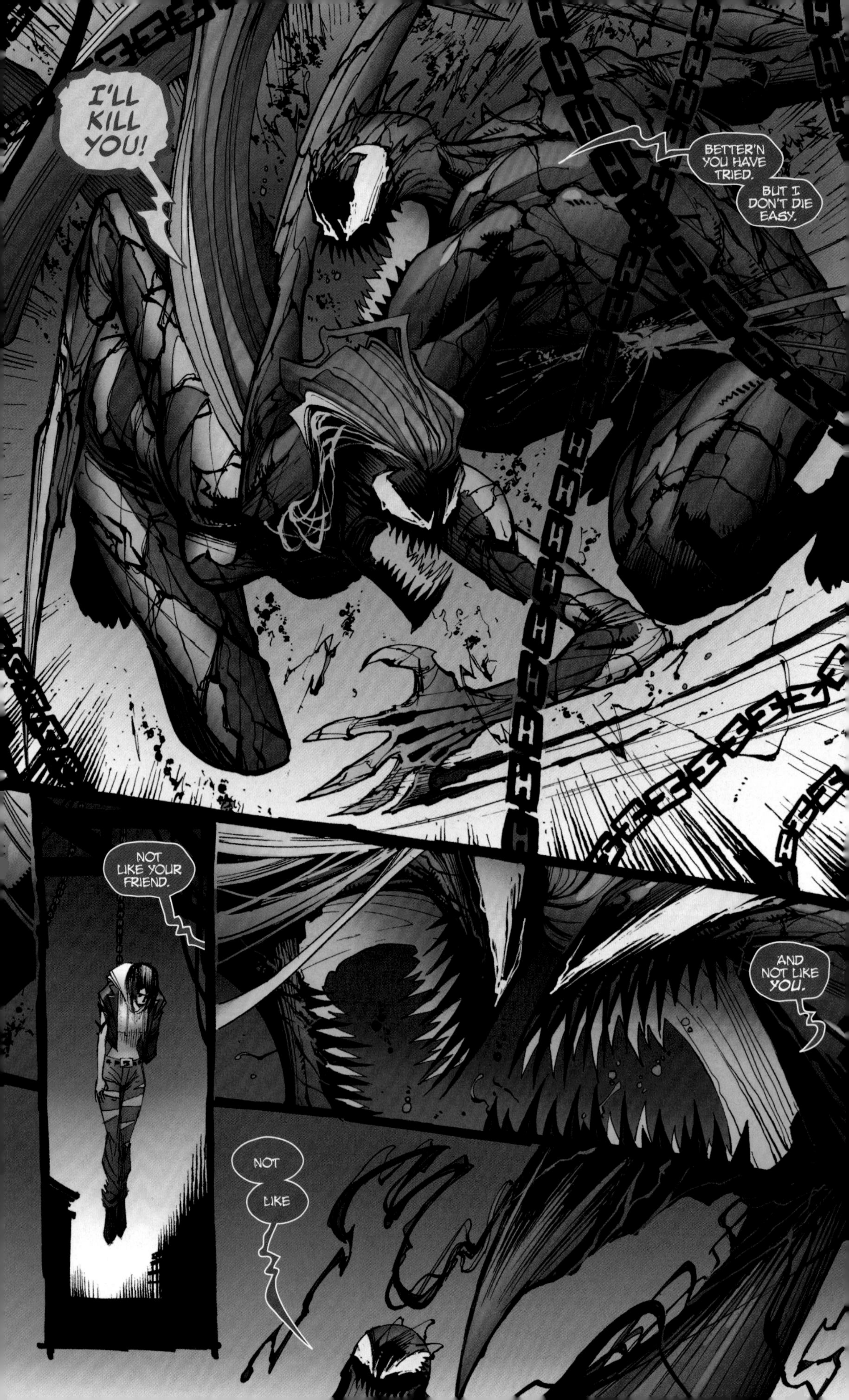
I'LL KILL YOU!
BETTER'N YOU HAVE TRIED.
BUT I DON'T DIE EASY.
NOT LIKE YOUR FRIEND.
AND NOT LIKE YOU.
NOT
LIKE

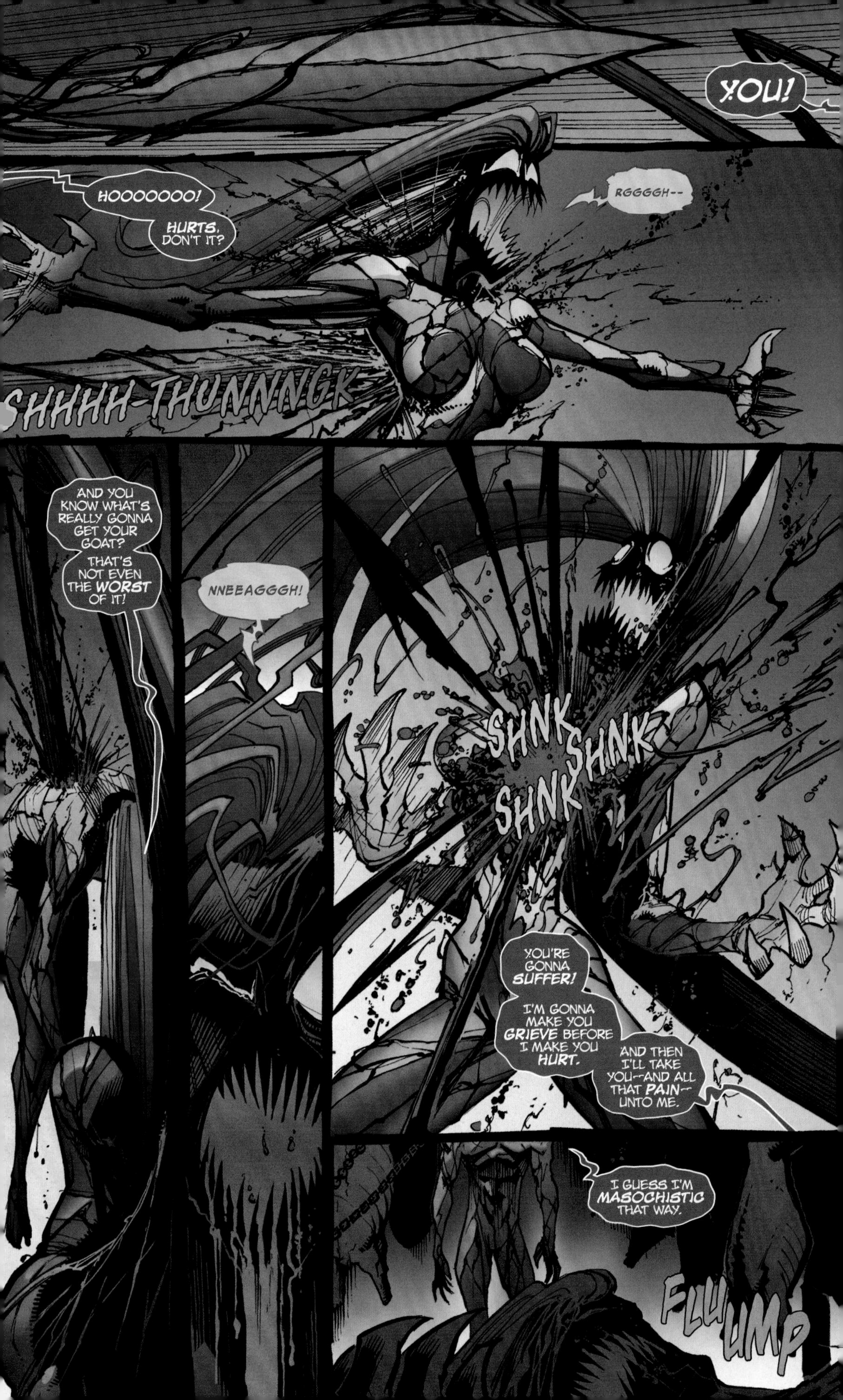
YOU!
HOOOOOOO!
HURTS, DON'T IT?
RGGGGH--
SHHHH-THUNNNGK
AND YOU KNOW WHAT'S REALLY GONNA GET YOUR GOAT?
THAT'S NOT EVEN THE WORST OF IT!
NNEEAGGGH!
SHNK SHNK SHNK
YOU'RE GONNA SUFFER!
I'M GONNA MAKE YOU GRIEVE BEFORE I MAKE YOU HURT.
AND THEN I'LL TAKE YOU--AND ALL THAT PAIN--UNTO ME.
I GUESS I'M MASOCHISTIC THAT WAY.
FLUUMP

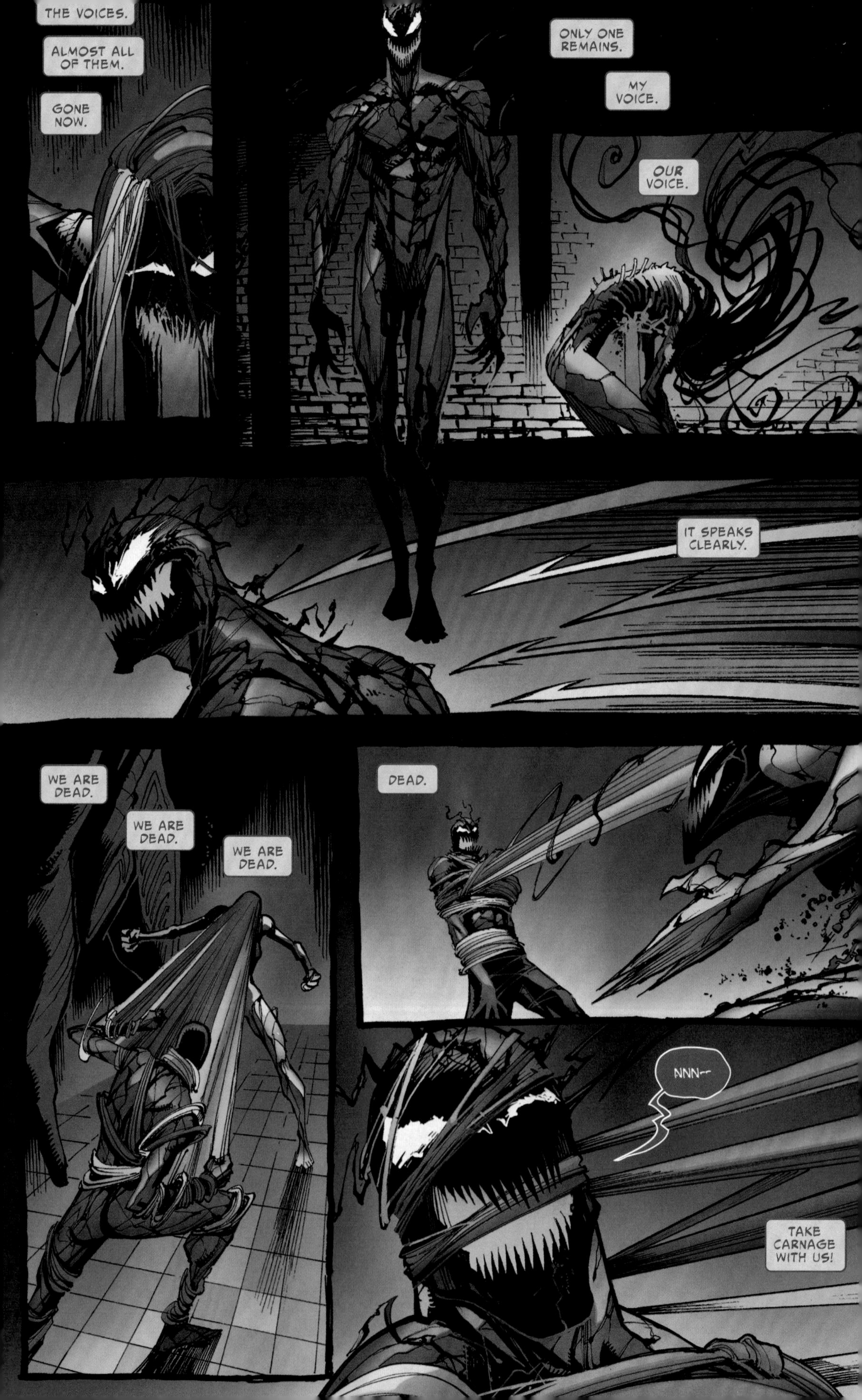

THE VOICES.
ALMOST ALL OF THEM.
GONE NOW.
ONLY ONE REMAINS.
MY VOICE.
OUR VOICE.
IT SPEAKS CLEARLY.
WE ARE DEAD.
WE ARE DEAD.
WE ARE DEAD.
DEAD.
NNN--
TAKE CARNAGE WITH US!

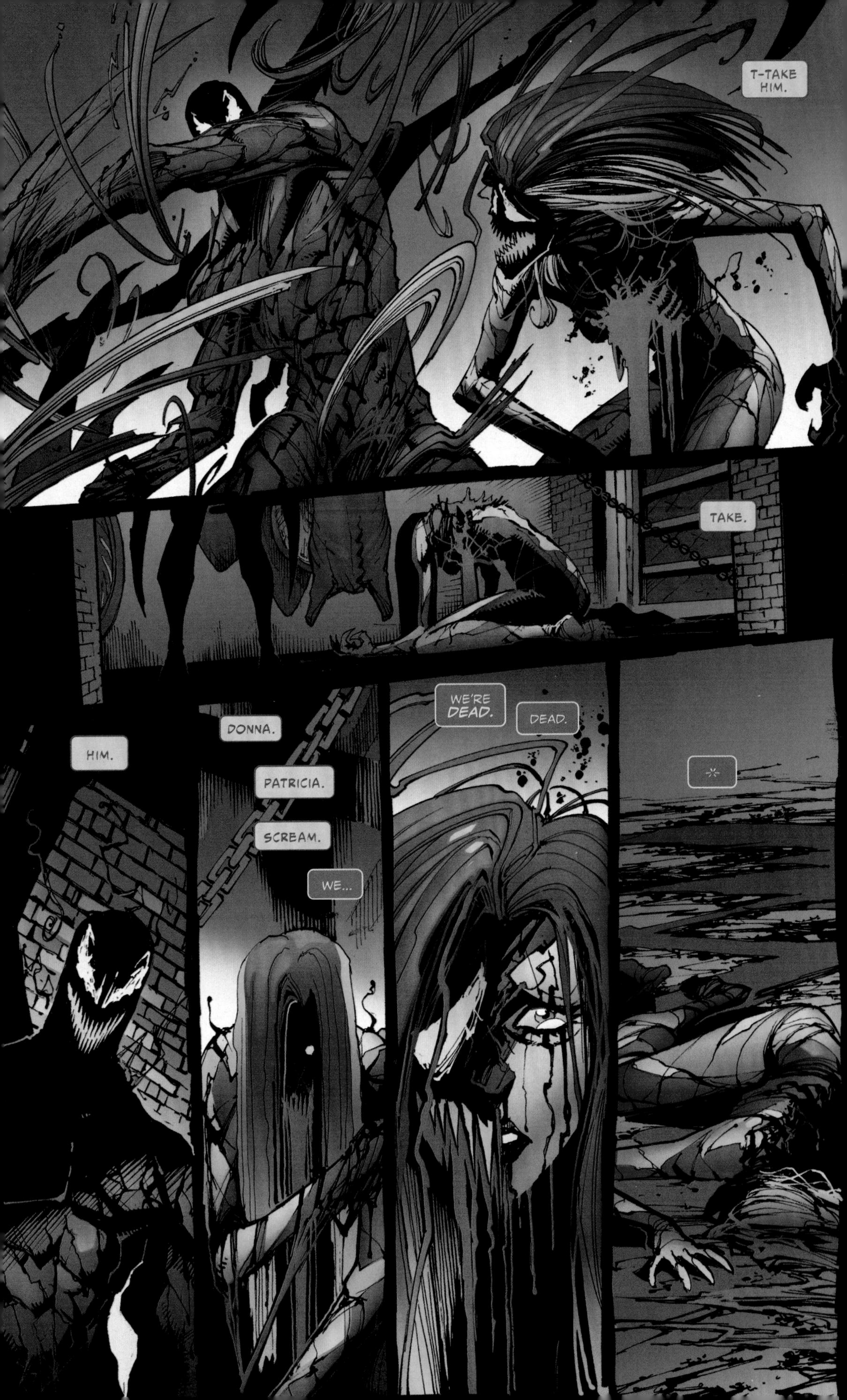
T-TAKE HIM.
TAKE.
HIM.
DONNA.
PATRICIA.
SCREAM.
WE...
WE'RE *DEAD.*
DEAD.

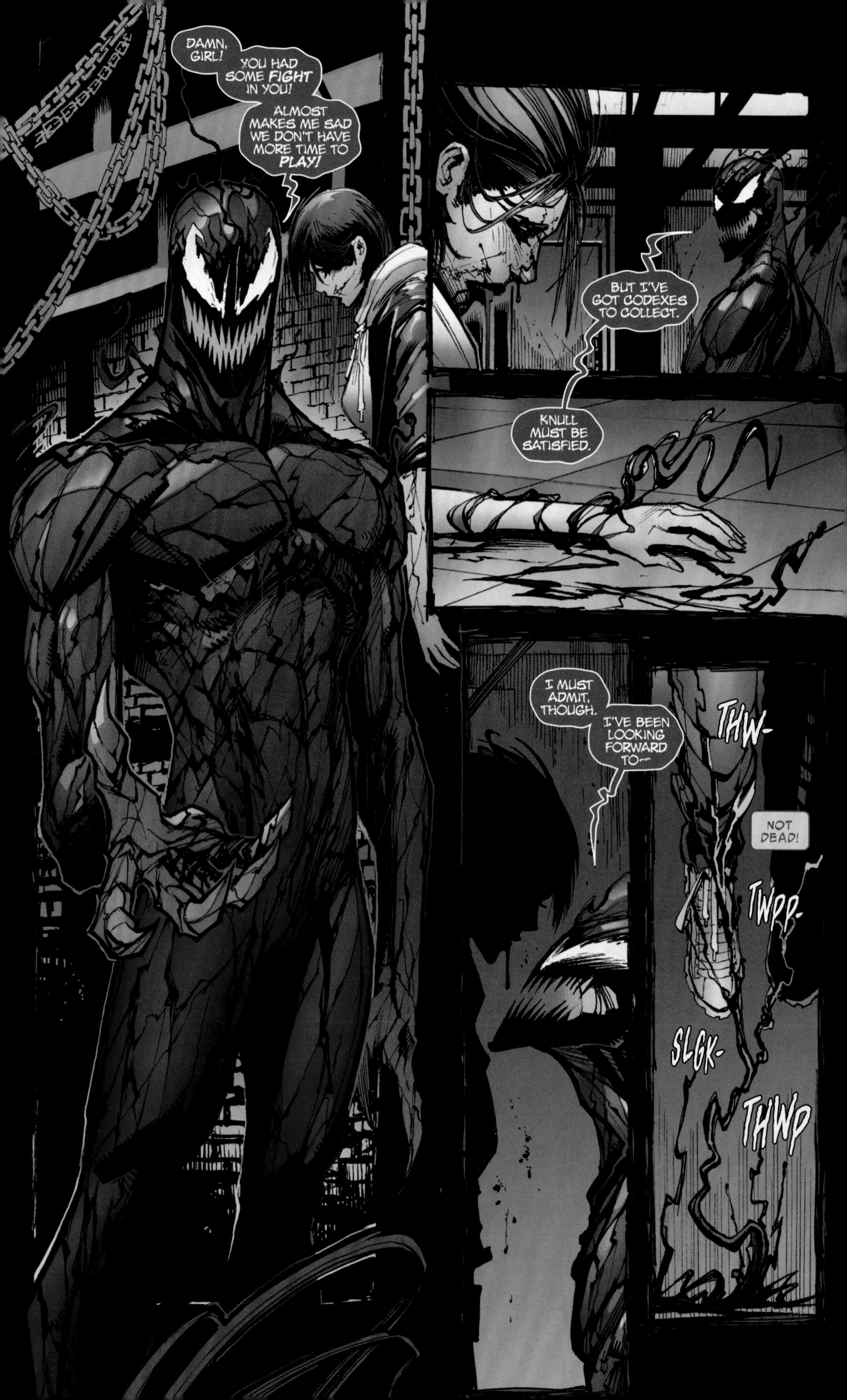
DAMN, GIRL!
YOU HAD SOME FIGHT IN YOU!
ALMOST MAKES ME SAD WE DON'T HAVE MORE TIME TO PLAY!
BUT I'VE GOT CODEXES TO COLLECT.
KNULL MUST BE SATISFIED.
I MUST ADMIT, THOUGH.
I'VE BEEN LOOKING FORWARD TO--
THW-
NOT DEAD!
TWPP-
SLGK-
THWP

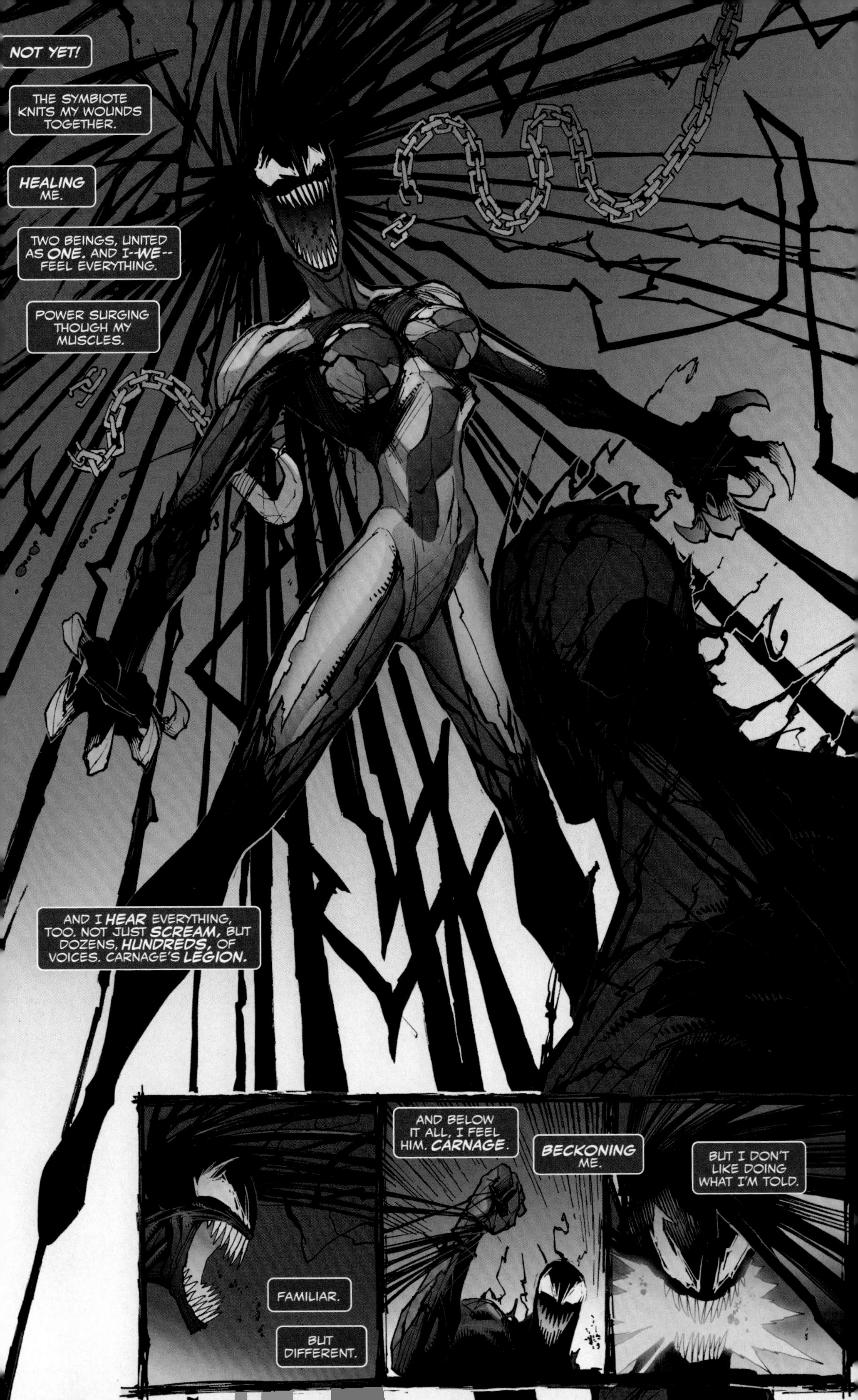
NOT YET!
THE SYMBIOTE KNITS MY WOUNDS TOGETHER.
HEALING ME.
TWO BEINGS, UNITED AS ONE. AND I--WE-- FEEL EVERYTHING.
POWER SURGING THOUGH MY MUSCLES.
AND I HEAR EVERYTHING, TOO. NOT JUST SCREAM, BUT DOZENS, HUNDREDS, OF VOICES. CARNAGE'S LEGION.
FAMILIAR.
BUT DIFFERENT.
AND BELOW IT ALL, I FEEL HIM. CARNAGE.
BECKONING ME.
BUT I DON'T LIKE DOING WHAT I'M TOLD.

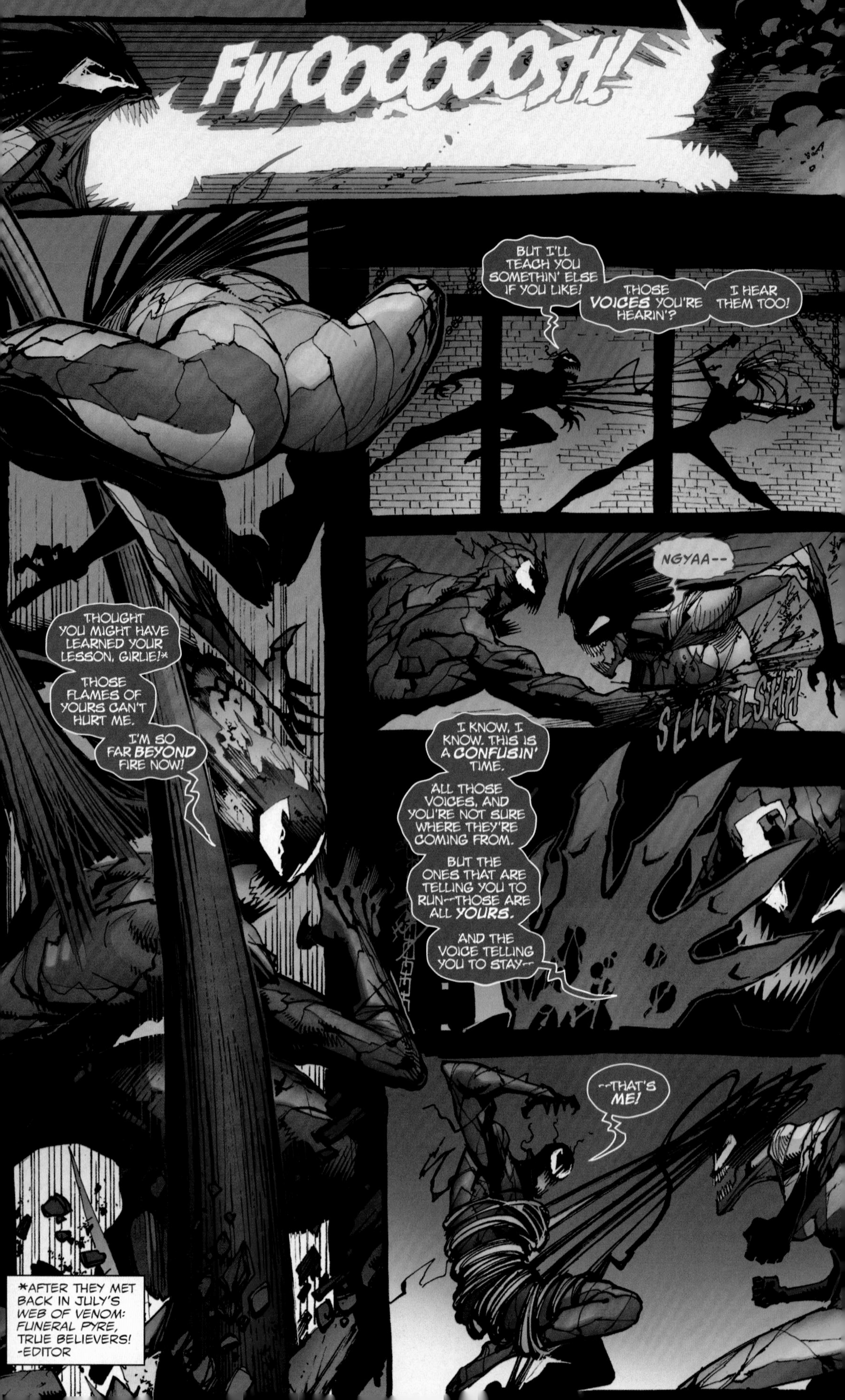
FWOOOOOOSH!
BUT I'LL TEACH YOU SOMETHIN' ELSE IF YOU LIKE!
THOSE VOICES YOU'RE HEARIN'?
I HEAR THEM TOO!
THOUGHT YOU MIGHT HAVE LEARNED YOUR LESSON, GIRLIE!*
THOSE FLAMES OF YOURS CAN'T HURT ME.
I'M SO FAR BEYOND FIRE NOW!
NGYAA--
SLLLLLSHH
I KNOW, I KNOW. THIS IS A CONFUSIN' TIME.
ALL THOSE VOICES, AND YOU'RE NOT SURE WHERE THEY'RE COMING FROM.
BUT THE ONES THAT ARE TELLING YOU TO RUN--THOSE ARE ALL YOURS.
AND THE VOICE TELLING YOU TO STAY--
--THAT'S ME!
*AFTER THEY MET BACK IN JULY'S WEB OF VENOM: FUNERAL PYRE, TRUE BELIEVERS! -EDITOR

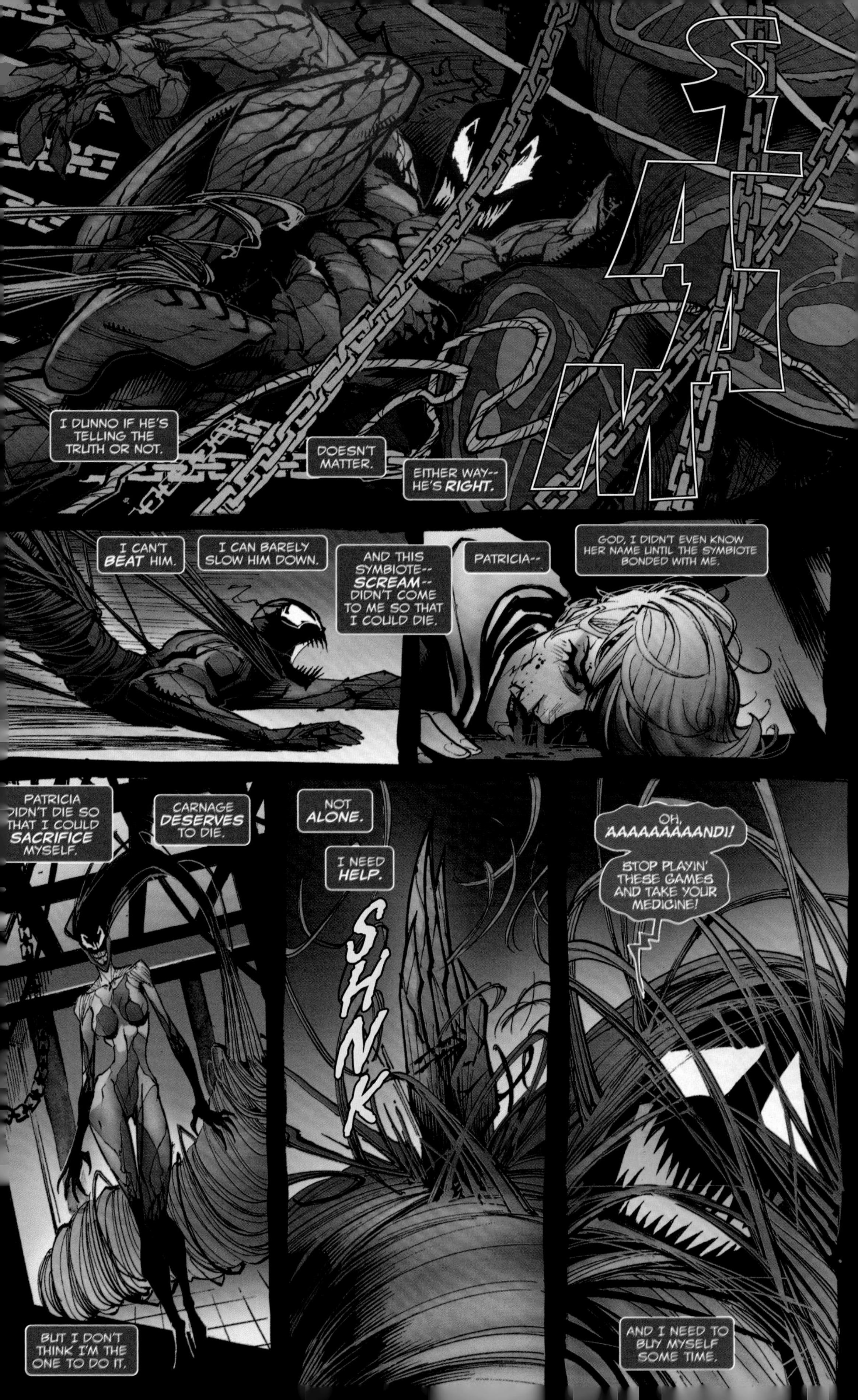

I DUNNO IF HE'S TELLING THE TRUTH OR NOT.
DOESN'T MATTER.
EITHER WAY-- HE'S RIGHT.
SLAM
I CAN'T BEAT HIM.
I CAN BARELY SLOW HIM DOWN.
AND THIS SYMBIOTE-- SCREAM-- DIDN'T COME TO ME SO THAT I COULD DIE.
PATRICIA--
GOD, I DIDN'T EVEN KNOW HER NAME UNTIL THE SYMBIOTE BONDED WITH ME.
PATRICIA DIDN'T DIE SO THAT I COULD SACRIFICE MYSELF.
CARNAGE DESERVES TO DIE.
BUT I DON'T THINK I'M THE ONE TO DO IT.
NOT ALONE.
I NEED HELP.
SHNK
OH, AAAAAAAAANDI!
STOP PLAYIN' THESE GAMES AND TAKE YOUR MEDICINE!
AND I NEED TO BUY MYSELF SOME TIME.

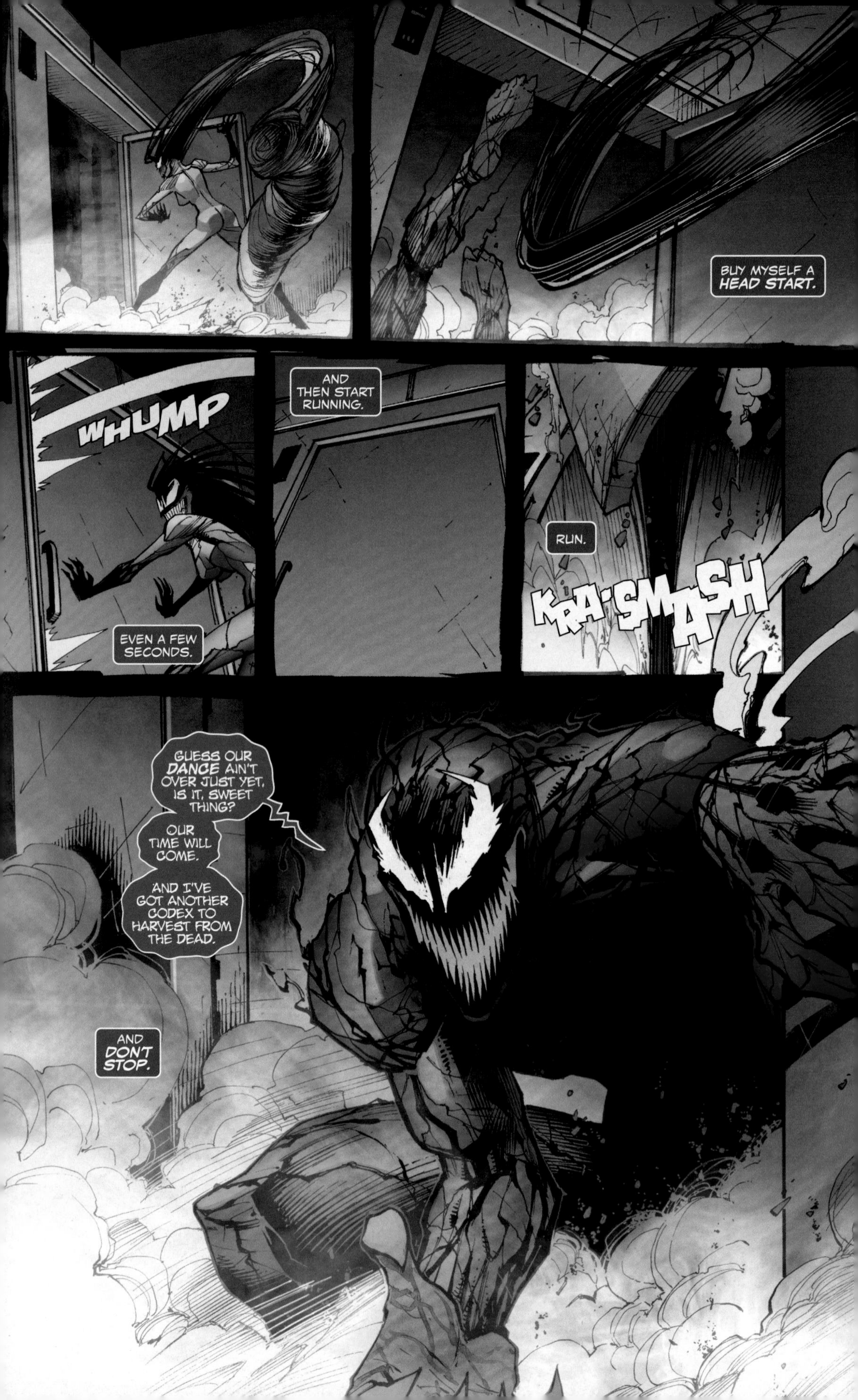
BUY MYSELF A HEAD START.
WHUMP
AND THEN START RUNNING.
EVEN A FEW SECONDS.
RUN.
KRA-SMASH
GUESS OUR DANCE AIN'T OVER JUST YET, IS IT, SWEET THING?
OUR TIME WILL COME.
AND I'VE GOT ANOTHER CODEX TO HARVEST FROM THE DEAD.
AND DON'T STOP.

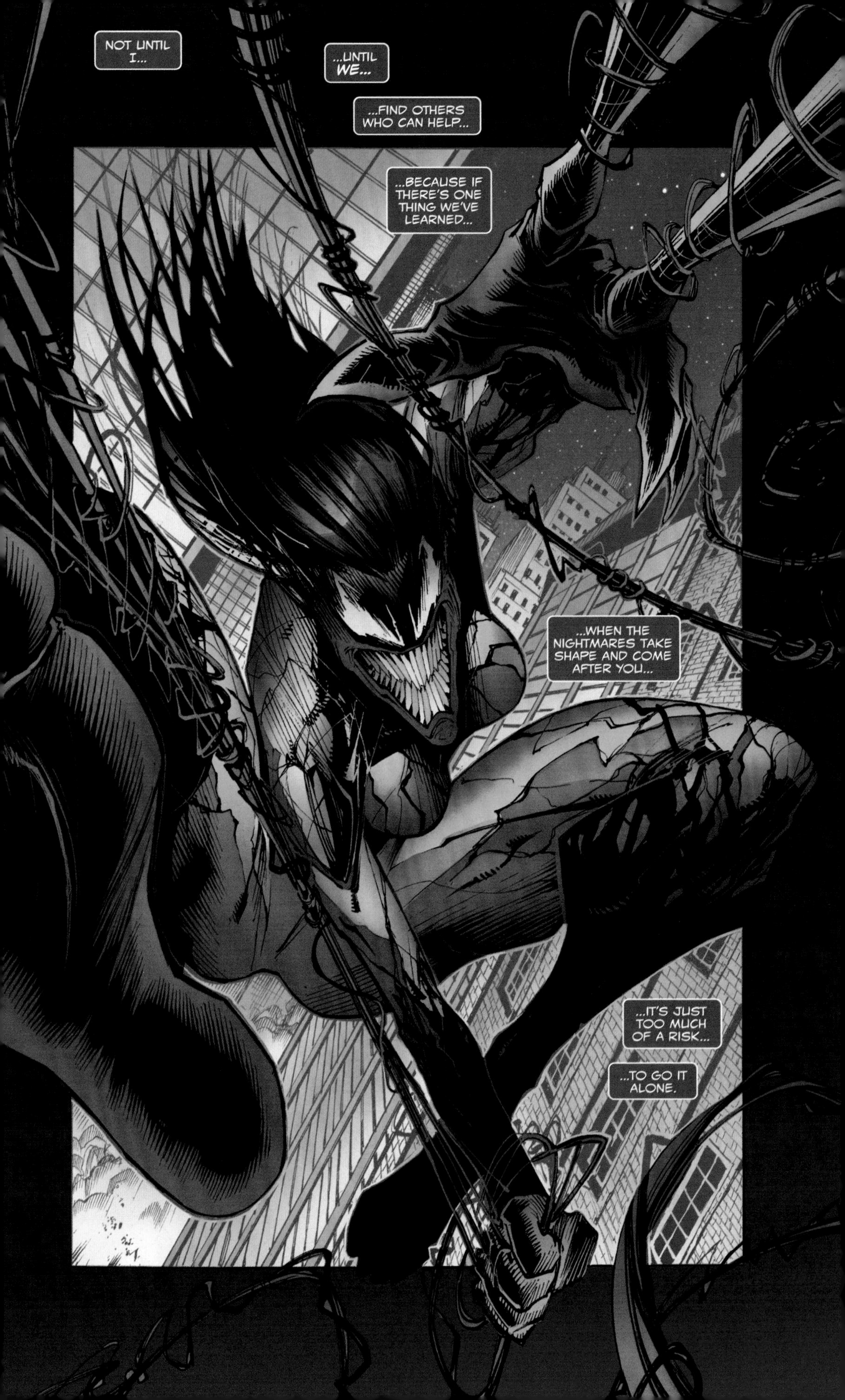
NOT UNTIL I...
...UNTIL WE...
...FIND OTHERS WHO CAN HELP...
...BECAUSE IF THERE'S ONE THING WE'VE LEARNED...
...WHEN THE NIGHTMARES TAKE SHAPE AND COME AFTER YOU...
...IT'S JUST TOO MUCH OF A RISK...
...TO GO IT ALONE.

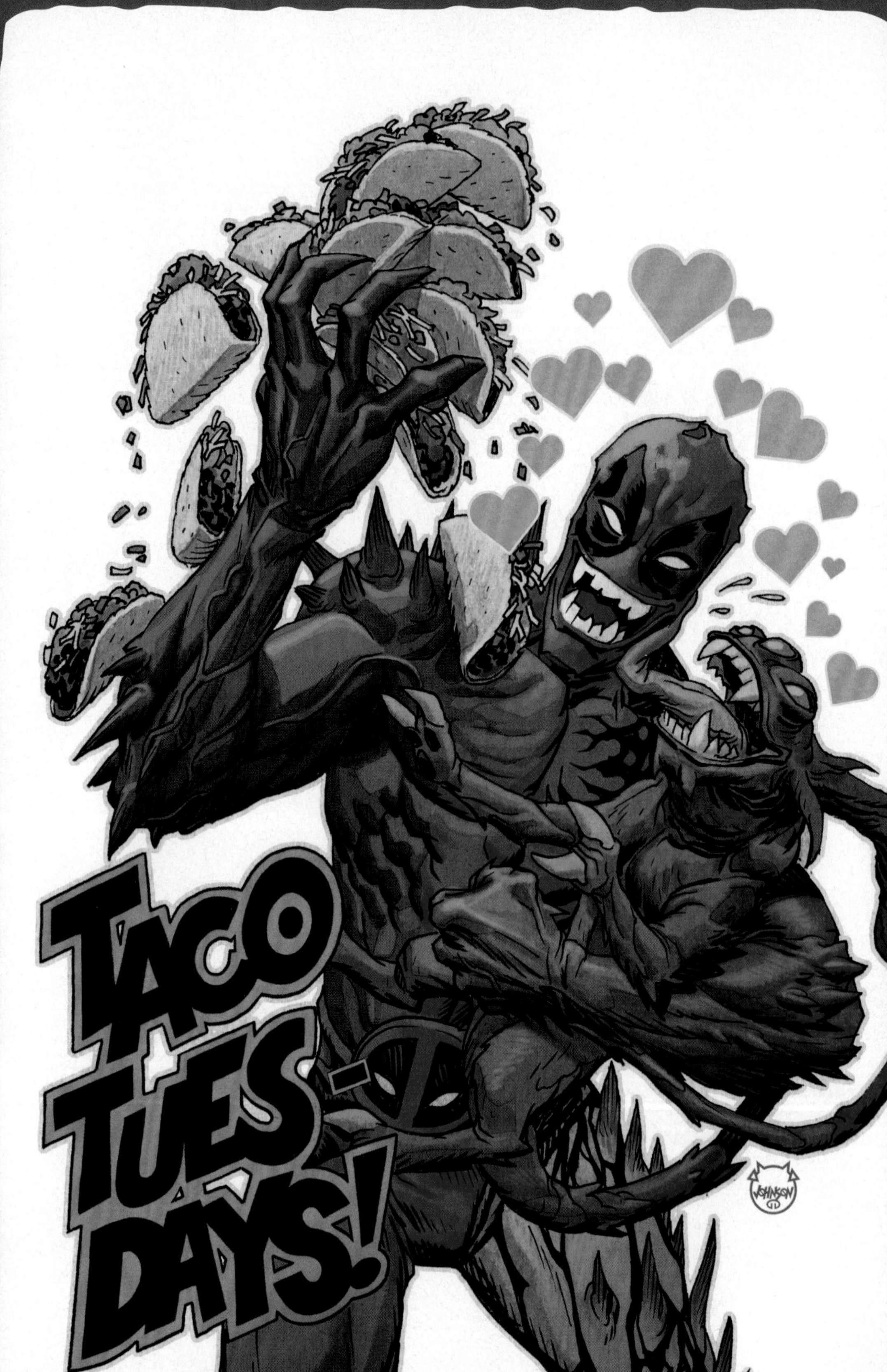
TACO TUES-DAYS!
JOHNSON GD

DAVE JOHNSON

SEPARATION ANXIETY Codex Variant

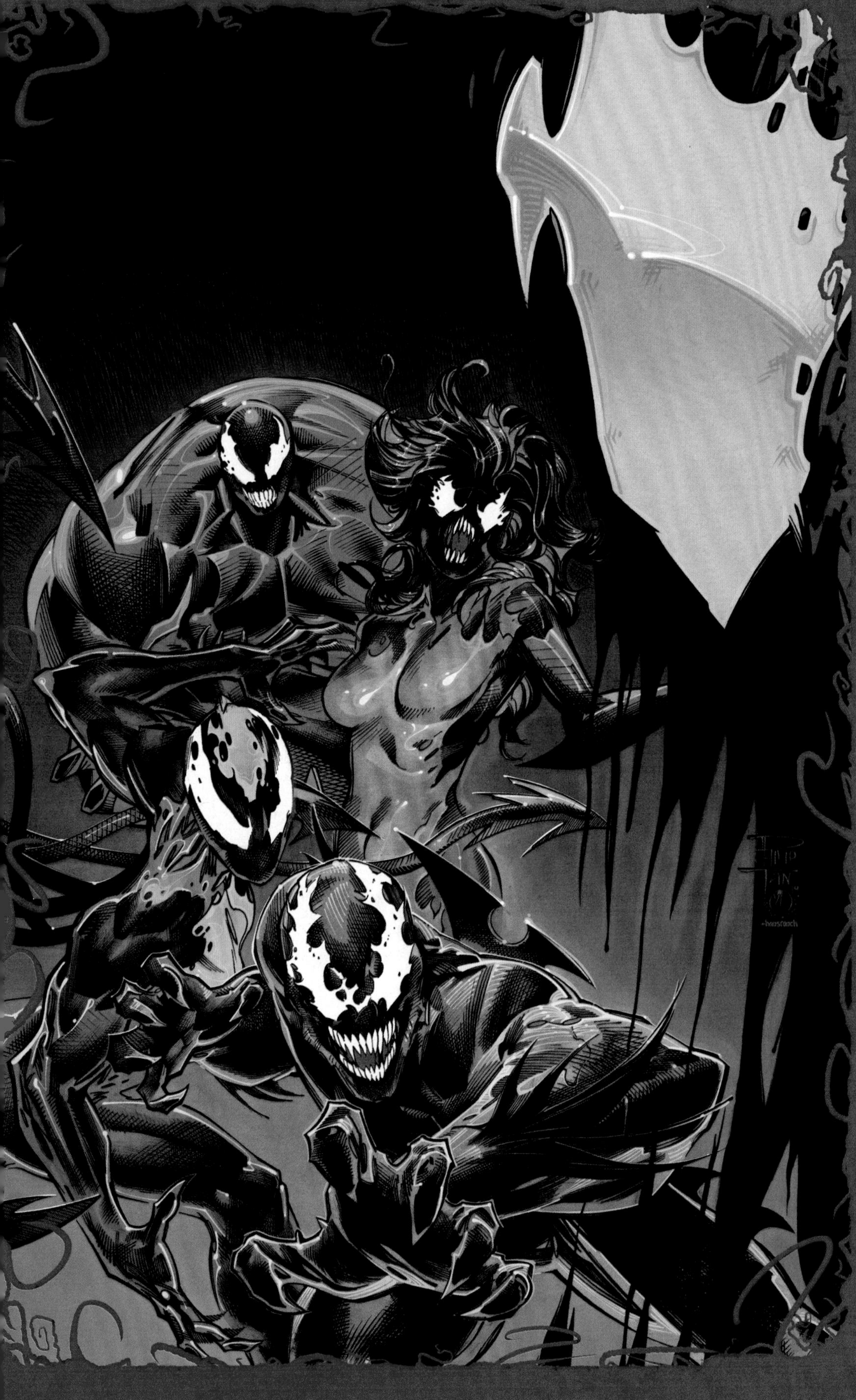

SEPARATION ANXIETY

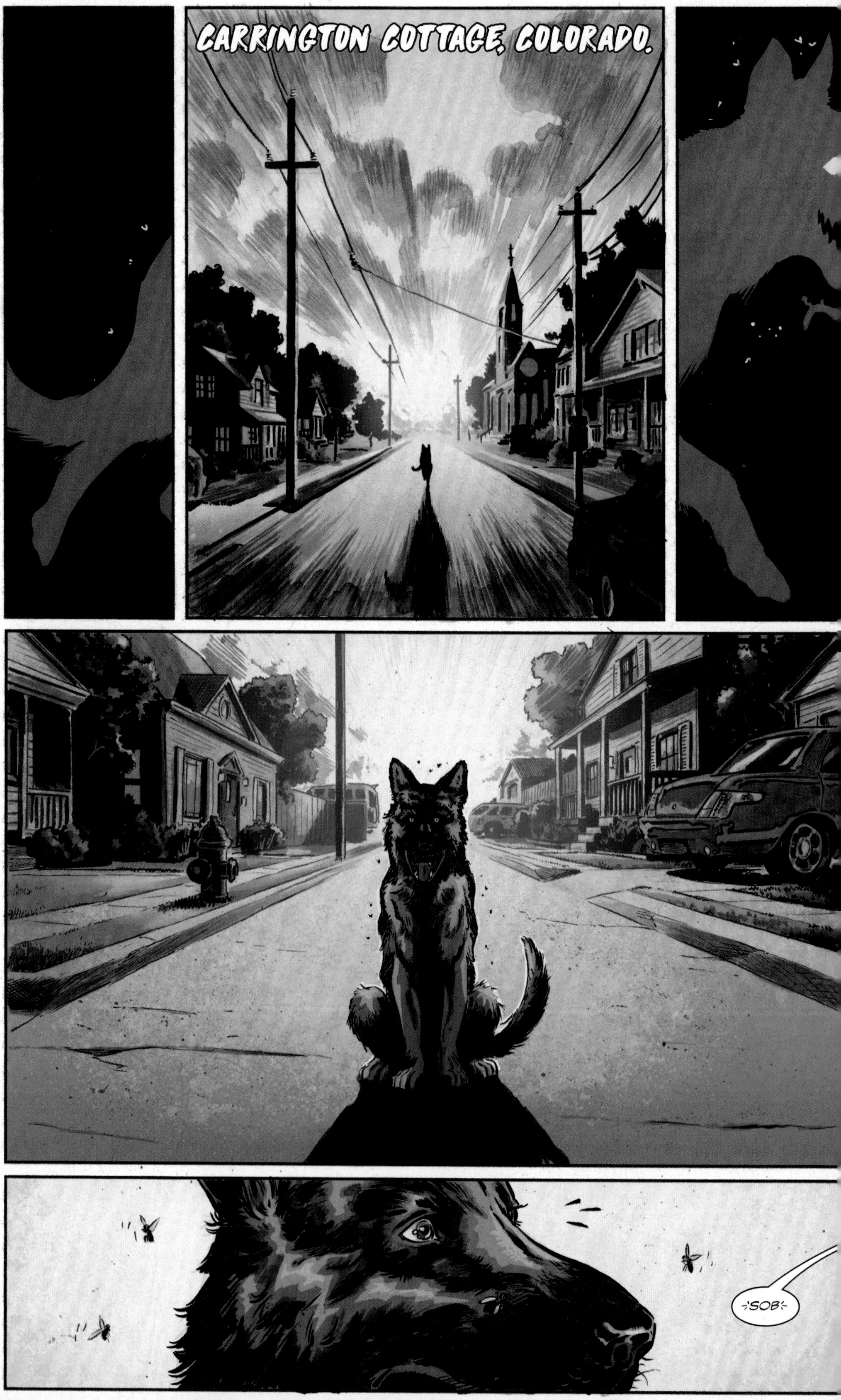
CARRINGTON COTTAGE, COLORADO.
SOB

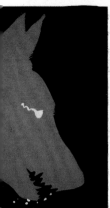

-:SOB SOB:-

-:GAASP:- WHERE DID YOU COME FROM?

WHAT'S THE MATTER? CAT GOT YOUR TONGUE?

snf

OKAY! OKAY! TAKE IT EASY, FELLA...

HAVEN'T SEEN YOU AROUND HERE BEFORE. WHERE'S YOUR HOME?

GOT NO COLLAR, HUH? THAT'S WEIRD... WHO DO YOU BELONG TO?

YOU MUST BE HUNGR--

SADIE! BACK INSIDE THE HOUSE! YOU'RE SUPPOSED TO BE PACKING!

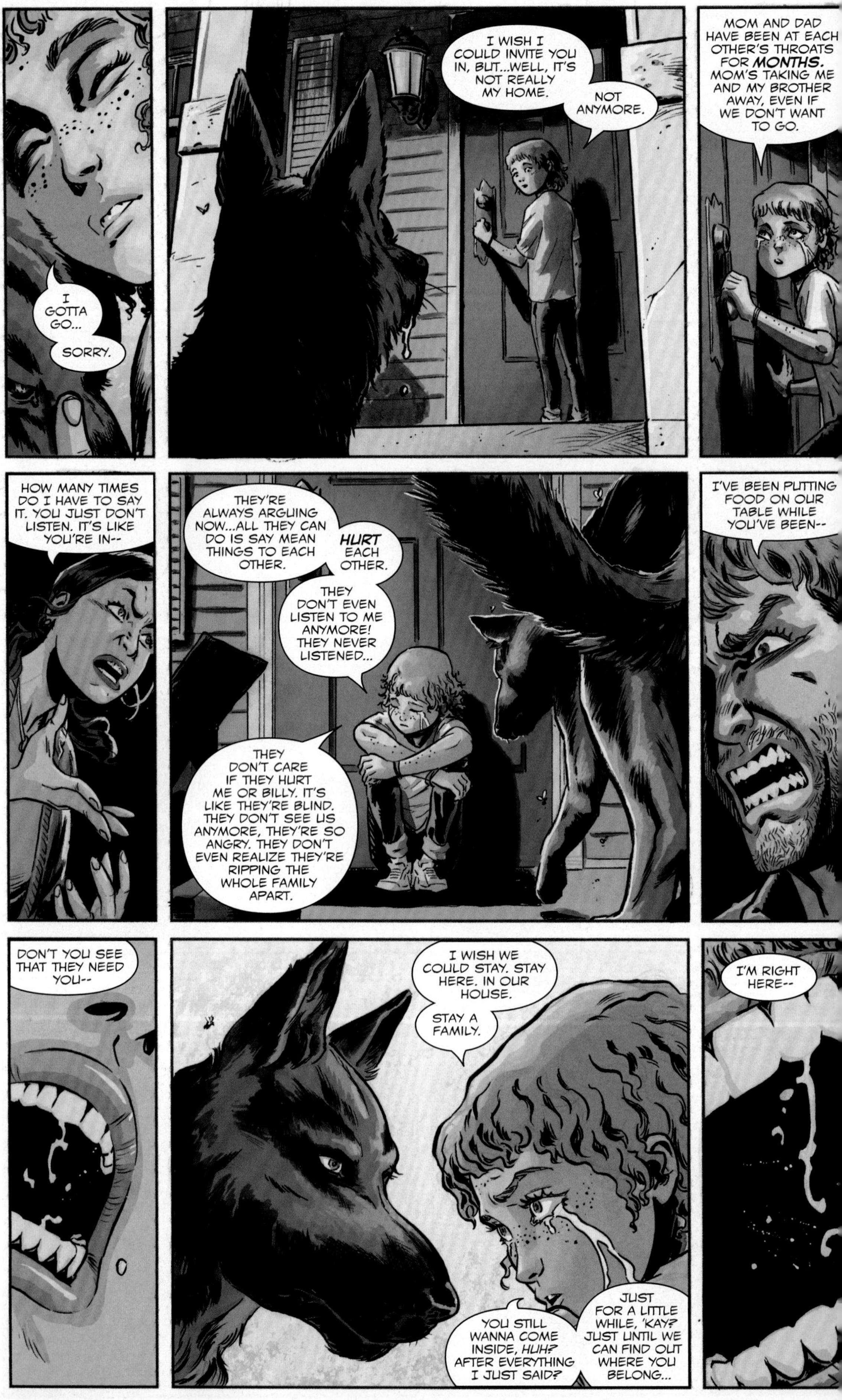
I GOTTA GO...
SORRY.
I WISH I COULD INVITE YOU IN, BUT...WELL, IT'S NOT REALLY MY HOME.
NOT ANYMORE.
MOM AND DAD HAVE BEEN AT EACH OTHER'S THROATS FOR **MONTHS.** MOM'S TAKING ME AND MY BROTHER AWAY, EVEN IF WE DON'T WANT TO GO.
HOW MANY TIMES DO I HAVE TO SAY IT. YOU JUST DON'T LISTEN. IT'S LIKE YOU'RE IN--
THEY'RE ALWAYS ARGUING NOW...ALL THEY CAN DO IS SAY MEAN THINGS TO EACH OTHER.
HURT EACH OTHER.
THEY DON'T EVEN LISTEN TO ME ANYMORE! THEY NEVER LISTENED...
THEY DON'T CARE IF THEY HURT ME OR BILLY. IT'S LIKE THEY'RE BLIND. THEY DON'T SEE US ANYMORE, THEY'RE SO ANGRY. THEY DON'T EVEN REALIZE THEY'RE RIPPING THE WHOLE FAMILY APART.
I'VE BEEN PUTTING FOOD ON OUR TABLE WHILE YOU'VE BEEN--
DON'T YOU SEE THAT THEY NEED YOU--
I WISH WE COULD STAY. STAY HERE. IN OUR HOUSE.
STAY A FAMILY.
YOU STILL WANNA COME INSIDE, *HUH?* AFTER EVERYTHING I JUST SAID?
JUST FOR A LITTLE WHILE, 'KAY? JUST UNTIL WE CAN FIND OUT WHERE YOU BELONG...
I'M RIGHT HERE--

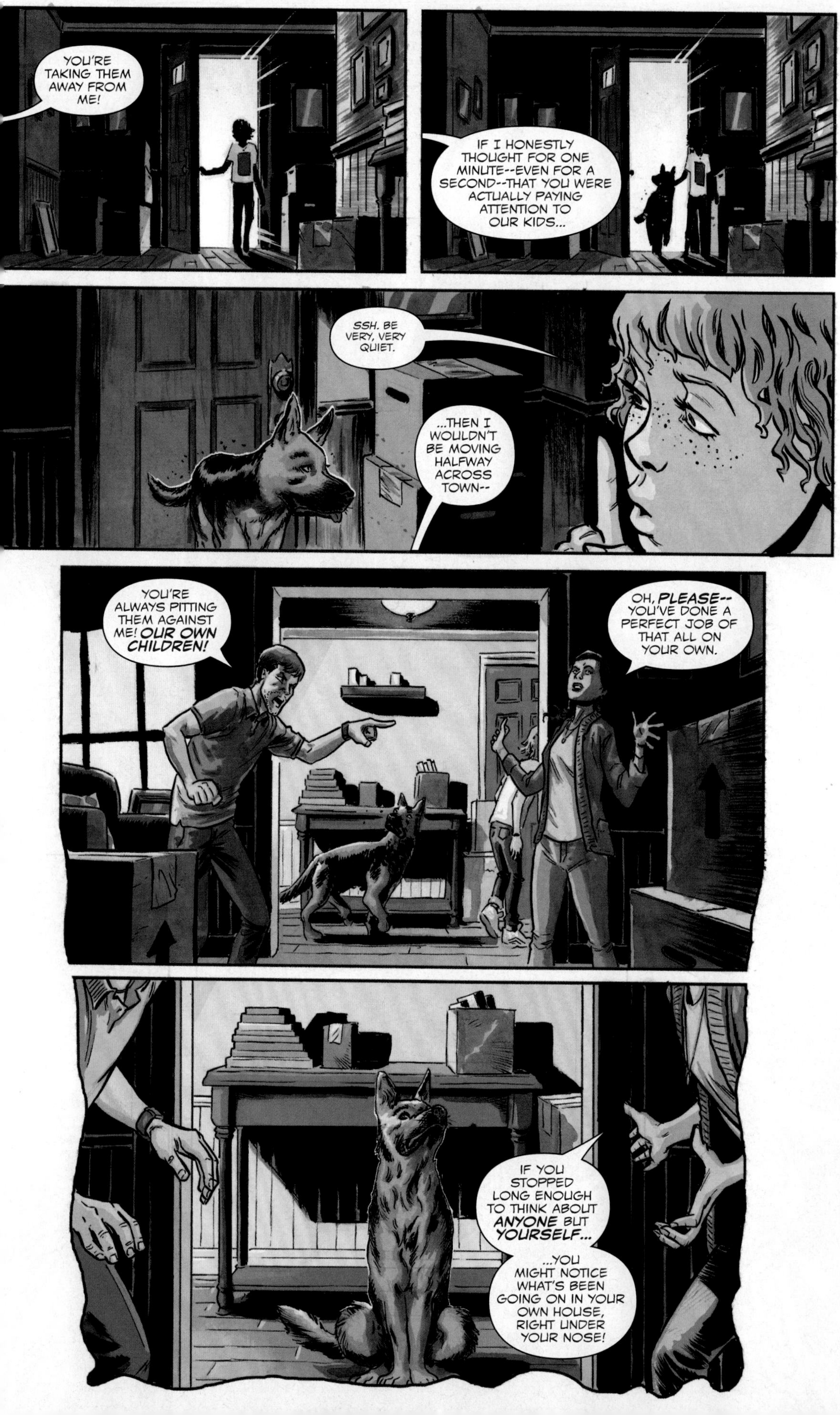

YOU'RE TAKING THEM AWAY FROM ME!
IF I HONESTLY THOUGHT FOR ONE MINUTE--EVEN FOR A SECOND--THAT YOU WERE ACTUALLY PAYING ATTENTION TO OUR KIDS...
SSH. BE VERY, VERY QUIET.
...THEN I WOULDN'T BE MOVING HALFWAY ACROSS TOWN--
YOU'RE ALWAYS PITTING THEM AGAINST ME! **OUR OWN CHILDREN!**
OH, **PLEASE--** YOU'VE DONE A PERFECT JOB OF THAT ALL ON YOUR OWN.
IF YOU STOPPED LONG ENOUGH TO THINK ABOUT **ANYONE** BUT **YOURSELF...**
...YOU MIGHT NOTICE WHAT'S BEEN GOING ON IN YOUR OWN HOUSE, RIGHT UNDER YOUR NOSE!

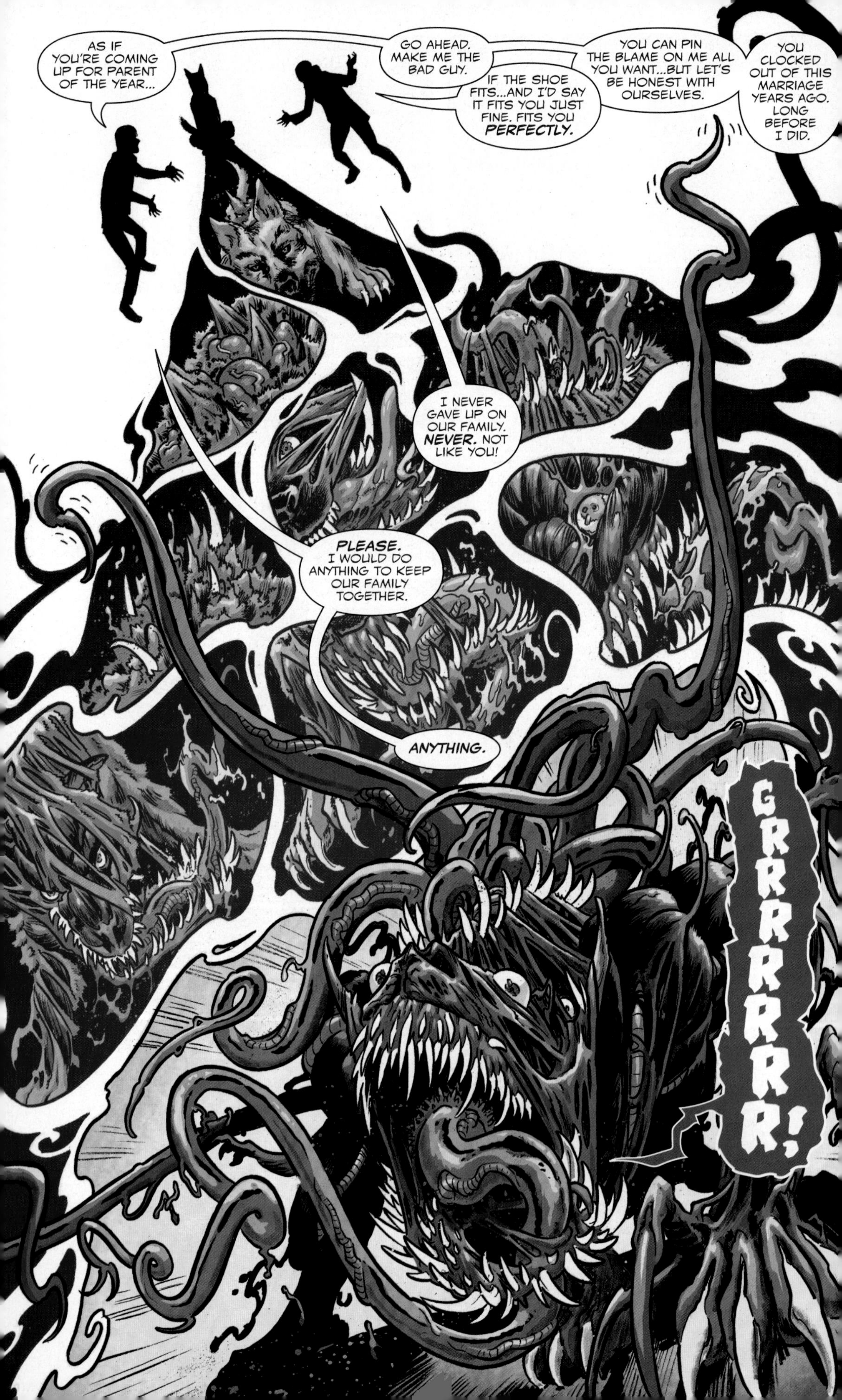
AS IF YOU'RE COMING UP FOR PARENT OF THE YEAR...
GO AHEAD. MAKE ME THE BAD GUY.
IF THE SHOE FITS...AND I'D SAY IT FITS YOU JUST FINE. FITS YOU PERFECTLY.
YOU CAN PIN THE BLAME ON ME ALL YOU WANT...BUT LET'S BE HONEST WITH OURSELVES.
YOU CLOCKED OUT OF THIS MARRIAGE YEARS AGO. LONG BEFORE I DID.
I NEVER GAVE UP ON OUR FAMILY. NEVER. NOT LIKE YOU!
PLEASE. I WOULD DO ANYTHING TO KEEP OUR FAMILY TOGETHER.
ANYTHING.
GRRRRRRR!

SEPARATION ANXIETY

For years, the **Life Foundation symbiotes**, as they came to be called,
existed separately — but when one of the organisms turned traitor and
began killing their hosts, the remaining four symbiotes had no choice
but to merge and form a new entity…called **Hybrid!**

As Hybrid, the symbiotes were most recently seen bonded
to a stray dog after an adventure involving Deadpool.

The whereabouts of the dog — and the four extraterrestrial
creatures bonded to it — remain unknown…

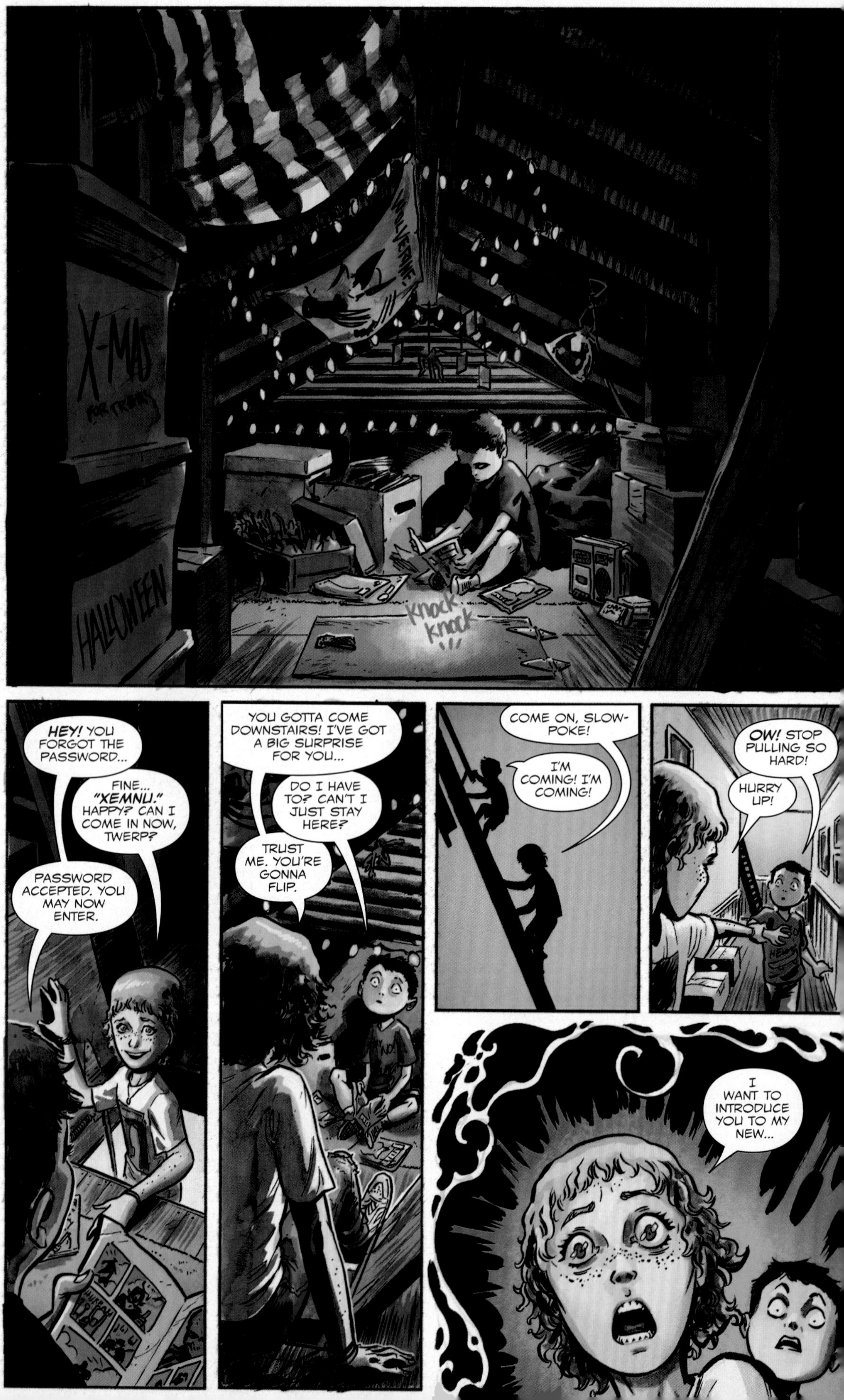
X-MAS
HALLOWEEN
KNOCK KNOCK !!!
HEY! YOU FORGOT THE PASSWORD...
FINE... "XEMNU." HAPPY? CAN I COME IN NOW, TWERP?
PASSWORD ACCEPTED. YOU MAY NOW ENTER.
YOU GOTTA COME DOWNSTAIRS! I'VE GOT A BIG SURPRISE FOR YOU...
DO I HAVE TO? CAN'T I JUST STAY HERE?
TRUST ME. YOU'RE GONNA FLIP.
COME ON, SLOW-POKE!
I'M COMING! I'M COMING!
OW! STOP PULLING SO HARD!
HURRY UP!
I WANT TO INTRODUCE YOU TO MY NEW...

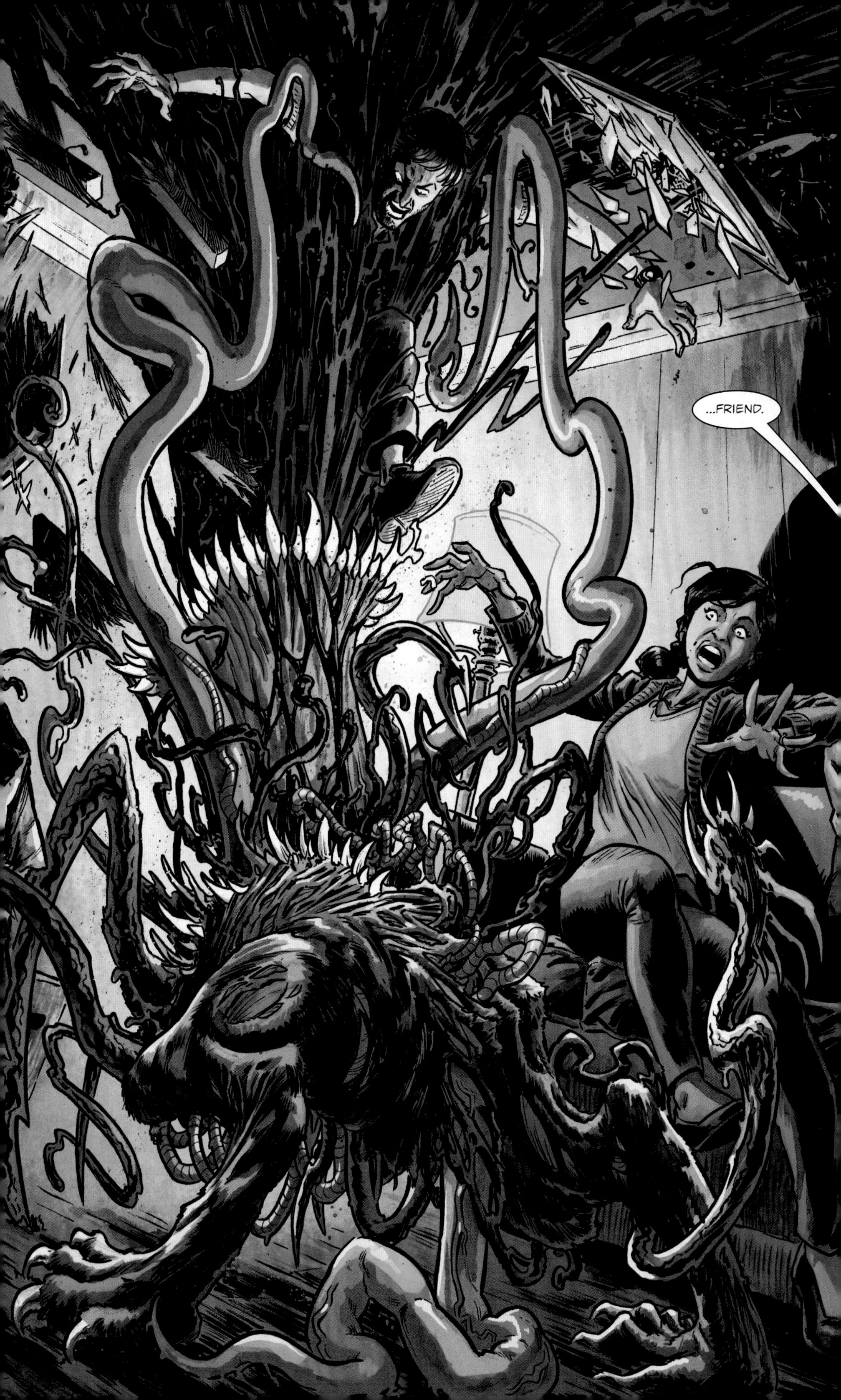
...FRIEND.

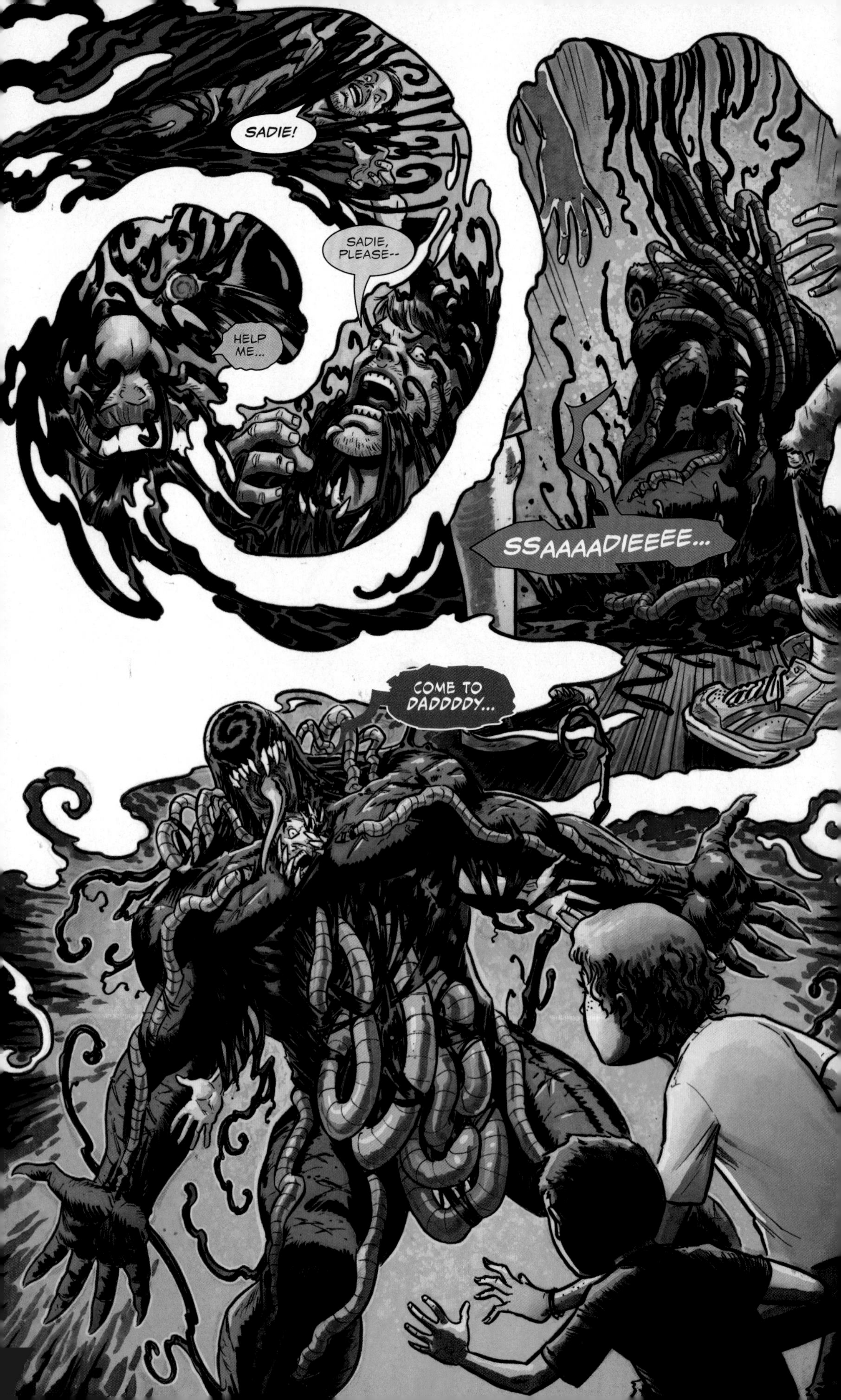
SADIE!
SADIE, PLEASE--
HELP ME...
SSAAAADIEEEE...
COME TO DADDDDY...

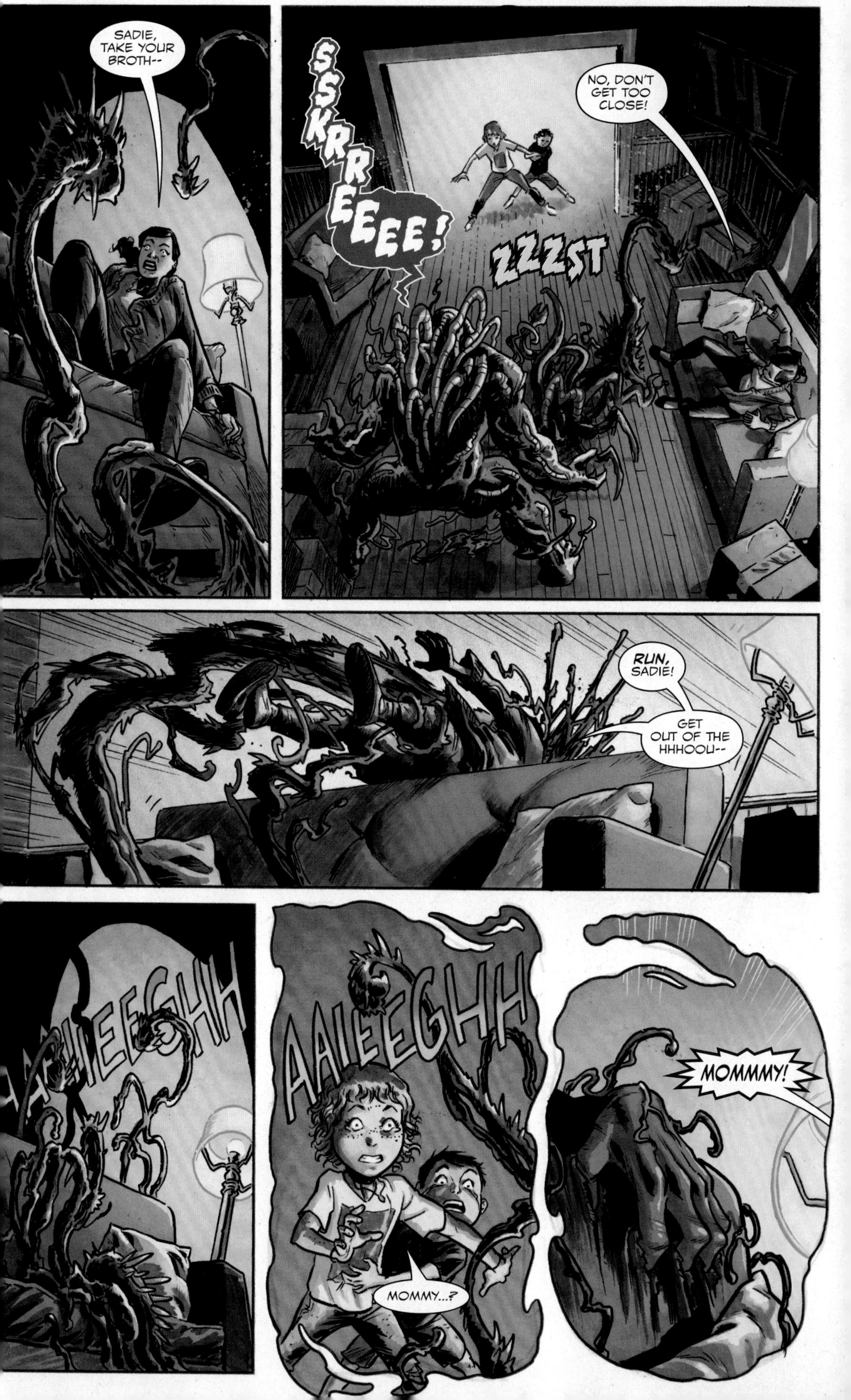
SADIE, TAKE YOUR BROTH--
SSKRREEEEE!
ZZZST
NO, DON'T GET TOO CLOSE!
RUN, SADIE!
GET OUT OF THE HHHOOU--
AAIEEGHH
AAIEEGHH
MOMMY...?
MOMMMY!

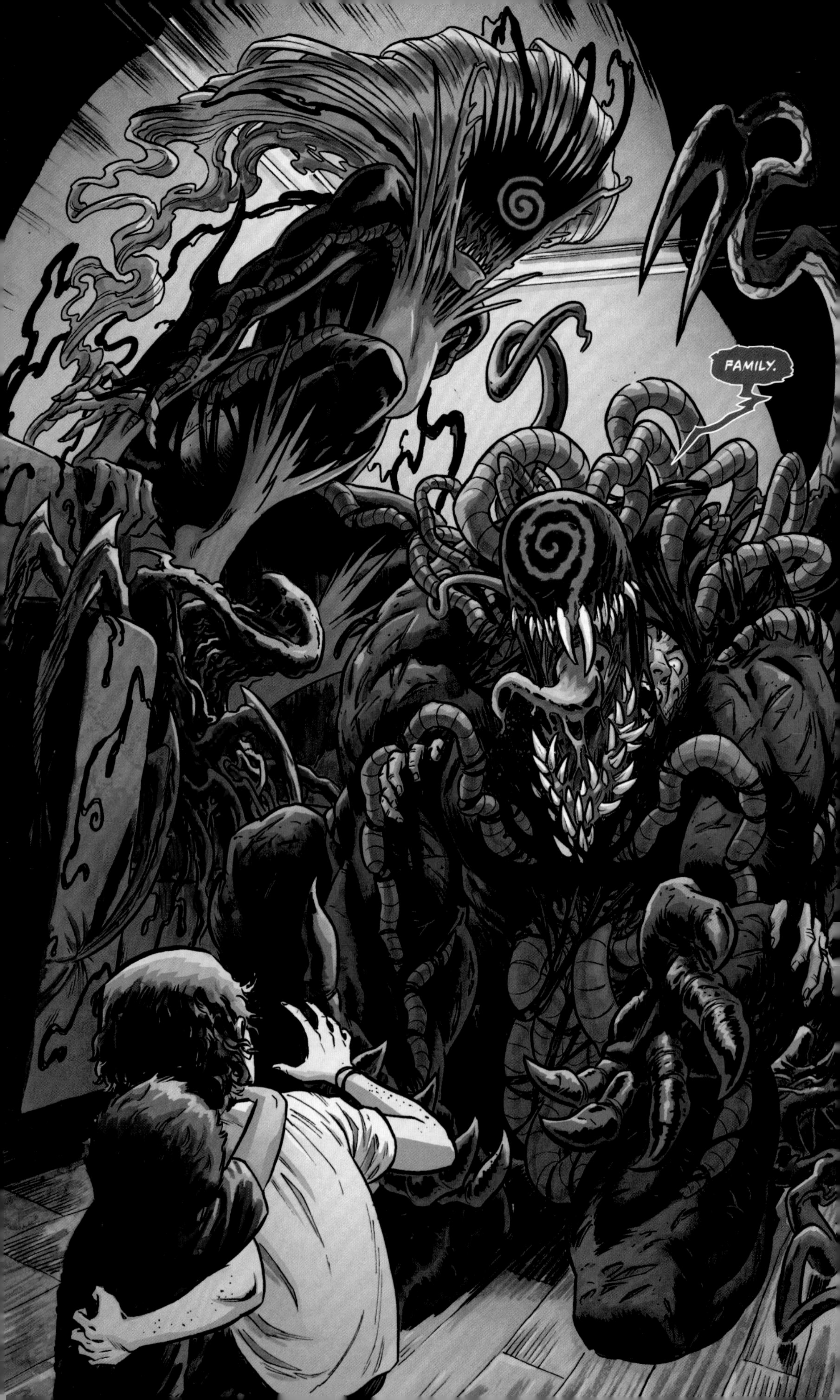
FAMILY.

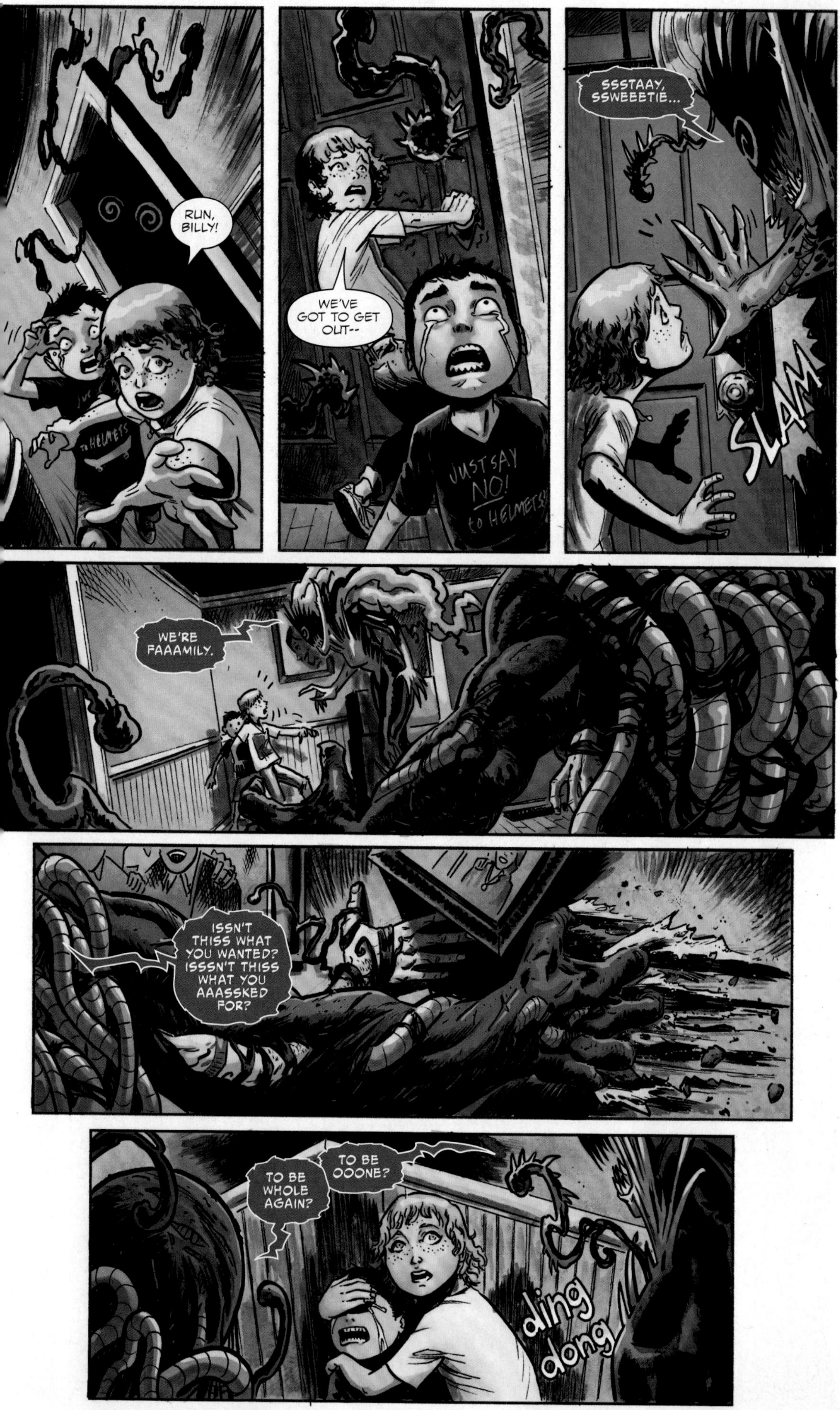
RUN, BILLY!
WE'VE GOT TO GET OUT--
JUST SAY NO! to HELMETS!
SSSTAAY, SSWEEETIE...
SLAM
WE'RE FAAAMILY.
ISSN'T THISS WHAT YOU WANTED? ISSSN'T THISS WHAT YOU AAASSKED FOR?
TO BE OOONE?
TO BE WHOLE AGAIN?
ding dong

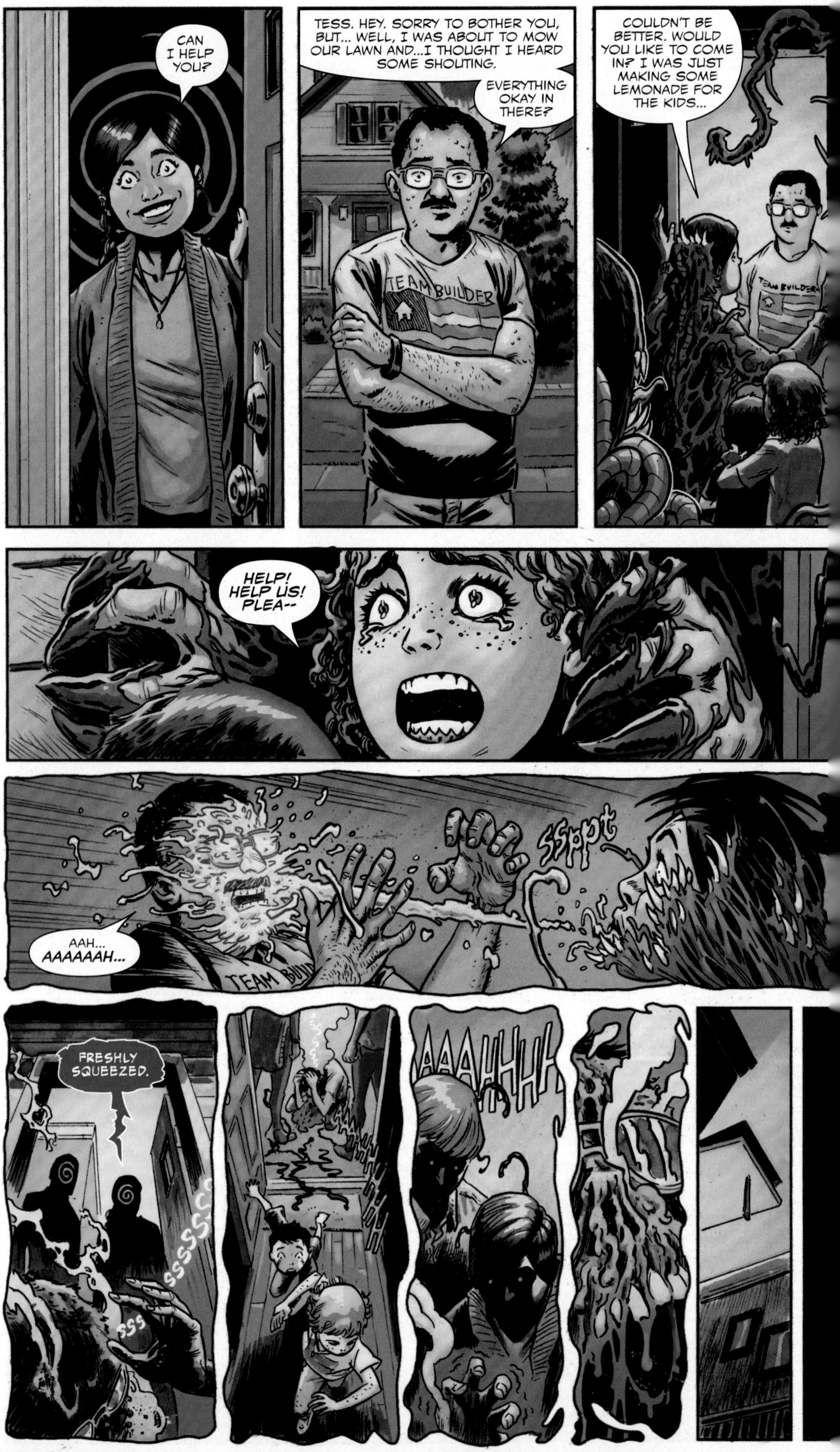
CAN I HELP YOU?
TESS. HEY. SORRY TO BOTHER YOU, BUT... WELL, I WAS ABOUT TO MOW OUR LAWN AND...I THOUGHT I HEARD SOME SHOUTING.
EVERYTHING OKAY IN THERE?
TEAM BUILDER
COULDN'T BE BETTER. WOULD YOU LIKE TO COME IN? I WAS JUST MAKING SOME LEMONADE FOR THE KIDS...
HELP! HELP US! PLEA--
SSPPT
AAH... AAAAAAH...
TEAM BUI
FRESHLY SQUEEZED.
SSSSSS
SSS
AAAAHHHH

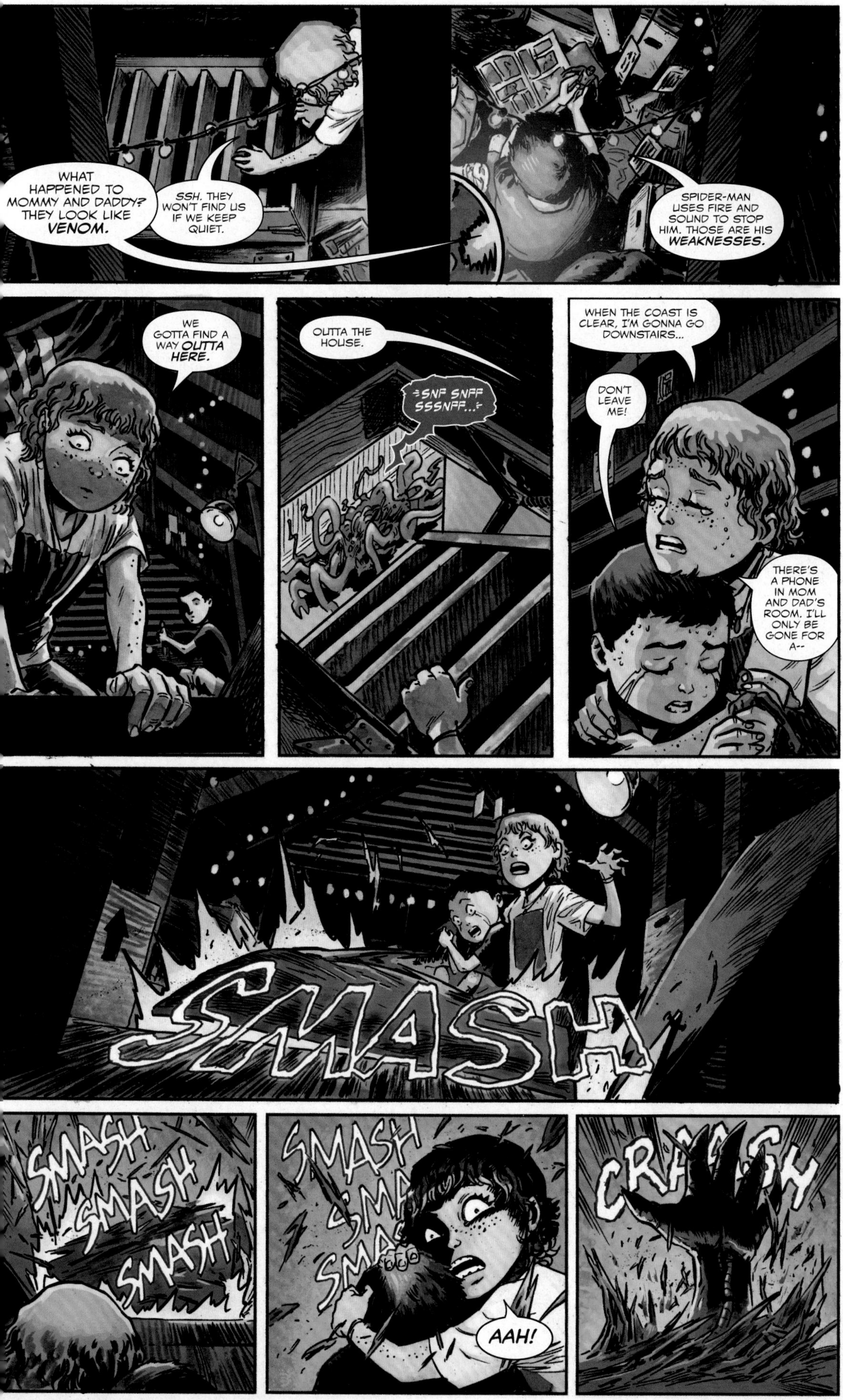
WHAT HAPPENED TO MOMMY AND DADDY? THEY LOOK LIKE VENOM.
SSH. THEY WON'T FIND US IF WE KEEP QUIET.
SPIDER-MAN USES FIRE AND SOUND TO STOP HIM. THOSE ARE HIS WEAKNESSES.
WE GOTTA FIND A WAY OUTTA HERE.
OUTTA THE HOUSE.
SNF SNFF SSSNFF...
WHEN THE COAST IS CLEAR, I'M GONNA GO DOWNSTAIRS...
DON'T LEAVE ME!
THERE'S A PHONE IN MOM AND DAD'S ROOM. I'LL ONLY BE GONE FOR A--
SMASH
SMASH SMASH SMASH
SMASH
AAH!

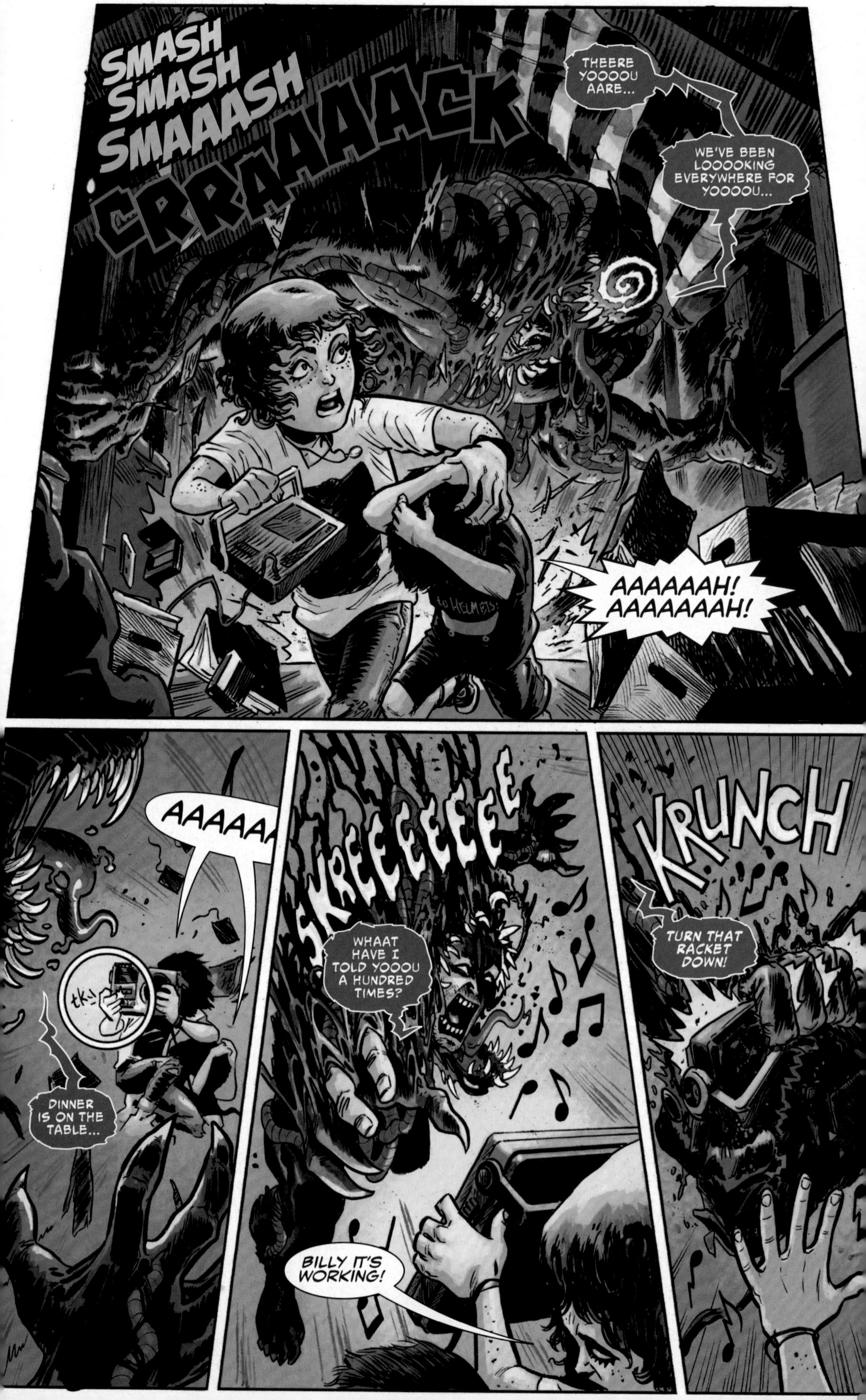
SMASH
SMASH
SMAAASH
CRRAAAACK
THEERE YOOOOU AARE...
WE'VE BEEN LOOOOKING EVERYWHERE FOR YOOOOU...
AAAAAAH! AAAAAAAAH!
AAAAAA
DINNER IS ON THE TABLE...
SKREEEEEEE
WHAAT HAVE I TOLD YOOOU A HUNDRED TIMES?
BILLY IT'S WORKING!
KRUNCH
TURN THAT RACKET DOWN!

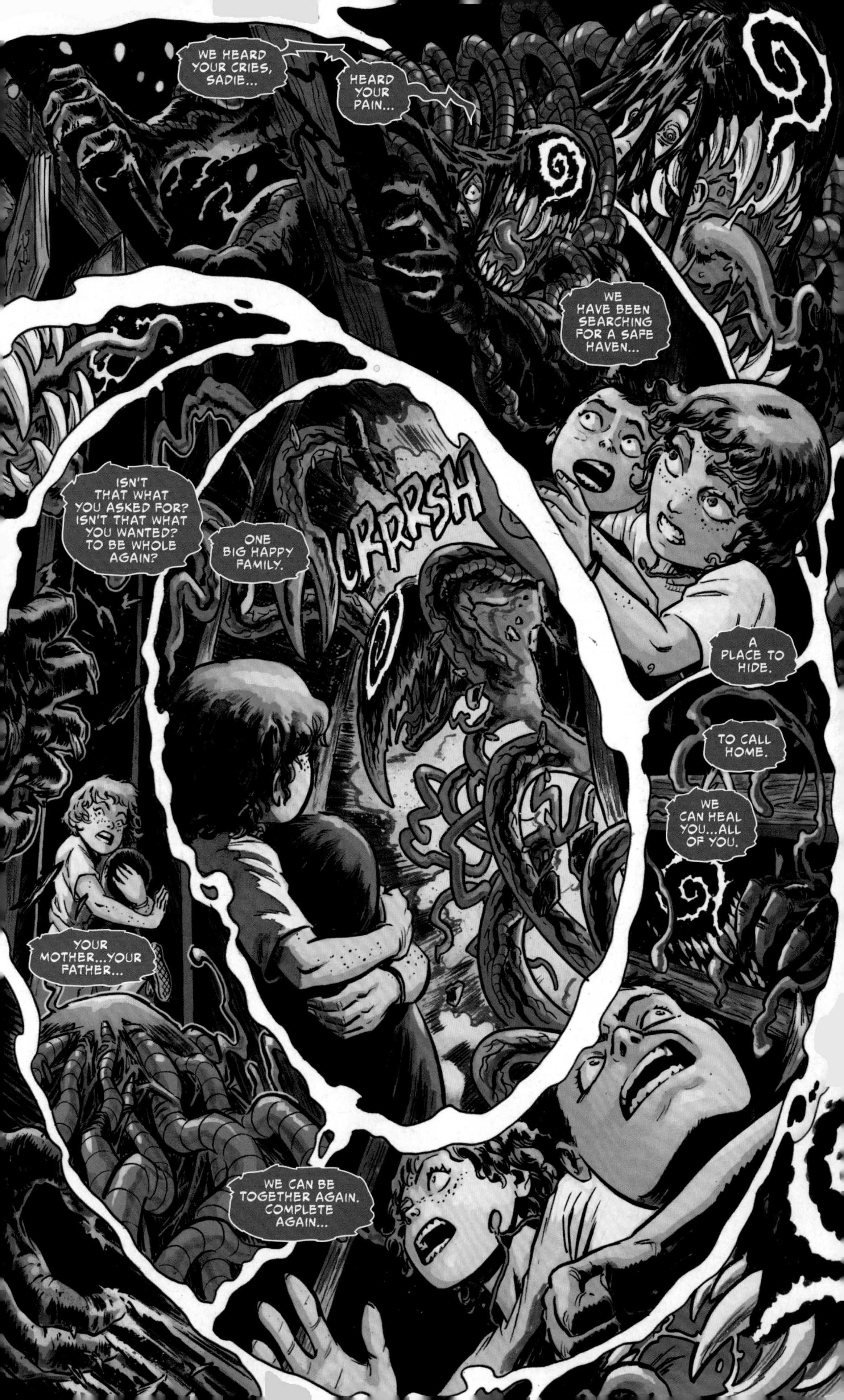
WE HEARD YOUR CRIES, SADIE...
HEARD YOUR PAIN...
WE HAVE BEEN SEARCHING FOR A SAFE HAVEN...
ISN'T THAT WHAT YOU ASKED FOR? ISN'T THAT WHAT YOU WANTED? TO BE WHOLE AGAIN?
ONE BIG HAPPY FAMILY.
CRRRSH
A PLACE TO HIDE.
TO CALL HOME.
WE CAN HEAL YOU...ALL OF YOU.
YOUR MOTHER...YOUR FATHER...
WE CAN BE TOGETHER AGAIN. COMPLETE AGAIN...

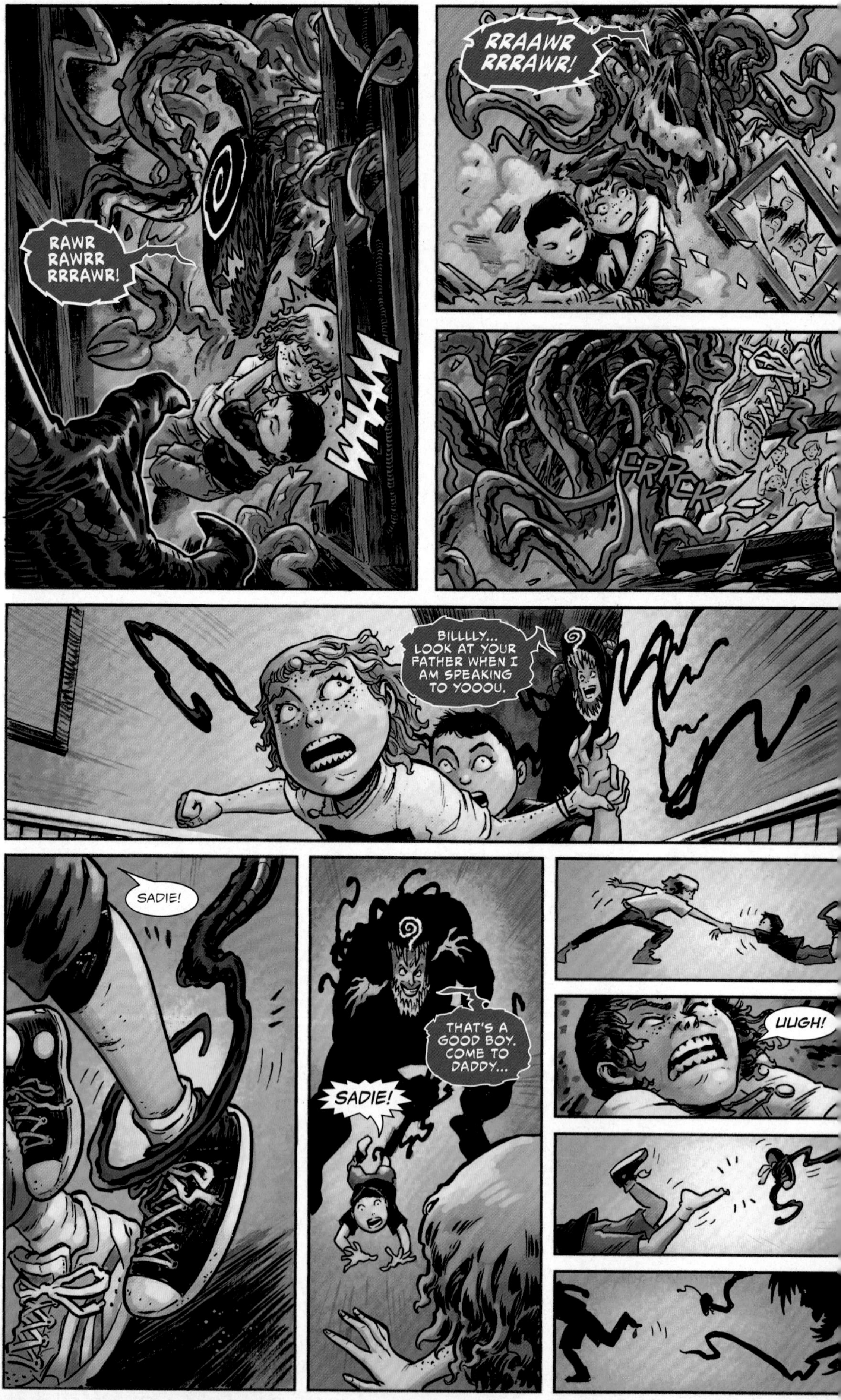

RAWR RAWRR RRRAWR!
WHAM
RRAAWR RRRAWR!
CRRCK
BILLLLY... LOOK AT YOUR FATHER WHEN I AM SPEAKING TO YOOOU.
SADIE!
THAT'S A GOOD BOY. COME TO DADDY...
SADIE!
UUGH!

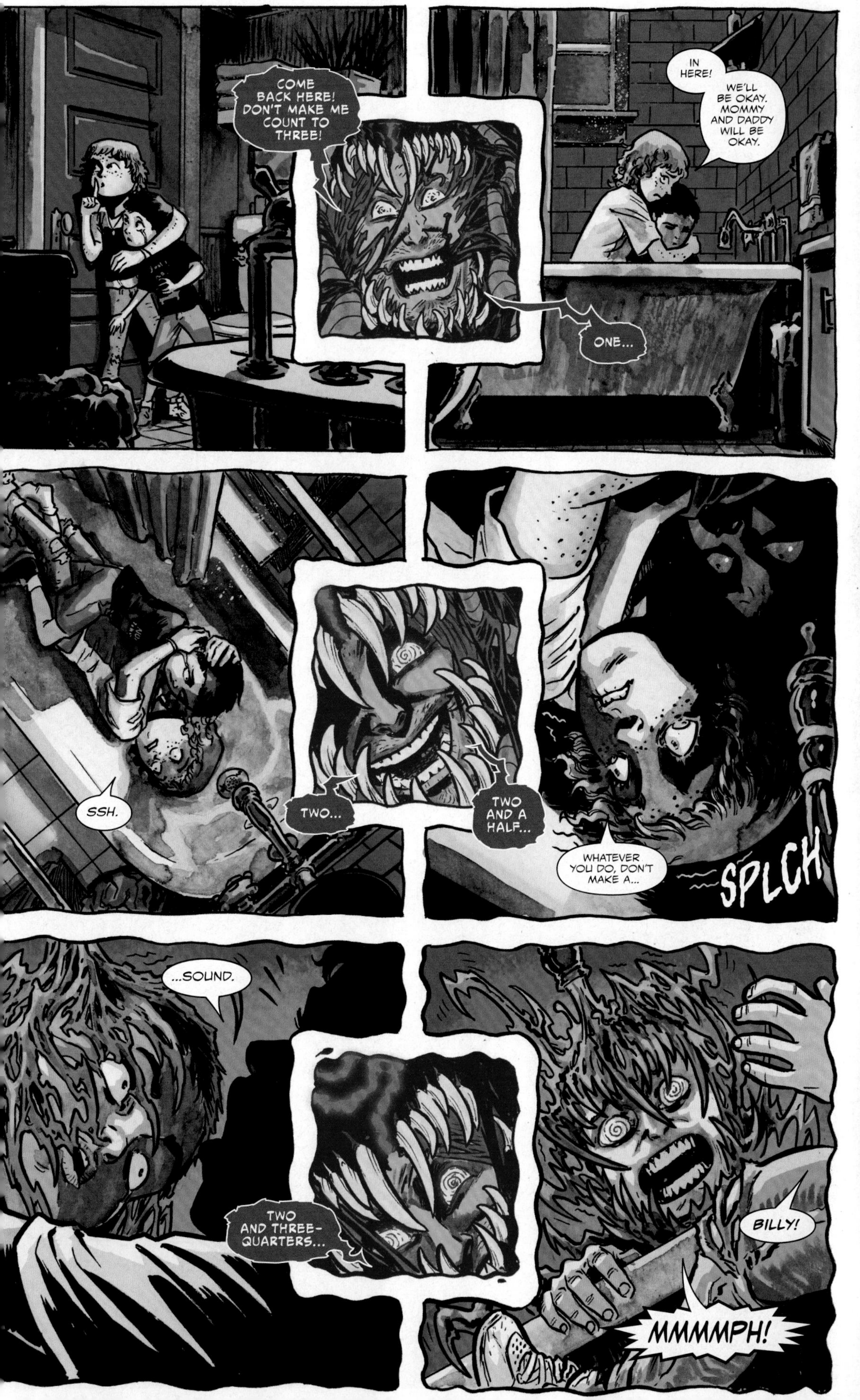
COME BACK HERE! DON'T MAKE ME COUNT TO THREE!
IN HERE!
WE'LL BE OKAY. MOMMY AND DADDY WILL BE OKAY.
ONE...
SSH.
TWO...
TWO AND A HALF...
WHATEVER YOU DO, DON'T MAKE A...
SPLCH
...SOUND.
TWO AND THREE-QUARTERS...
BILLY!
MMMMPH!

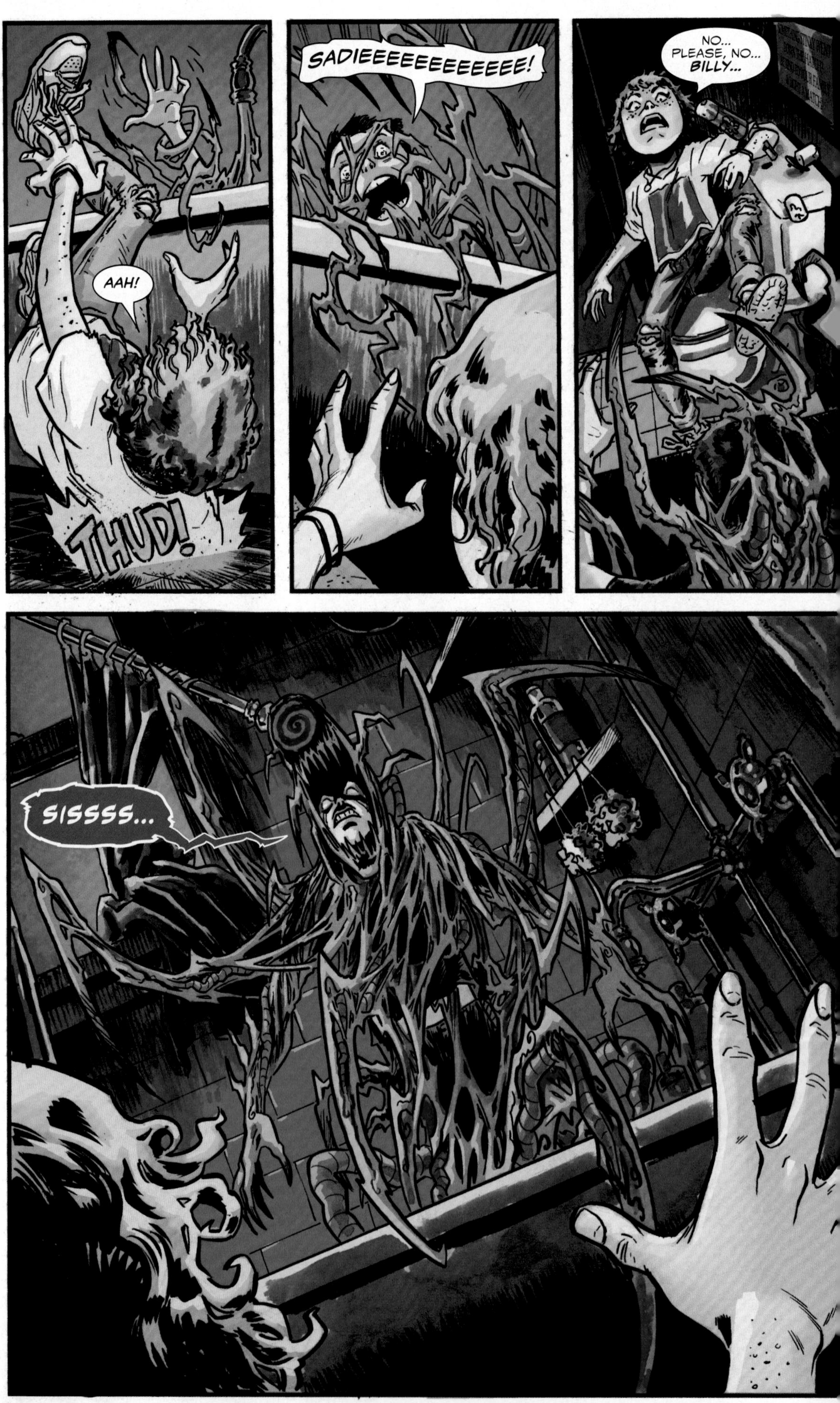
AAH!
THUD!
SADIEEEEEEEEEEEEE!
NO... PLEASE, NO... BILLY...
SISSSS...

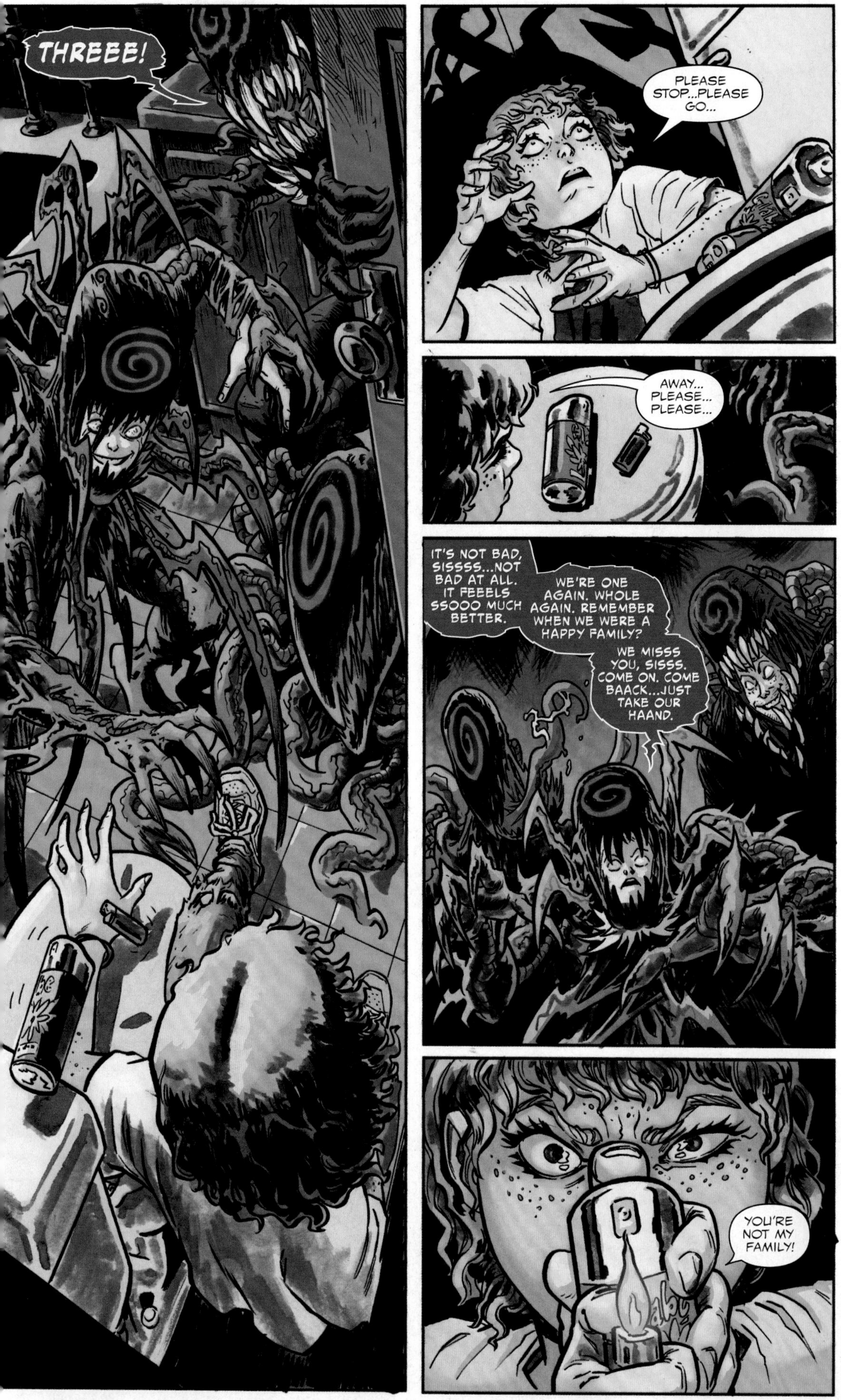
THREEE!
PLEASE STOP...PLEASE GO...
AWAY... PLEASE... PLEASE...
IT'S NOT BAD, SISSSS...NOT BAD AT ALL. IT FEEELS SSOOO MUCH BETTER.
WE'RE ONE AGAIN. WHOLE AGAIN. REMEMBER WHEN WE WERE A HAPPY FAMILY?
WE MISSS YOU, SISSS. COME ON. COME BAACK...JUST TAKE OUR HAAND.
YOU'RE NOT MY FAMILY!

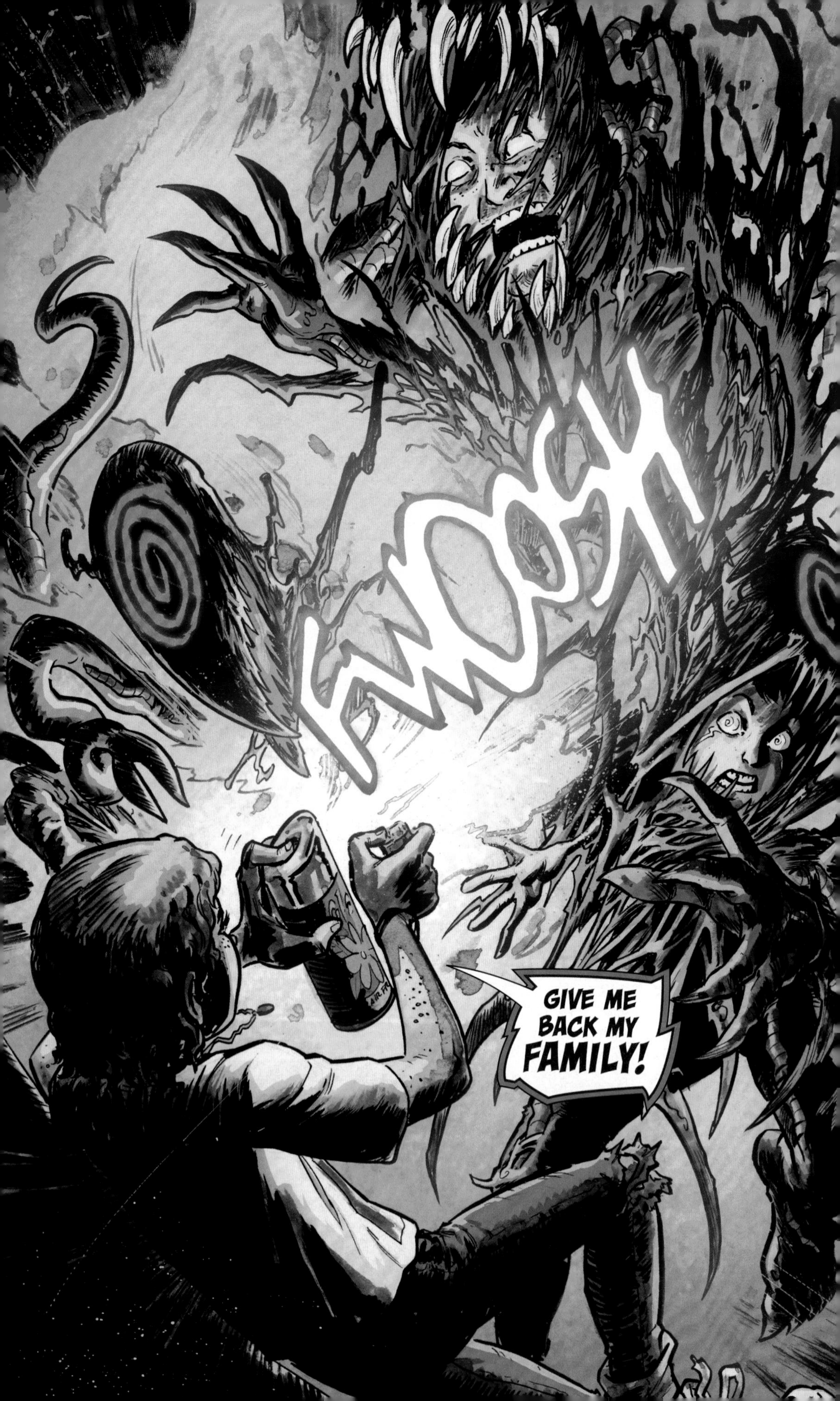
FWOOSH
GIVE ME BACK MY FAMILY!

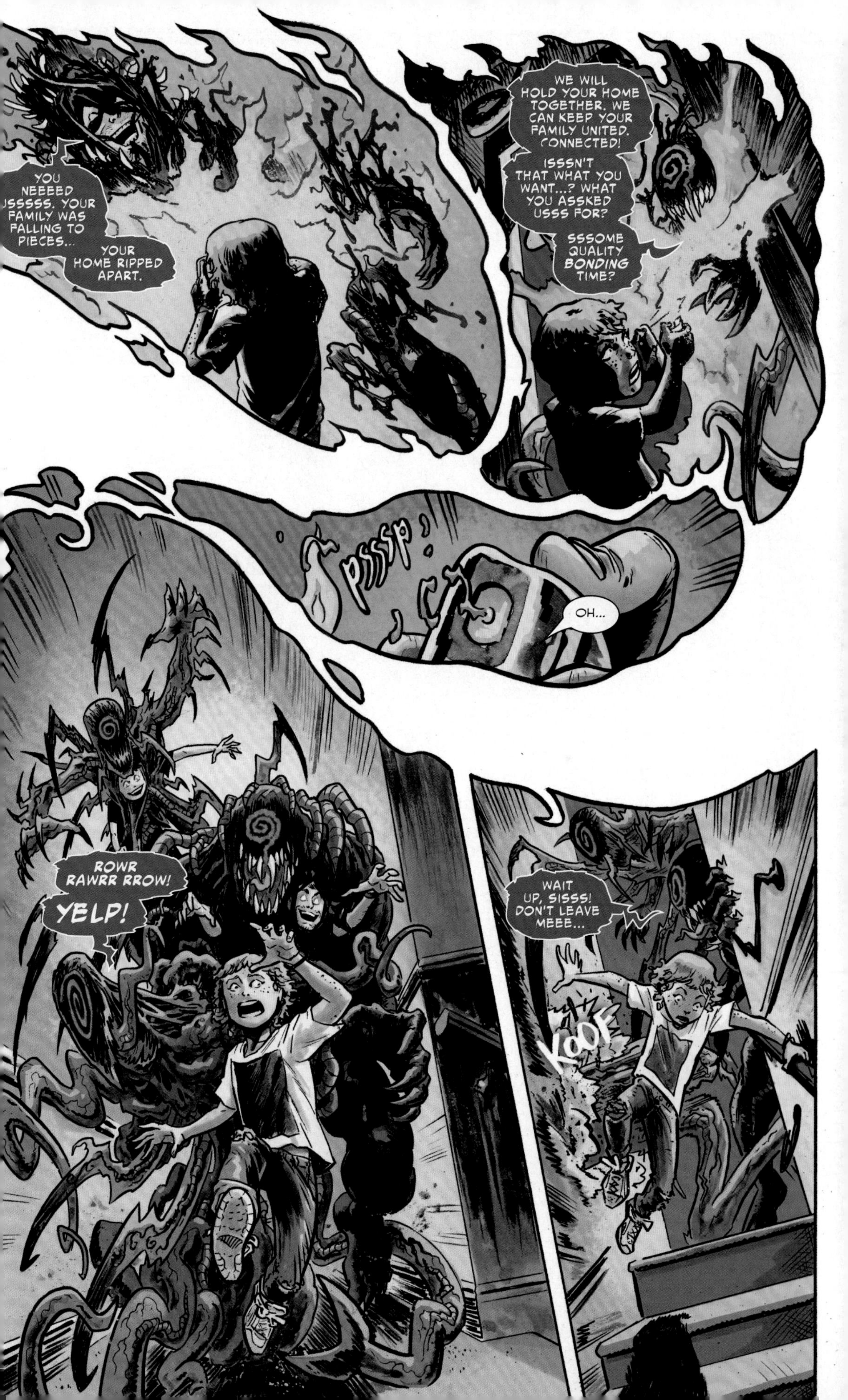
YOU NEEEED USSSSS. YOUR FAMILY WAS FALLING TO PIECES...
YOUR HOME RIPPED APART.
WE WILL HOLD YOUR HOME TOGETHER. WE CAN KEEP YOUR FAMILY UNITED. CONNECTED!
ISSSN'T THAT WHAT YOU WANT...? WHAT YOU ASSKED USSS FOR?
SSSOME QUALITY BONDING TIME?
PSSSP!
OH...
ROWR RAWRR RROW!
YELP!
WAIT UP, SISSS! DON'T LEAVE MEEE...
KOOF

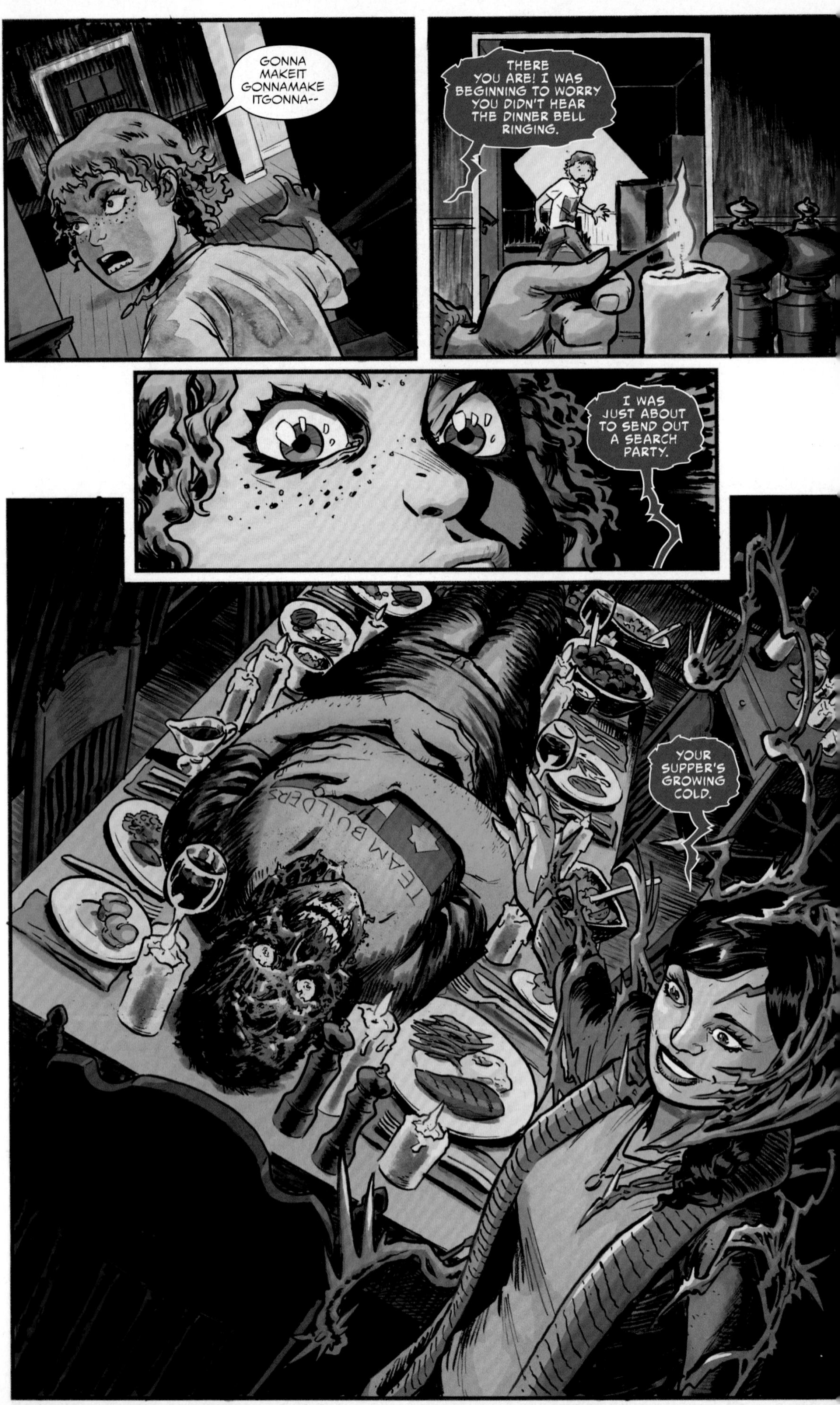
GONNA MAKEIT GONNAMAKE ITGONNA--
THERE YOU ARE! I WAS BEGINNING TO WORRY YOU DIDN'T HEAR THE DINNER BELL RINGING.
I WAS JUST ABOUT TO SEND OUT A SEARCH PARTY.
TEAM BUILDERS
YOUR SUPPER'S GROWING COLD.

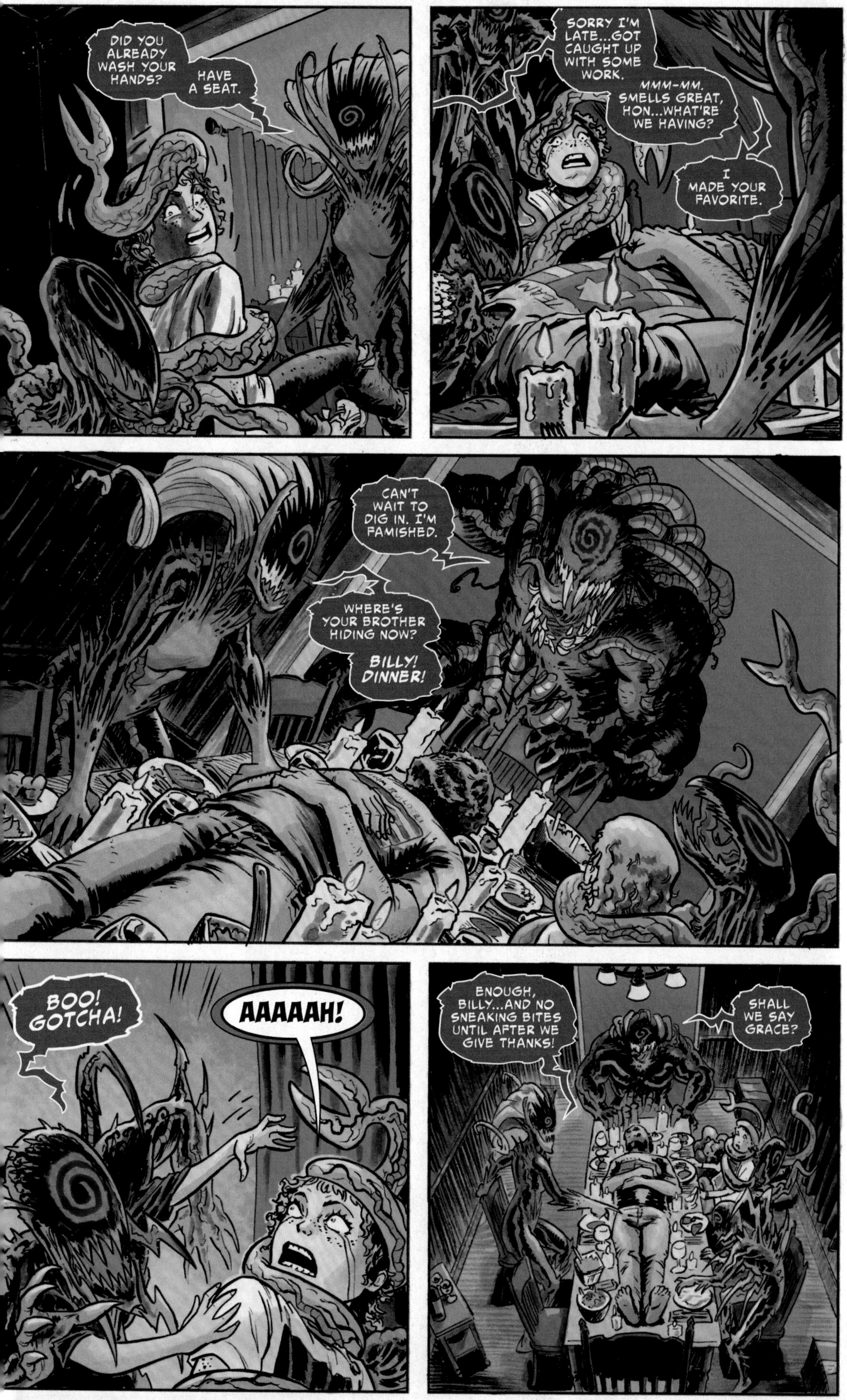
DID YOU ALREADY WASH YOUR HANDS?
HAVE A SEAT.
SORRY I'M LATE...GOT CAUGHT UP WITH SOME WORK.
MMM-MM. SMELLS GREAT, HON...WHAT'RE WE HAVING?
I MADE YOUR FAVORITE.
CAN'T WAIT TO DIG IN. I'M FAMISHED.
WHERE'S YOUR BROTHER HIDING NOW?
BILLY! DINNER!
BOO! GOTCHA!
AAAAAH!
ENOUGH, BILLY...AND NO SNEAKING BITES UNTIL AFTER WE GIVE THANKS!
SHALL WE SAY GRACE?

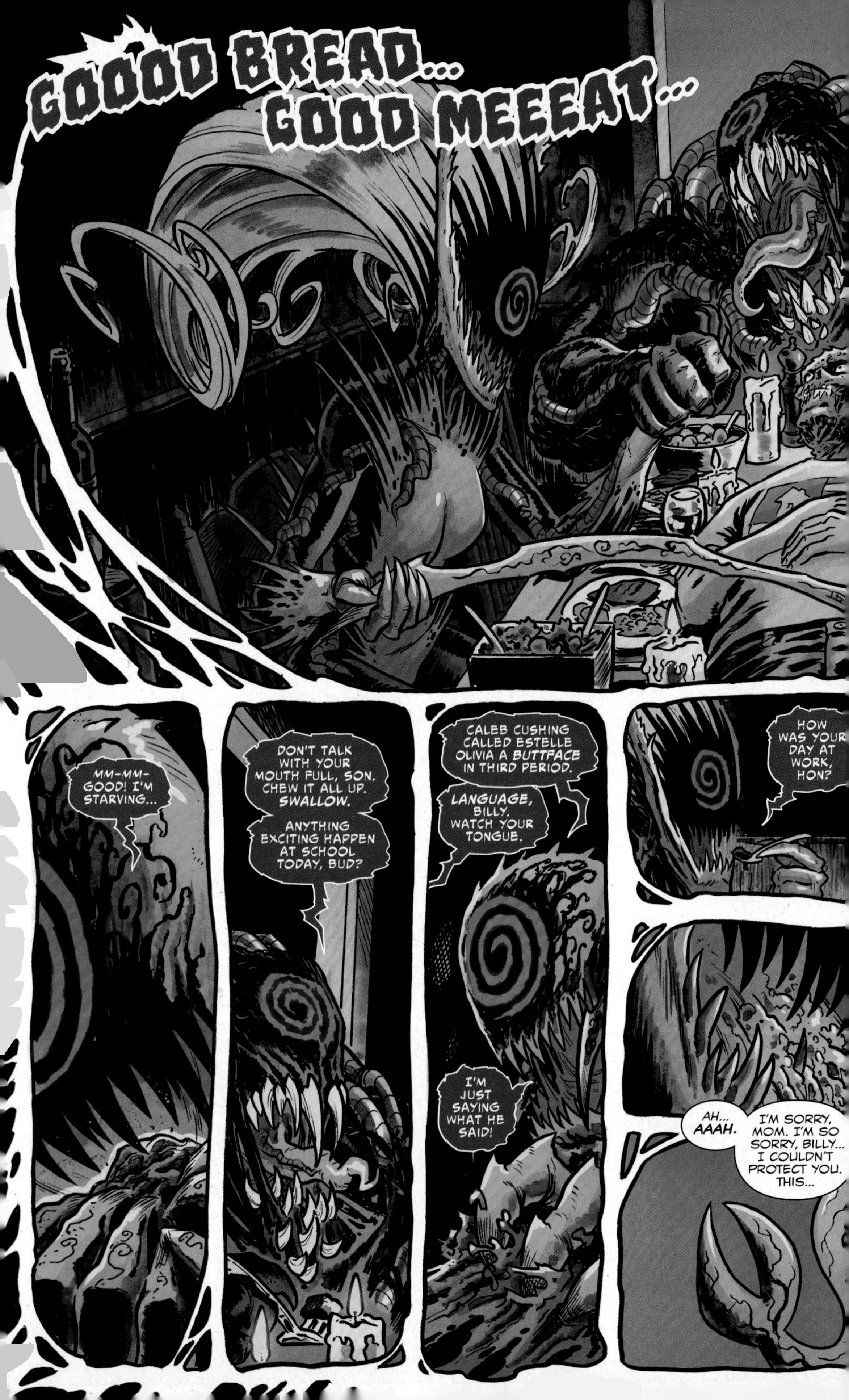
GOOOD BREAD... GOOD MEEEAT...
MM-MM-GOOD! I'M STARVING...
DON'T TALK WITH YOUR MOUTH FULL, SON. CHEW IT ALL UP. SWALLOW.
ANYTHING EXCITING HAPPEN AT SCHOOL TODAY, BUD?
CALEB CUSHING CALLED ESTELLE OLIVIA A BUTTFACE IN THIRD PERIOD.
LANGUAGE, BILLY. WATCH YOUR TONGUE.
I'M JUST SAYING WHAT HE SAID!
HOW WAS YOUR DAY AT WORK, HON?
AH... AAAH.
I'M SORRY, MOM. I'M SO SORRY, BILLY... I COULDN'T PROTECT YOU. THIS...

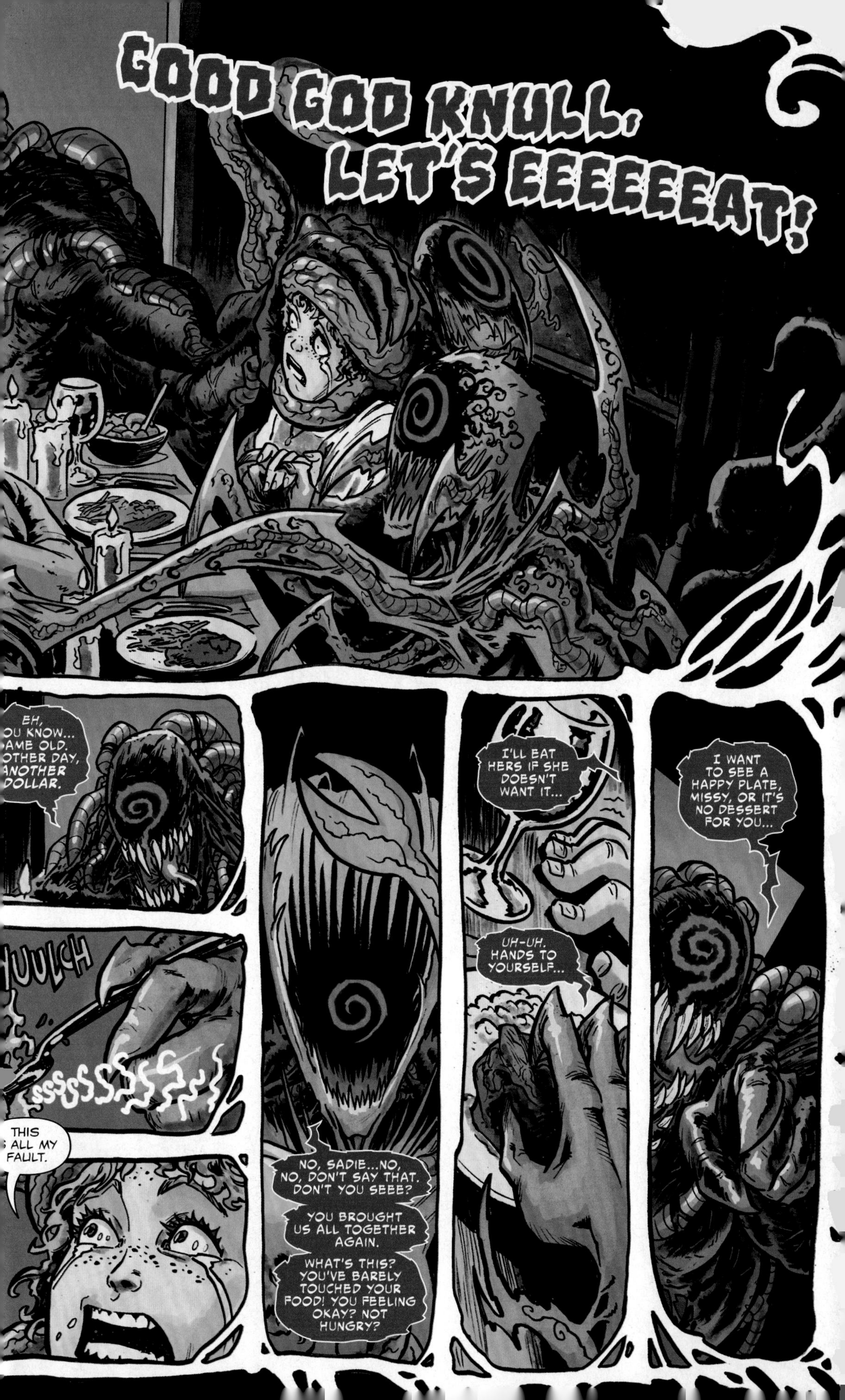
GOOD GOD KNULL. LET'S EEEEEEAT!
EH, YOU KNOW... SAME OLD. OTHER DAY, ANOTHER DOLLAR.
HUULCH
SSSSSSSSS
THIS ALL MY FAULT.
NO, SADIE...NO, NO, DON'T SAY THAT. DON'T YOU SEEE?
YOU BROUGHT US ALL TOGETHER AGAIN.
WHAT'S THIS? YOU'VE BARELY TOUCHED YOUR FOOD! YOU FEELING OKAY? NOT HUNGRY?
I'LL EAT HERS IF SHE DOESN'T WANT IT...
UH-UH. HANDS TO YOURSELF...
I WANT TO SEE A HAPPY PLATE, MISSY, OR IT'S NO DESSERT FOR YOU...

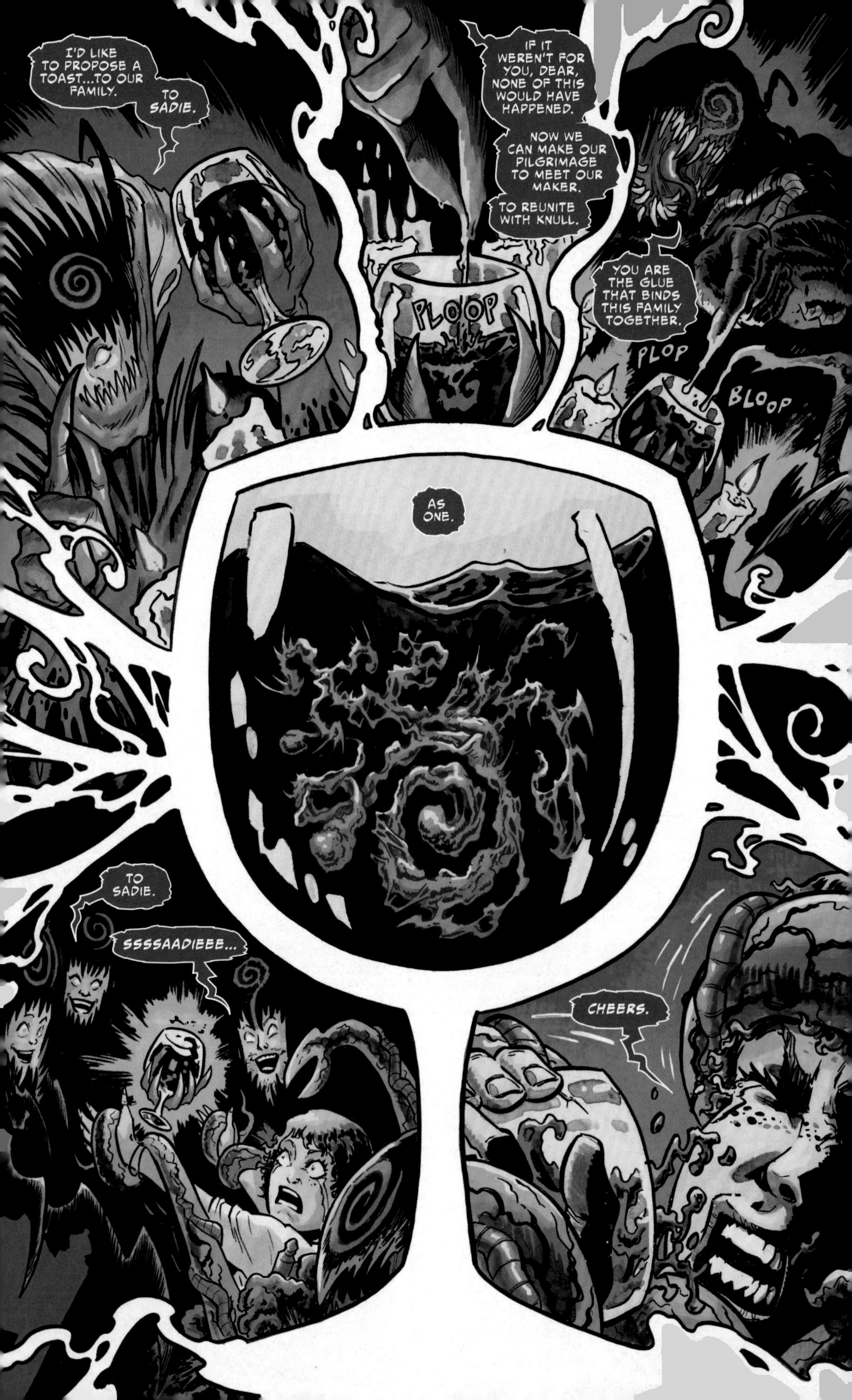

I'D LIKE TO PROPOSE A TOAST...TO OUR FAMILY.
TO SADIE.
IF IT WEREN'T FOR YOU, DEAR, NONE OF THIS WOULD HAVE HAPPENED.
NOW WE CAN MAKE OUR PILGRIMAGE TO MEET OUR MAKER.
TO REUNITE WITH KNULL.
PLOOP
YOU ARE THE GLUE THAT BINDS THIS FAMILY TOGETHER.
PLOP
BLOOP
AS ONE.
TO SADIE.
SSSSAADIEEE...
CHEERS.

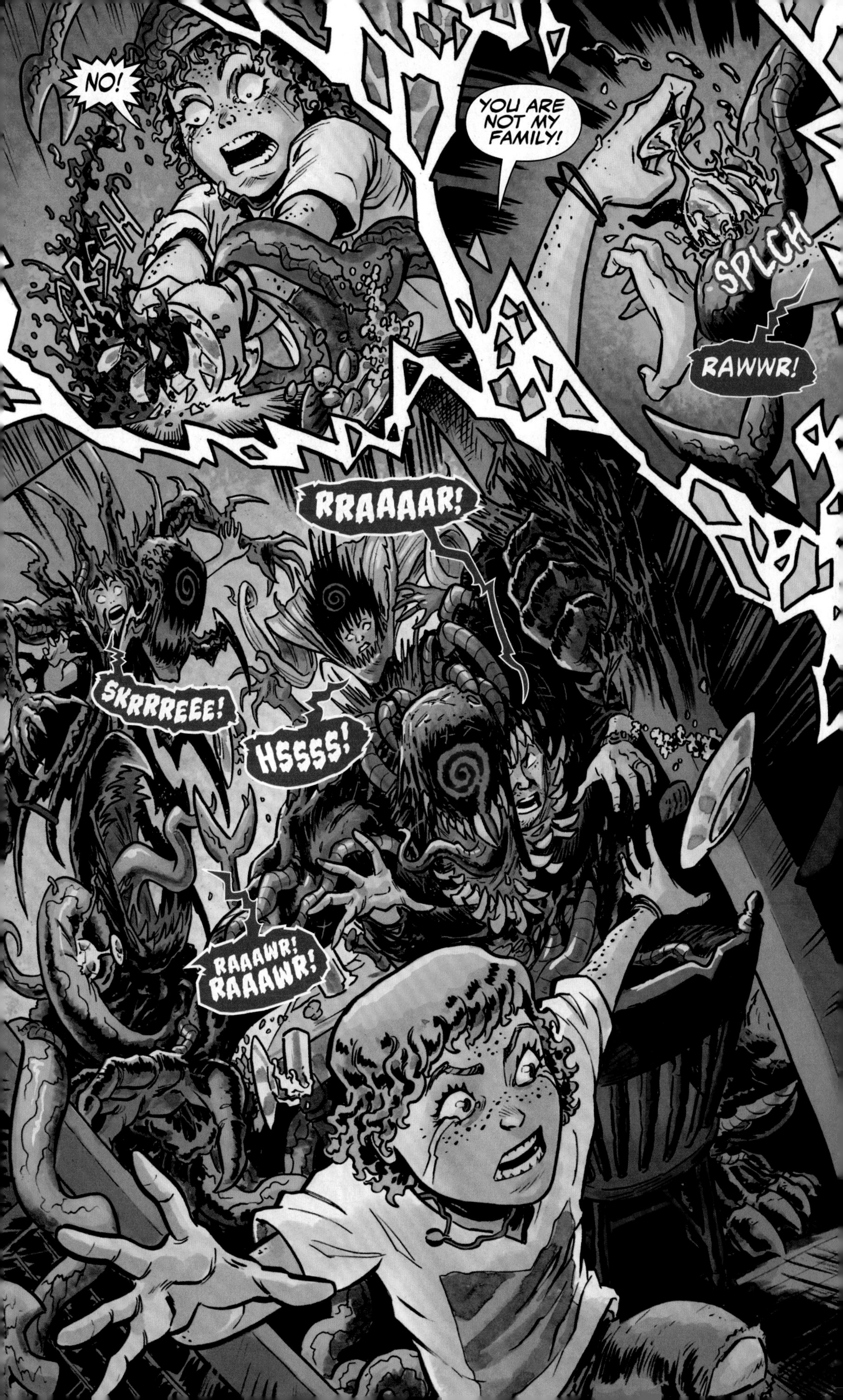
NO!
KRSSH
YOU ARE NOT MY FAMILY!
SPLCH
RAWWR!
RRAAAAR!
SKRRREEE!
HSSSS!
RAAAWR! RAAAWR!

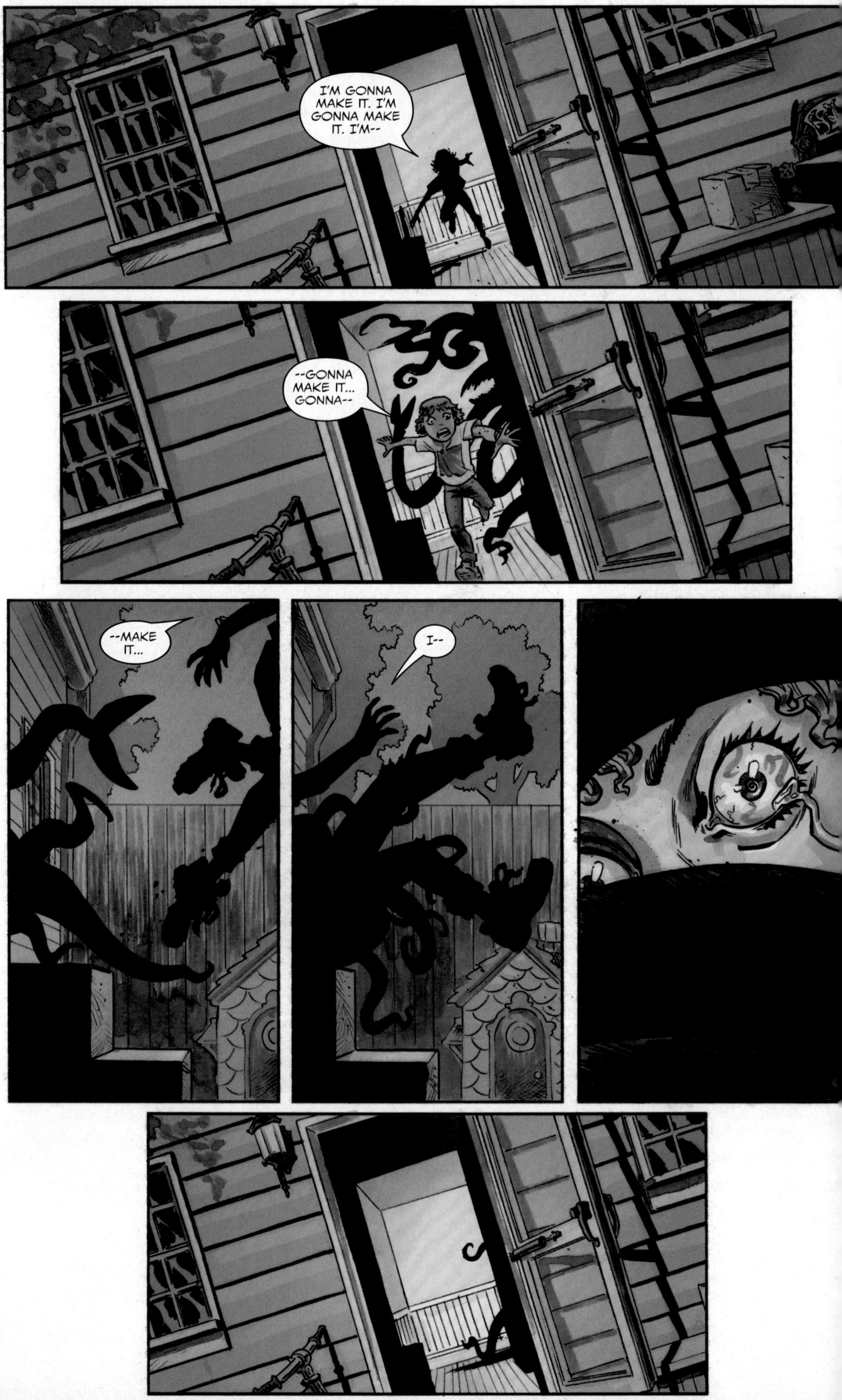
I'M GONNA MAKE IT. I'M GONNA MAKE IT. I'M--
--GONNA MAKE IT... GONNA--
--MAKE IT...
I--

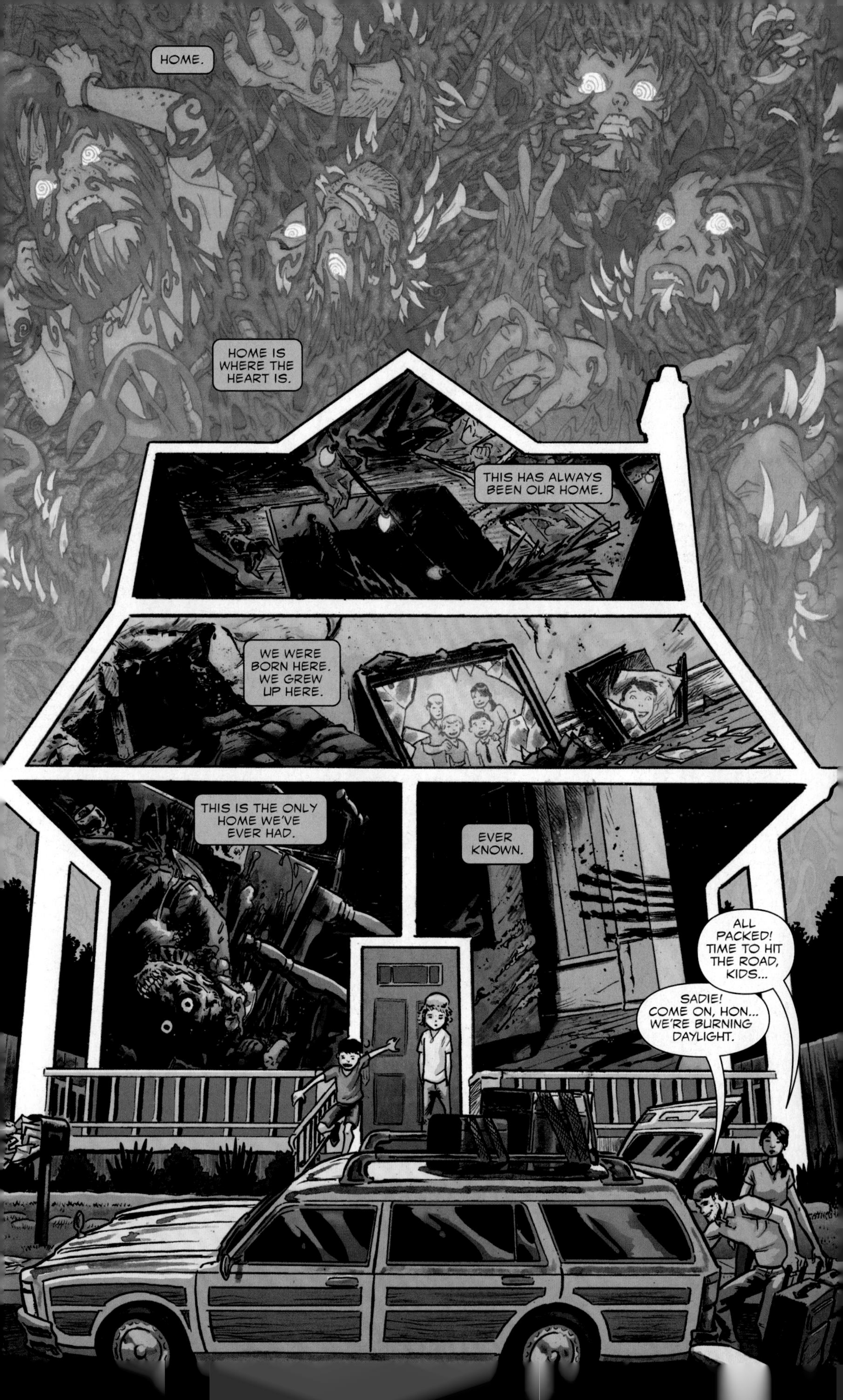
HOME.
HOME IS WHERE THE HEART IS.
THIS HAS ALWAYS BEEN OUR HOME.
WE WERE BORN HERE. WE GREW UP HERE.
THIS IS THE ONLY HOME WE'VE EVER HAD.
EVER KNOWN.
ALL PACKED! TIME TO HIT THE ROAD, KIDS...
SADIE! COME ON, HON... WE'RE BURNING DAYLIGHT.

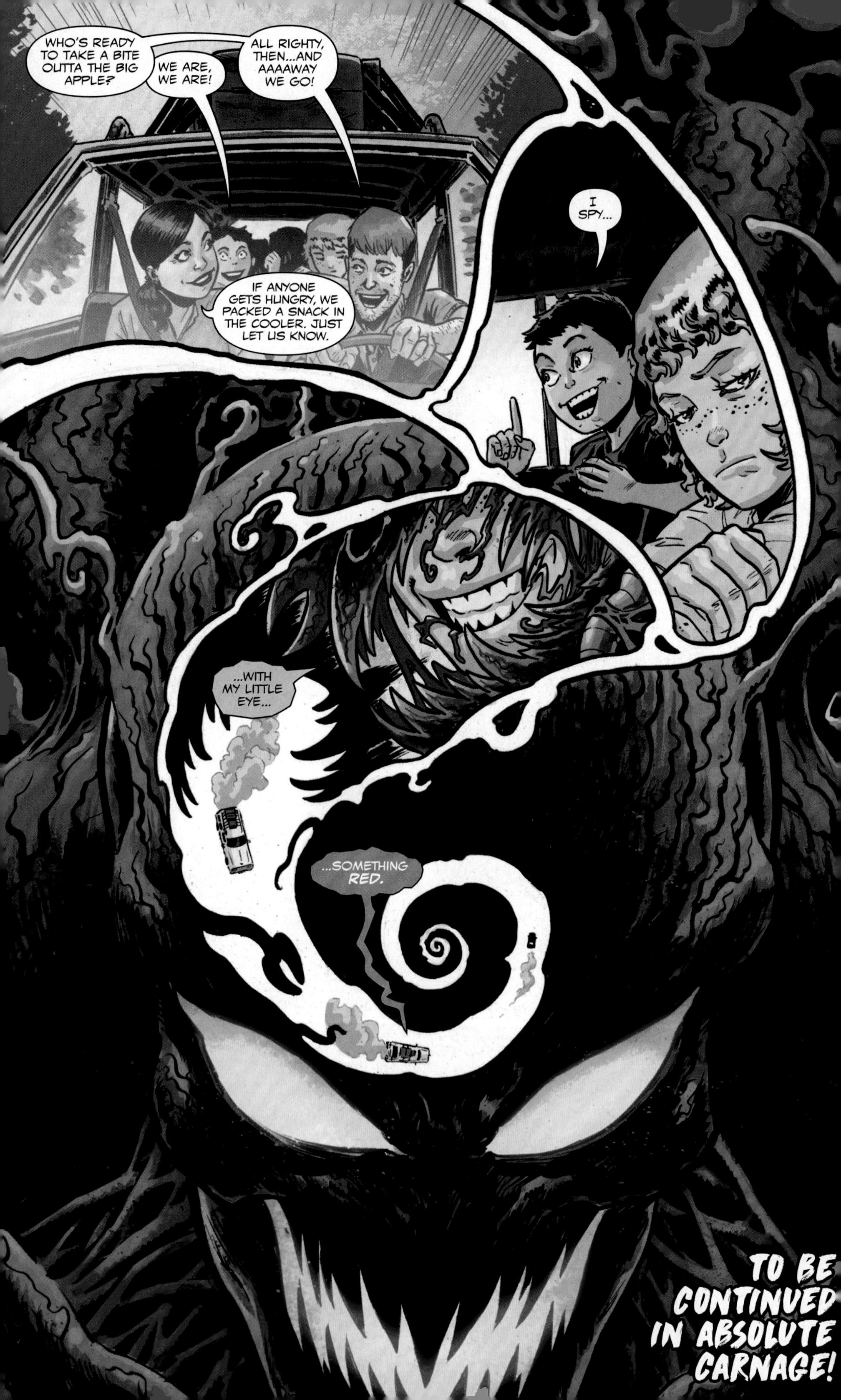
WHO'S READY TO TAKE A BITE OUTTA THE BIG APPLE?
WE ARE, WE ARE!
ALL RIGHTY, THEN...AND AAAAWAY WE GO!
IF ANYONE GETS HUNGRY, WE PACKED A SNACK IN THE COOLER. JUST LET US KNOW.
I SPY...
...WITH MY LITTLE EYE...
...SOMETHING RED.
TO BE CONTINUED IN ABSOLUTE CARNAGE!

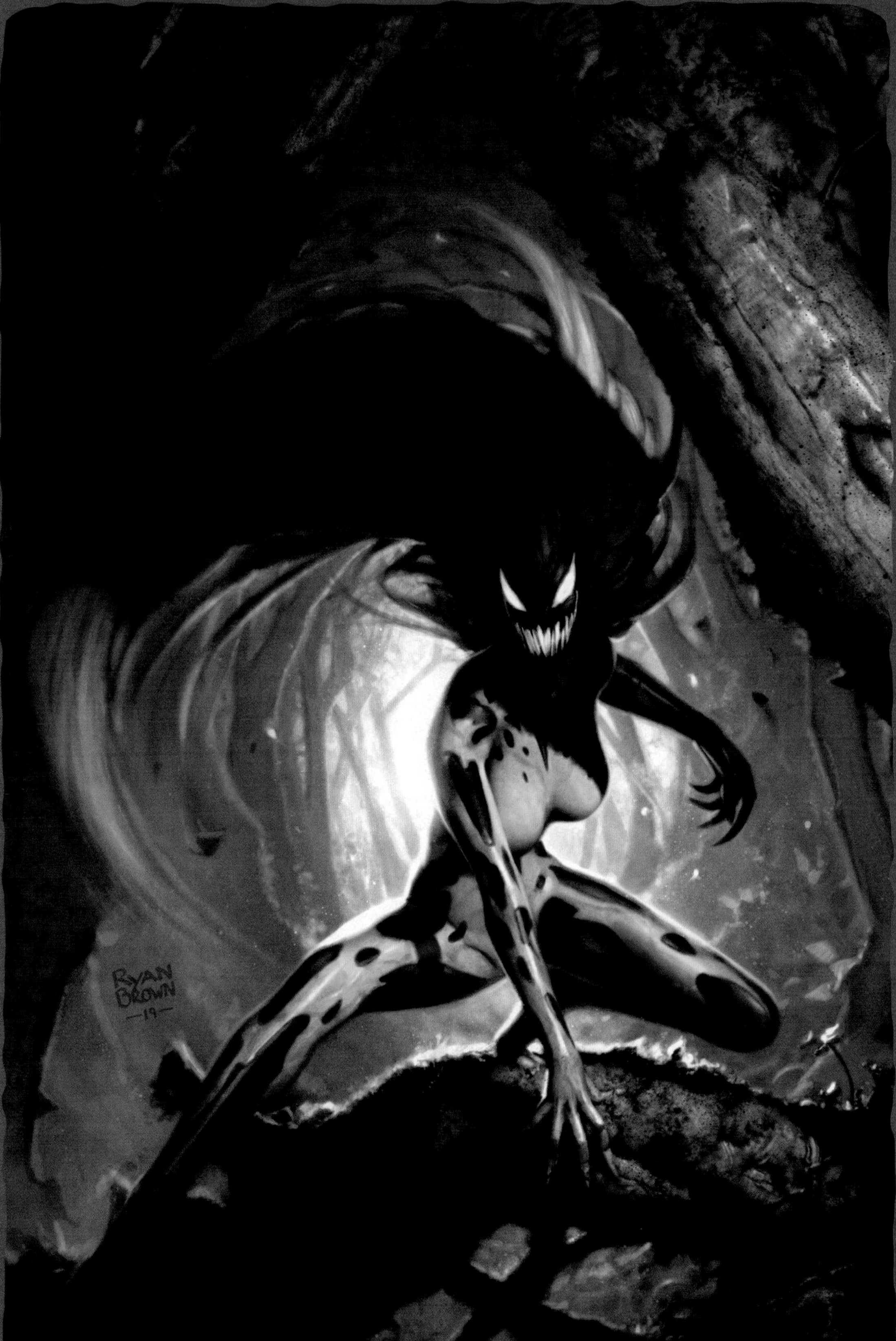
RYAN BROWN
-19-

RYAN BROWN

SCREAM #1 Variant

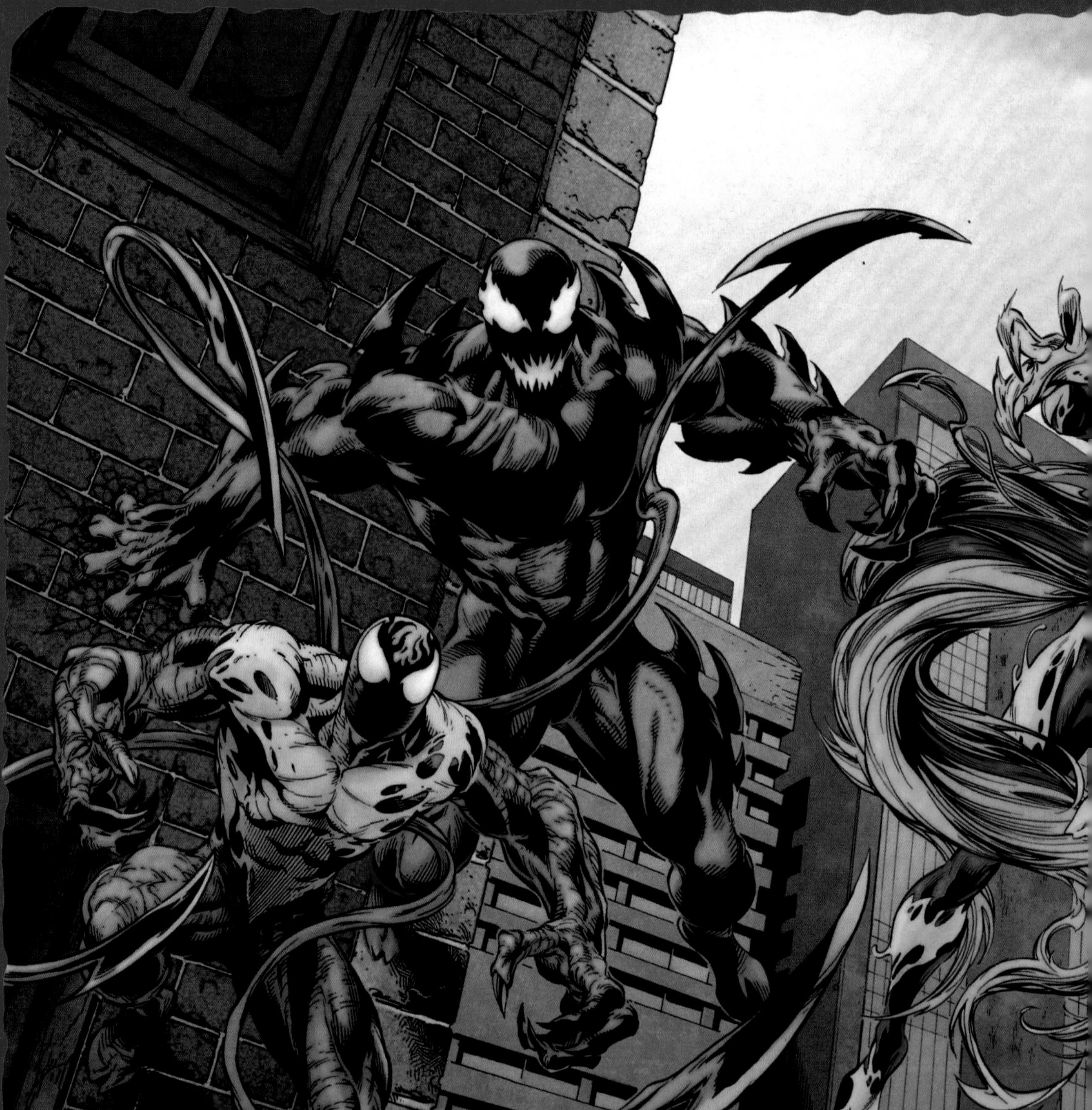

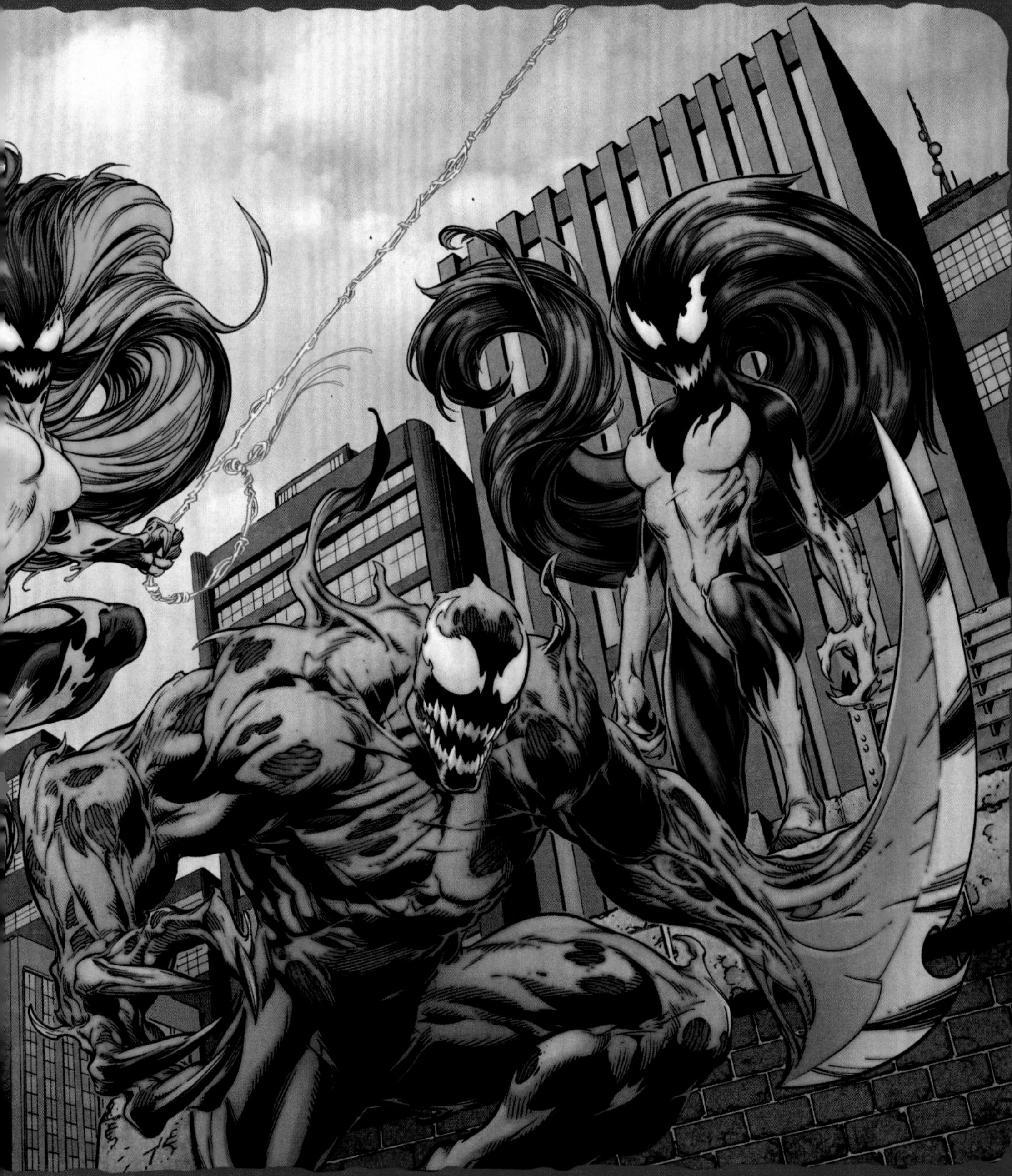

MARK BAGLEY, JOHN DELL & MORRY HOLLOWELL

SCREAM #1-3 Connecting Variants

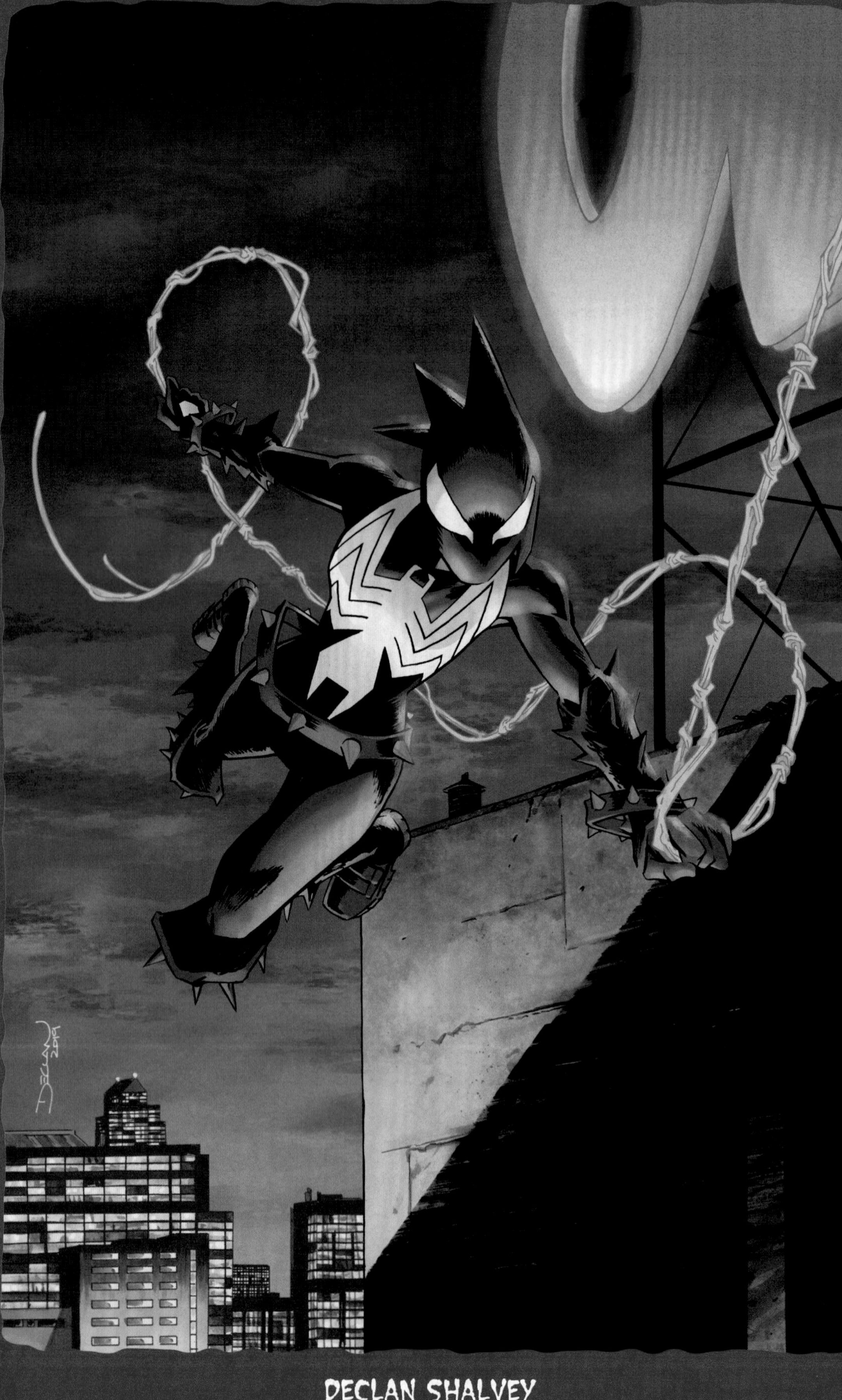
DECLAN 2019

DECLAN SHALVEY

SCREAM #2 Codex Variant

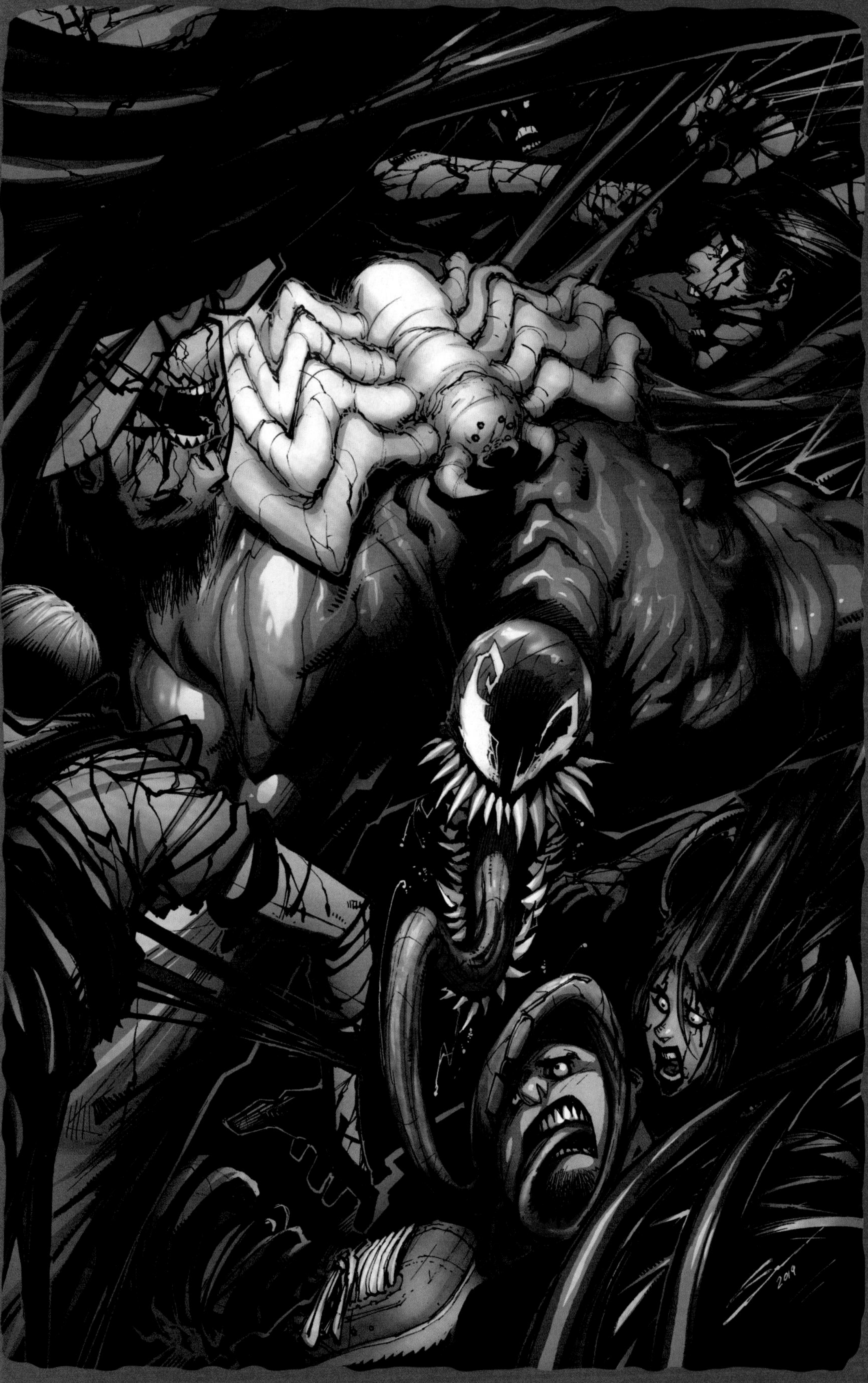

GERARDO SANDOVAL & JASON KEITH

***SCREAM* #3** Codex Variant

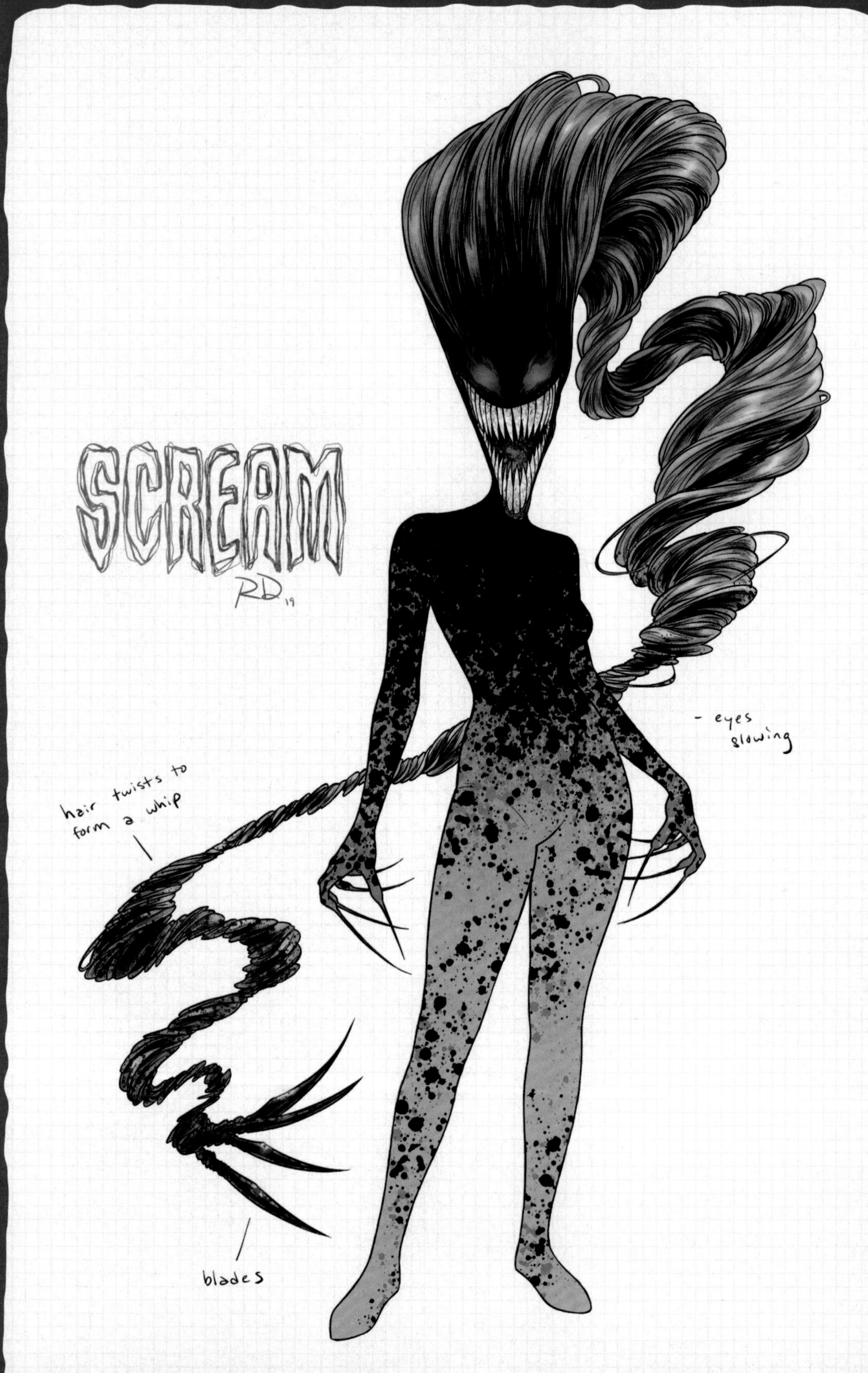
SCREAM
RD 19
- eyes glowing
hair twists to form a whip
blades

RUSSELL DAUTERMAN

SCREAM #1 Young Guns Design Variant

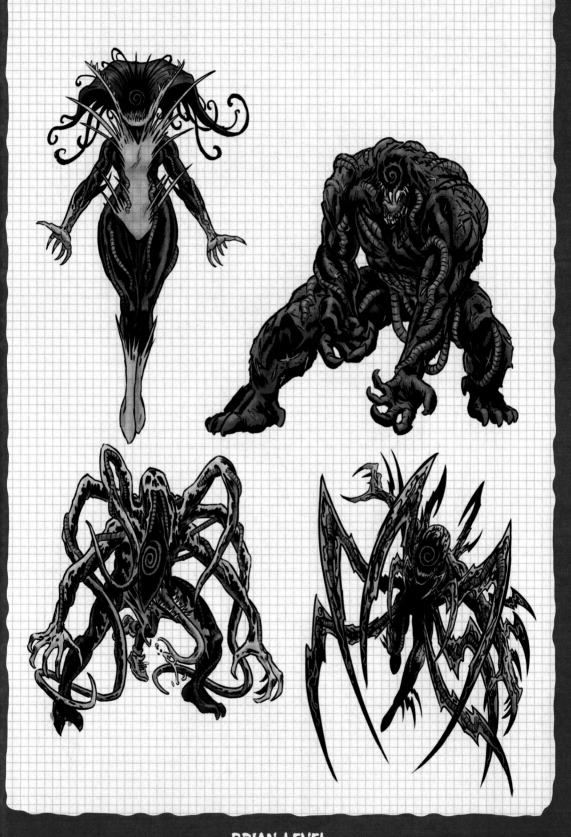

BRIAN LEVEL
SEPARATION ANXIETY Design Variant

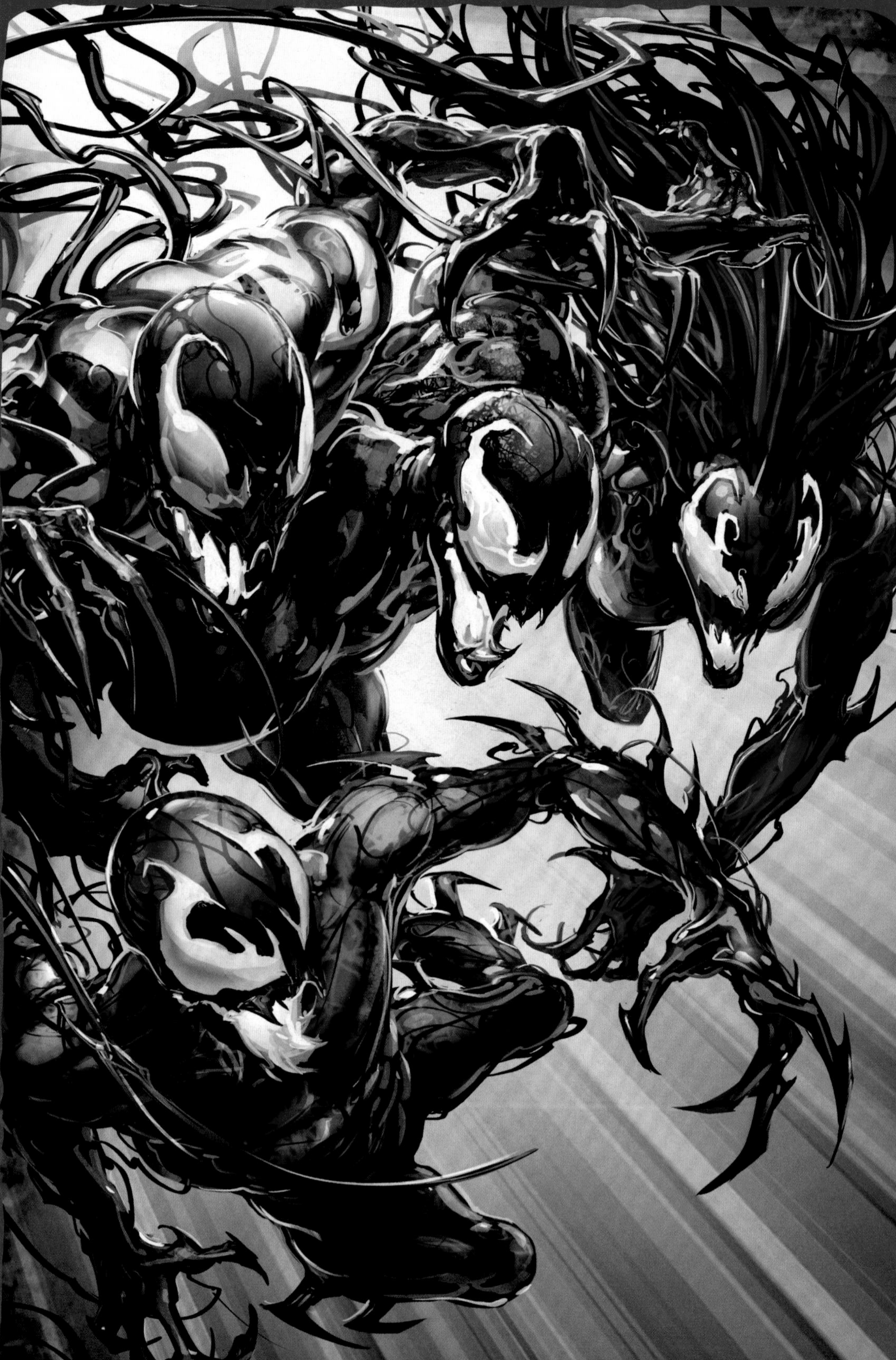

CLAYTON CRAIN
***SEPARATION ANXIETY* Variant**

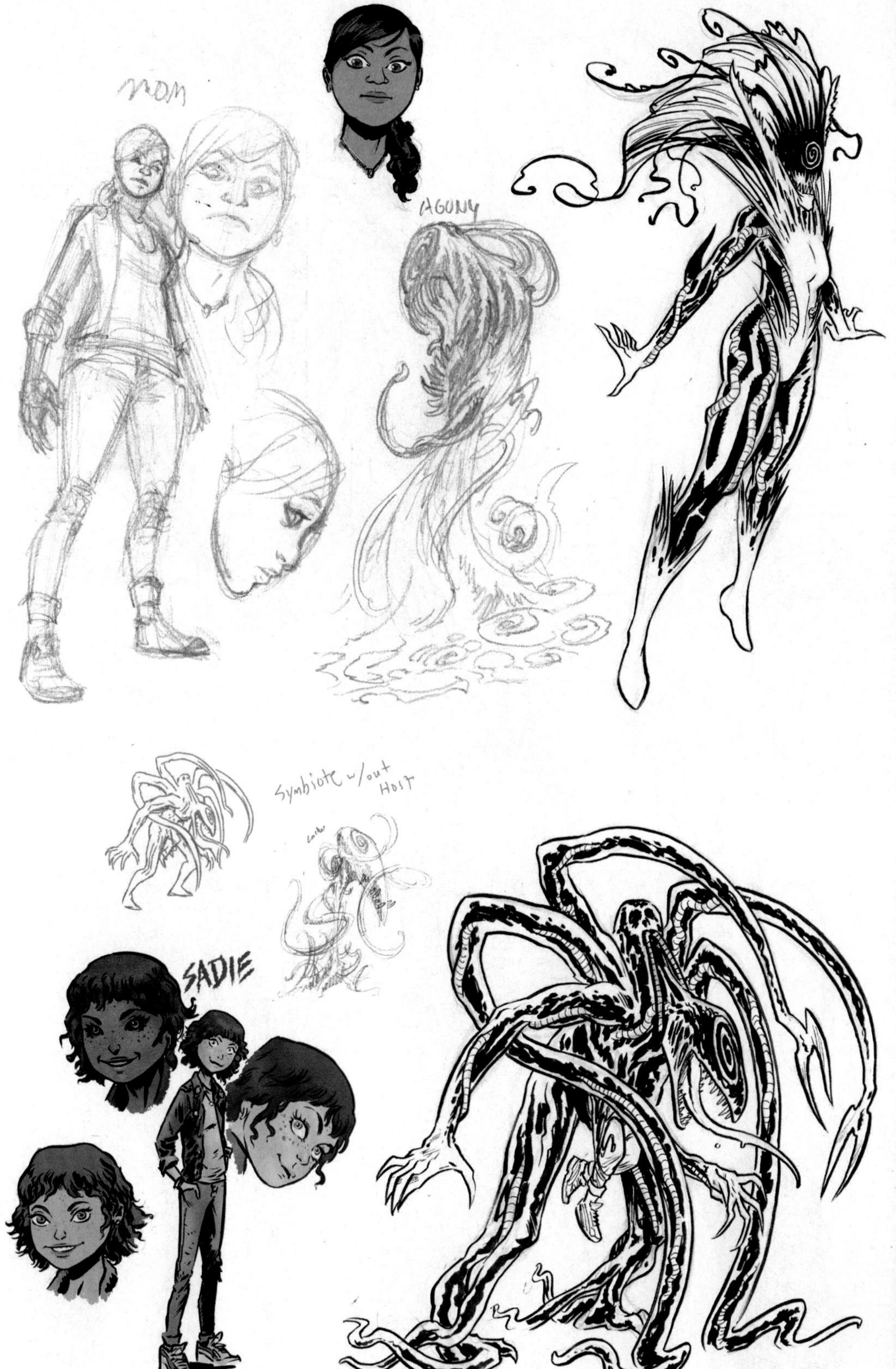
MOM
AGONY
Symbiote w/out Host
SADIE

BRIAN LEVEL

Character Designs

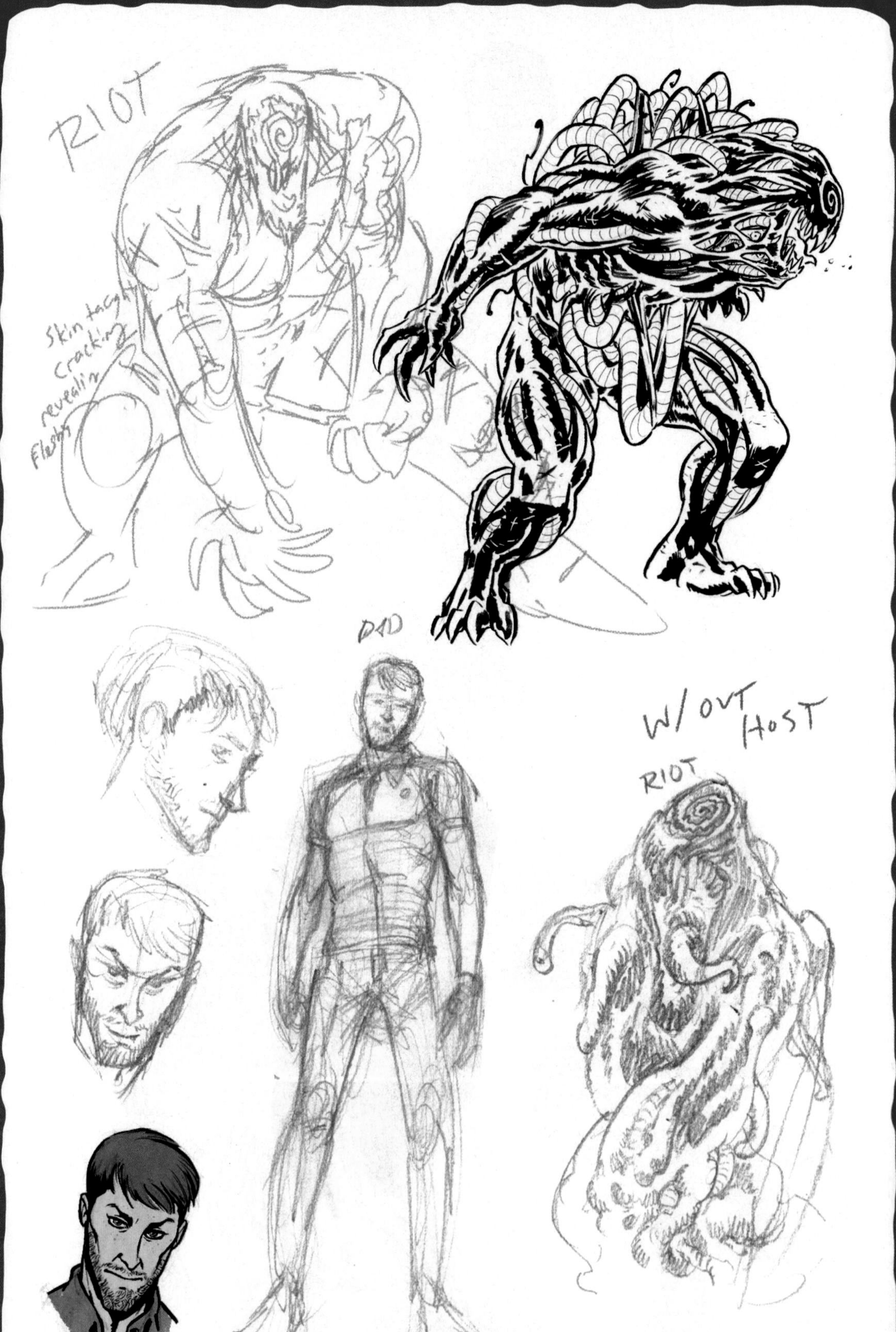
RIOT
Skin tearing cracking revealing Flesh
DAD
W/OUT HOST
RIOT

BRIAN LEVEL
Character Designs

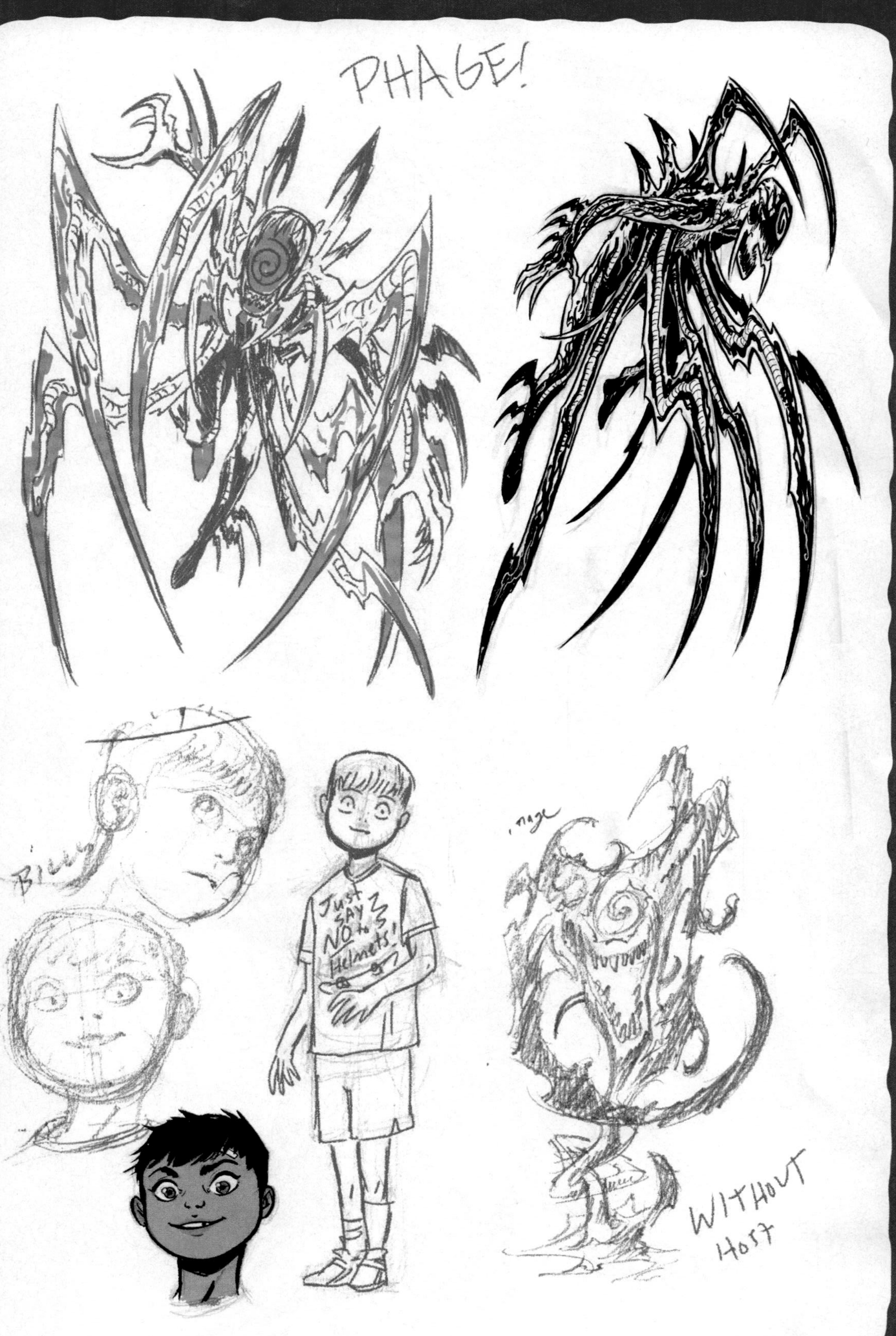
PHAGE!
Just SAY NO to Helmets!
WITHOUT Host

BRIAN LEVEL
Character Designs

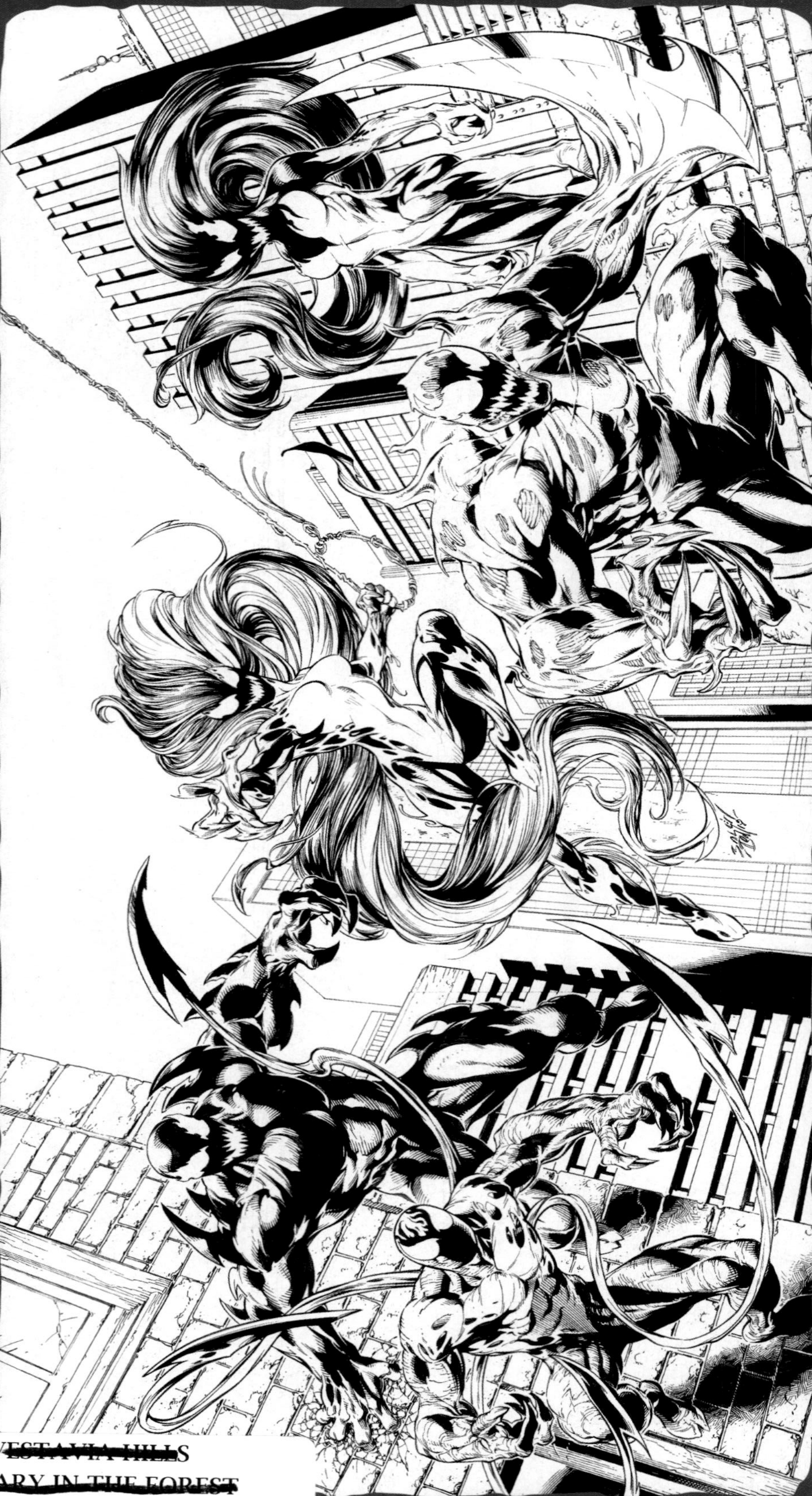

AGLEY & JOHN DELL
AM #1-3 Connecting Variant Art